Competing with Knowledge

The information professional in the knowledge management age

Competing with Knowledge

The information professional in the knowledge management age

Angela Abell
Principal Consultant and Director, TFPL Ltd

Nigel Oxbrow
Chief Executive, TFPL Ltd

 tfpl

LIBRARY ASSOCIATION PUBLISHING
LONDON

Published by
Library Association Publishing
7 Ridgmount Street
London WC1E 7AE

Library Association Publishing is wholly owned by The Library Association.

First published 2001

British Library Cataloguing in Publication Data

A catalogue record for this book is available from the British Library.

ISBN 1-85604-339-8

Typeset in 11/14pt New Baskerville and Swiss 721 by Library Association Publishing. Printed and made in Great Britain by MPG Books Ltd, Bodmin, Cornwall.

Contents

Introduction

Over the next twenty years, companies, government and individuals will face increasing difficulties in an environment of increasing complexity.

   . . . we have enormous positive potential, including technology, improvements in communications, availability of capital, and great increases in the quantity and availability of information . . .

Open Horizons: three scenarios for 2020
The 1998 report from the Chatham House Forum

During the Industrial Revolution, capital was in short supply and labour was comparatively cheap. In the 21st Century, financial capital will become the commodity and intellectual capital will be in short supply. Already in the IT industry, the value of software now exceeds that of the hardware. Most of the worth of the pharmaceutical industry is locked up in its patents. Knowledge is the key.

   To succeed in this new, competitive, global economy, Britain's businesses need to be knowledge driven. That applies not just to high-tech business but to all businesses in all sectors.

Rt Hon Tony Blair MP, Prime Minister,
CBI Annual Conference, October 1999

This book is about the emerging knowledge economy, how that economy is changing the way people live and work, and the environments and organizations in which they move. It has a specific focus on how these environments are changing, the mix of skills required and the future role of information professionals. It is based on research and client work over the last five years, and draws on the case studies we have built up as part of this work. Our intention is to provide a background for those intrigued by knowledge management and the emerging knowledge economy. By summarizing the drivers and features of emerging knowledge environments and discussing our views of the impact of information skills in these environments, we hope to stimulate information professionals to continue to explore the potential impact on their careers and work. We also hope to engage further the interest of those from other professions and backgrounds in the relevance and value of information management skills.

In 1995 we had an American visitor to TFPL who was enthusiastic about a new idea, 'knowledge management'. He brought the idea to us because he judged that our views about information management within corporate organizations, its use and value, the issues and barriers connected with trying to build and sustain corporate information strategies, would make us sympathetic to the idea. Knowledge management, he told us, was about taking a completely different approach to managing an organization. It was an holistic approach which addressed all aspects of creating and using knowledge. This meeting coincided with a range of new management books and articles on the topic of knowledge management that caught our imagination and made us think about how these new ideas would affect our clients and the information profession.

So we started researching the concept of knowledge management (KM), a journey that was to take us into fascinating areas and introduce us to a whole new language. During 1996 we started counting how many times we said and heard the word 'holistic'. Since then we have become used to a language that contains not only intellectual capital but also human capital and structural capital; that has intangible assets and knowledge assets, knowledge navigators and knowledge terrorists. We have become convinced that new environments are emerging based round building and exploiting knowledge and that the 'KM approach' is part of the ongoing development in thinking about management and organizations. Some people will claim that it is all about organizational development, others that it is primarily a human resources issue. Obviously some believe it to be an exemplar of the effective use of IT. But we have come firmly to believe that knowledge initiatives within organizations are about achieving the next level in the continuous process of improving the business. The KM label is not important but the concept and strategies behind it are vital to future survival and growth. They are about the success of the organization, linking business strategy to the way that the organization works.

So while KM is a buzz-word that is already showing signs of losing its buzz, many organizations are recognizing the value of knowledge and are adapting to the new knowledge economy. They are already changing the way that they operate and the way that their people work – and are reaping the benefits. They are also presenting a unique opportunity for a profession that is based on the theory of information management and use. The skills found in the library and information professions have never been so explicitly valued in corporate bodies. It is up to members of those professions to understand and demonstrate that they have those skills and to show how they can be applied.

There are many drivers of change, and many outcomes. For example: the changing nature of competition – for organizations, professions and people; increased collaboration between clients/suppliers; the recognition of a range of stakeholders in the enterprise in addition to the financial ones; cooperation between individuals from different professions and functions to build creative environments; corporate capability becoming acknowledged as the key to success for all organizations – public, private, academic.

The experience of work is changing. People are far more mobile, with less expectation of, or perhaps even desire for, long service with one firm, and with temporary and contract working being employed at all levels, as exemplified in Handy's shamrock organization. Roles are changing, becoming far more ambiguous with a focus on outcomes and process, rather than input and control. Employers are still grappling with the new mix of skills required in knowledge environments and for them this book explores how far the management of information and knowledge can benefit from applying an existing body of theory and skills across the enterprise. It discusses how these skills mix with other professional and technical skills to create a sophisticated corporate capability in managing corporate knowledge.

The changing environments present a challenge to individuals, professions and functions. Developing a culture that effectively uses knowledge requires collaboration and cooperation and a reassessment of individual contribution. How can individuals take the opportunity offered – improve the impact of their skills on business objectives – improve their capability? The opportunity is to develop creative environments for the benefit of the organization – thus generating competitive advantage, and, for individuals working within the organization, more productive, stimulating and enjoyable environments.

We set out to demonstrate the impact that information professionals can have in these environments – and how information skills need to be dispersed throughout organizations, by focusing on information management within a knowledge environment.

We hope that the following chapters will be of interest to all readers and will inspire others to consider how their expertise can be applied in new and exciting ways. Most of all we hope to demonstrate our belief that information professionals have a unique opportunity in the knowledge economy to add value and to have fun.

Thanks are due to many people who have helped, directly or indirectly, to create this work. We acknowledge our debt to all the organizations who have shared ideas, problems and solutions with us as they have developed their thinking about KM, and especially to those people who have read sections of this book for accuracy and clarity, and to Donald Abell for coining the phrase 'Fad, Fashion or Fact', later to become the 'Rhetoric, fashion or fact' of our opening chapter.

We are also continually grateful to our colleagues at TFPL who work with us to develop our thinking and ideas, generously sharing their contacts and experiences.

Special thanks are due to Barry Mahon and Rosemary Raddon who not only applied editing skills but also contributed ideas and common sense. Without their help the book would never have left our office. Thanks also to David Madden, who applied bibliographic and proofreading skills.

Angela Abell and Nigel Oxbrow

Part 1

The knowledge context

1

The changing nature of competition

Change – rhetoric, fashion or fact

In industrial societies the future is brought to us by technological change. This was recognized in the 1940s and described evocatively as 'waves of creative destruction' (Schumpeter, 1943). Technology was then an issue of mechanization and its impact on traditional crafts. In our own times the waves of future change manifest themselves through information technologies which have created the means of instant communication. Ideas, policies and visions can be stated firmly and confidently and be reported throughout the media, via the Internet, through publication, conferences and networks. A skilful and articulate politician, management guru, author or influential consultancy can quickly make their ideas seem like facts. Surveys and market research have become a respectable public relations tool and we are constantly presented with the latest concerns of corporate leaders, of market analysts, of employees, through sound bites to gain media attention. Politicians propose policies that they wish to see adopted, backed up by the research and opinions of those employed to develop them. Management thinkers present an idea that is then explored by those organizations that see themselves as early adopters and a management fashion is born. 'Another management fad.' Somewhere between the rhetoric and fashion, organizations adopt, or pay lip service to, the ideas that seem to be robust and make sense. How many individual working practices have changed and how far some of the ideas presented in this book are penetrating organizations will be the subject of much future research. What we are setting out to do is to summarize some of the influences that are affecting the way in which information professionals may work and develop in the coming decade.

The knowledge economy

The knowledge economy has become a reality for many organizations and nation states. The rapid development of information and communications technology (ICT) has changed the basis of trading and doing business. The wealth of a nation no longer depends on its ability to acquire and convert raw materials, but on the abilities and intellect of its citizens and the skills with which organizations harness and develop those abilities. The success of organizations depends on their ability to operate in this fast moving and global marketplace. Customers are increasingly knowledgeable about competing products, have a rich landscape of choice, have a range of economic, ethical and environmental values that may influence their choice of supplier, and expect and demand quality products and services. Effective relationships between supplier and client are seen to be crucial to the success or failure of an organization, changing the basis of the supply chain. Organizations cannot necessarily rely on keeping costs low by virtue of their buying power as a means of maintaining attractive margins and market share. Competition in the 1990s requires collaboration between supplier and client to enable the development of sophisticated and novel products. Regulation in some sectors has changed: in many cases, such as the financial sector, freeing up the market and increasing competition; in others, such as pharmaceuticals, both increasing the control and the requirement for communication with their marketplace. Corporate survival depends on the extent to which organizations understand their clients and their environment(s), and their ability to provide innovative and competitive services and products.

These pressures are not confined to the private sector. In the UK, for example, the Citizen's Charters of the early 1990s made explicit the need for government departments to interact more successfully with their clients. More recent developments include the 'joined-up government' initiative to facilitate easier 'one-stop' access to public information and services. The creation of bodies such as the Environment Agency, the Health and Education Agency and the Higher Education Council for England are part of a perceived need to make the delivery of services more directly responsive to their marketplace

– both customers and suppliers. Government policy and executive delivery are separated in order to improve contact and delivery.

One core theme has emerged through the changes. It is not particularly new, as a quotation from the 1930s, attributed to Andrew Carnegie, indicates:

> The only irreplaceable capital an organisation possesses is the knowledge and ability of its people. The productivity of that capital depends on how effectively people share their competence with those who can use it.

Annual reports have for many years contained an acknowledgment of the quality of the people employed and their intrinsic value to the operation, but this has not necessarily reflected the way these people were managed. A number of studies, the views of some management gurus, and the realization that human resources, not materials, really do provide the competitive edge have influenced the way that these resources are managed in organizations.

In 1993 the Royal Society for the encouragement of Arts, Manufactures and Commerce (RSA) launched the Tomorrow's Company Programme, which set out to explore how organizations need to respond to this changing environment. It concluded that there is an interwoven mix of stakeholders who all contribute to the success of the organization, and who all need to share the same values and have a commitment to its survival. The Tomorrow's Company Centre, formed in 1996, advocates an 'inclusive approach', taking account of the needs and future of all communities involved with and affected by the operations of the organization. These communities include customers, suppliers, staff, and the community in which it operates. This is just one example of the arguments that are changing the way in which organizations and individuals think about competition.

Changing organizations

Corporate bodies have to deal with change in order to survive and at any time the primary concerns of senior management will reflect the elements of change that most affect their business. Two of the many elements pressing for attention are ICT and globalization.

Information and Communications Technology (ICT)

The development of information and communications technology has produced opportunities and challenges. Early applications of technology offered the prospect of increased production and less reliance on people. The integration of communications and information technology introduces opportunities to operate in new markets, to change ways of working, to deliver different products and to develop business relationships with a variety of suppliers. It enables flexibility, allowing information to be exchanged across geographical and time barriers. Virtual offices, mobile work forces and innovative partnerships have all been enabled by ICT. It also brings new problems. While technical directors and their staff wrestle with problems of compatible IT platforms and software applications and lobby for international standards and faster and cheaper communications, chief executives are being urged to adopt leadership styles suitable for dispersed and mobile workforces, information-aware communities and flexible, creative organizations.

Globalization

As ICT enables organizations to increase their horizons, globalization has emerged as a major concern for many chief executives. Large corporate bodies may have offices in many countries or be, in effect, a federation of many national organizations. The interaction of different cultures, the integration of processes and procedures, of values and commitment, of knowledge and best practice, whilst nurturing a sense of corporate identity, present practical and philosophical problems. Smaller organizations are able to form ad hoc international networks, responding to opportunities and presenting themselves as new players in the marketplace. Equally, the fact that alternative suppliers can be based anywhere in the world is threatening local supply networks reliant on the large neighbourhood corporate. Customers are enabled to access a wide range of information, select new solutions for their requirements and be tempted by new approaches. They have more choice and have become more demanding.

Globalization also means that the effect of a change in trading conditions (regulation, economic downturn, changes in government) in one place is felt more immediately and acutely by organizations in many other places   Decisions made at global HQ will have direct effects in the rest of that organization. Similarly, decisions made by national governments may affect many organizations in many countries. Understanding the market environment takes on a new and real meaning when an organization reflects on the potential causal effect of changes across the world.

This dimension is not confined to the private sector. The public sector also reflects global interaction. The directives of the European Union have a direct effect on UK government departments, legislation and organizations as, for example, the current debate on the Working Time Directive illustrates. The increased mobility of people for employment or lifestyle, the use of trade regulation as a bargaining power, the transfer of best practices across geographical boundaries, all impact on the public sector.

The development of capability

Global management, virtual offices, flatter management structures and a focus on business processes are some of the responses to this changing context and they can be seen as part of organizational development. The theory of organizations, the way they work and learn, is an established academic field that has much to offer to organizations in a knowledge-based economy. From the beginning of the 20th century, behavioural theories of motivation of individuals and groups have challenged the economic theories and scientific principles of management. In the last four decades techniques such as group engineering, flexible manufacturing, total quality management and empowerment gradually turned the focus to recognizing the need for the individual to be involved in, and take responsibility for, their part in the business process. Knowledge Management (KM), the most influential management philosophy of the second half of the 1990s, can be seen as the practical application of many of these theories. It can be argued that KM was the natural outcome of a continuum of management trends – it was going to happen anyway and just needed a label under which to draw together a number of relevant and significant developments.

Hubert Saint Onge (1999) argues that KM is about the development of corporate capability, which is essential if an organization is to develop and lead its market rather than endlessly work to keep up with the demand (see Figure 1.1).

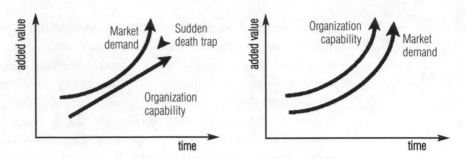

Fig 1.1 *Market demand and corporate capability (Saint Onge, 1999)*

Corporate capability, he argues, is the integration of:

- Strategy: the goals of the organization and the ways it seeks to serve them
- Structure: the grouping of accountabilities; structures that define the position of the relationship between members of the organization
- Systems: the ways in which processes (information, communication, decision making) and flows (products/services and capital) proceed
- Culture: the combined sum of the individual opinions, shared mindsets, values and norms.

Whether or not all organizations would recognize this as their approach to success, it reflects a current focus on the need to develop a business approach that gives an organization the capability to respond to rapidly changing markets and conditions through innovative approaches, channels and products. The knowledge economy requires that organizations have the ability to identify the change signals and the flexibility and agility to respond rapidly. Their management must inspire and enable innovation, ensure that they learn from success and failure, and provide the infrastructure to support a radically new way of working.

Networked organizations

Networked organizations recognize that capability is built through individuals, groups and processes. While ICT has enabled individuals to be geographically mobile and facilitated remote working, the interaction of people outside controlled hierarchical structures is proving to be the real strength. Team and project-based working, multidisciplinary groups, formal and informal conversations, are all emerging as the platform for developing corporate flexibility. Such approaches cut across departmental loyalties and organizational structures and are challenging attitudes to management, motivation, reward and recognition. People move between teams and are members of several. Team members may be geographically dispersed and their roles reflect their contribution to the team rather than organizational seniority. Communication channels between team members cross those of their function or business unit. Fellow team members may include representatives of suppliers, customers or business partners. Individuals gain new experience and increase their own capability. The challenge for the organization is to encourage this development of individuals and groups and to build it into corporate capability.

However, the reality of team working in practice may differ from ideal models. The 1998 Workplace Employee Relations Survey (based on a survey of 30,000 managers, worker representatives and employees) found that team working is now extensive and is regarded as a key element of work organization. 'Overall, 83 per cent of managers stated that at least some employees in the largest occupational group worked in formally designated teams, and in 65 per cent of workplaces most employees in the group worked in teams' (Cully et al, 1999). In 54% of cases the team had responsibility for a product or service, and in 35% of cases also jointly decided how the work was to be done. However in only 3% of these workplaces did teams correspond to the model of autonomous team working (see Figure 1.2).

E-economy – the development of knowledge trading

Information and communication technology has not only enabled global connection and information exchange. It has resulted in new ways of doing business. In his speech to the Confederation of British Industry (CBI) conference in October 1999 UK Prime Minister Tony Blair used the phrase e-economy, which is fast becoming the catch-all phrase for the use of electronic networks for trading. Estimating that more than 13 million people have access to the Internet in Britain (100 million in the USA) he went on to predict that the revenue from e-commerce would top £10 bn in the UK in the year 2000, 'a three-fold increase' on 1999. He also noted that e-mail is a vital tool of business life, and suggested that

The real challenge is in transactions which are business-to-business – B2B as it's known in the jargon. Like BT's new move to get all its suppliers to conduct their business with BT through the Internet; an initiative BT thinks will save it as much as $1 billion a year. Other prominent British companies are thinking of doing the same. US estimates suggest business-to-business transactions on the net could total $400 billion by 2003.

E-commerce, as a part of the e-economy, is becoming a reality for a significant part of the population, creating new businesses and new

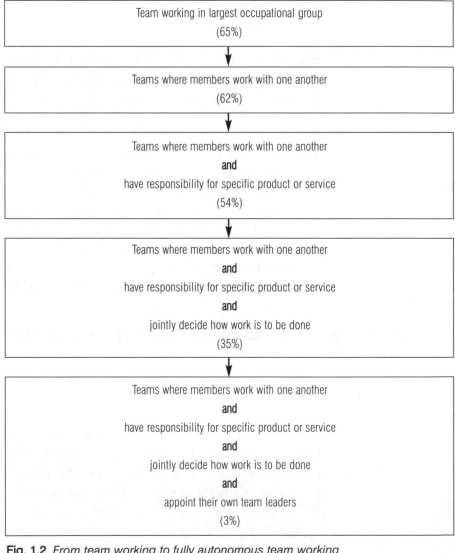

Fig. 1.2 *From team working to fully autonomous team working*
(From Cully (1999), reproduced with permission)

opportunities for existing ones. Many everyday items and services can be purchased online. The activity was, ironically, led by the very traditional business of bookselling, and continues to provide access to many traditional products, such as toys and wine, as well as to new and innovative products – such as animated digital greetings cards and virtual bouquets.

E-commerce

'E-commerce is a generic term used to describe a range of technologies and applications for buying and selling goods and services digitally' (ETHOS, 1999). Although electronic interchange of data has been established for some time, it is the Internet that has fuelled its growth, offering access to global markets without time or geographic restrictions. It enables low-cost access to the market, makes business set-up comparatively easy, provides new ways for businesses to track customers and potential customers, and creates mechanisms for suppliers to maintain communication with, and provide additional services to, customers. E-commerce is building new business models, requiring partnerships between communications, finance and trading companies, and presenting a way for customers to buy, with a rapidly expanding range of choice, without leaving their homes or offices. The changes occurring as a result of the rapid development of e-commerce are also affecting the public sector. The UK government is increasingly providing mechanisms for businesses and citizens to conduct their business with them via the Internet and academic institutions are exploiting the potential for the delivery of distance learning and online education packages.

Evidence of the conviction that e-commerce will become a crucial part of the trading environment can be seen by the appointment in 1999 of a minister of e-commerce within the Department of Trade and Industry. Changes to the policy, regulation and commercial environment to support the growth of e-commerce are also beginning to emerge, with, for example, the publication in the UK of the White Paper outlining a Consumer Strategy (*Modern Markets*, 2000), and directives expected from the EU.

E-business

Direct sales to customers are only part of the picture. Businesses are increasingly using ICT to conduct business-to-business transactions. Paper transactions between businesses are increasingly being replaced by electronic in the manufacturing, service and financial sectors. Tourism and travel industries have already moved a long way down this path. Electronic records are gradually emerging in the health sector with laboratory results being made available to GPs electronically. Individual and business transactions with government departments will become possible electronically.

Customer relationship marketing

The use of the data generated by ICT has increased the potential to develop closer customer relationships and to exploit new markets. Loyalty cards in supermarkets, air miles and bonus points are new marketing tools reliant on data collected electronically. The planning of sites of retail outlets, delivery of customized products, and target marketing of loans and credit cards reflect the data collected about buying and lifestyle habits. Knowing what the customer is likely to want before they do is a competitive advantage in direct client and business-to-business trading.

A further development has been the recognition by a few companies that their corporate website can be the route to maintain customer intimacy through providing access to value-added products. Packaging knowledge generated by the business gives clients access to information that has been assessed and placed in context by experts. The Blue Flag product of the law firm Linklaters & Paine is an example. Their corporate finance practice interprets law, regulations and changes which are relevant to their client base and makes the information available as a value-added service to existing clients.

Competing with information and knowledge

The recognition of knowledge as a primary competitive advantage focuses attention on both people and information. While people are seen as the crucial ingredient to the building and application of knowledge, the outcome, the intellectual capital of the organization, is the result. A well-understood expression of intellectual capital in a scientific and technical organization is in the patents it holds, which both protect its right to exploit the efforts of its research and development activities and provide an information store on which future development work can be built. As organizations recognize that their success is equally reliant on their knowledge of the customer base, their knowledge of the marketplace, their know-how and processes, the concept of intellectual capital is applied more broadly and organizations make decisions about the value of what they know and their plans to exploit it. Increasingly, financial institutions assess corporate knowledge and its exploitation as part of their decisions on the financial health of their clients or their value as takeover targets. While the Internet, electronic commerce, new commercial partnerships, customer interaction and the development of extranets are producing an environment where more information is made available to a diverse range of audiences, there is also more thought given to the value of information as a competitive weapon which will produce competitive advantage. Microsoft is not the only organization to protect details of its next product until it is ready to launch and gain control of the market, or to use controlled leakage of information to influence the competitive environment. 'Vapourware' is a term applied to many new product announcements, particularly in IT.

The Internet has also enabled information suppliers to penetrate client organizations through electronic platforms. Where the delivery of online information sources was once controlled by an intermediary, direct desktop access has changed the perception of the ultimate client and forced the suppliers to concentrate on user-friendly delivery of their product. Where once the problem was persuading individuals within an organization that information from external sources could be useful to them, access to the Internet has brought a confusing array of sources and problems of selection and control. While the corporate response to these changes has been variable, the information supply sector has seen numerous mergers and acquisitions, resulting in the owner of a business information supplier being listed as one of the top e-millionaires in a 1999 newspaper survey (Dan Wagner, *Sunday Times*, 3 October 1999).

In a typical new development brought about by this atmosphere of change, 1999 saw the launch of IQ Port, an Internet service designed to trade in knowledge. Based on the concept that individuals have valuable knowledge to share, and will do so for financial reward, IQ Port provided a platform for the publication of knowledge 'assets'. These could be purchased online at a price fixed by the supplier, or the value could be assigned by the purchasers. The service also fostered the concept of knowledge communities, groups of individuals who signed up to the site for discussion and to review 'assets' of particular interest to them. Launched as a pilot through the UK bank NatWest's electronic trading division, it attracted interest, including a group of academics who presented themselves as a knowledge community in order to sell their expertise. Although it did not survive the bank's reassessment of its business focus, it is an indication of the increasing view of knowledge 'assets', both tangible and intangible, as a tradeable commodity.

Changing work groups

Individuals are operating in increasingly complex environments. Their ability to navigate and utilize information, learn new skills and feel comfortable in ambiguous work situations has become as important to success as academic achievement. Flexible and mobile working arrangements, contract and short-term employment and the concept of portfolio careers have changed the relationship between employer and employee. There has also been a subtle shift in the power base. After a period of full employment in the 1960s when power seemed to rest with employees and trade unions, subsequent economic downturns with resulting high unemployment appeared to shift power to employers. There was emerging, at the same time, an increasing need for a high- and multi-skilled, flexible workforce, which led to apparent skills shortages and an increasing gap between those in and out of employment. The organizations that flourished in the 1990s needed knowledgeable people – people who were able to learn. At the same time they were not offering jobs for life, or even, necessarily, for more than a few years. Mobility and flexibility meant that individuals had to be prepared to change roles within their organizations, change employers or change careers.

The individuals who flourish in this climate are those who are able to apply their skills in many environments, are able to learn and develop and who are able to deal with change. These individuals also recognize that they and their knowledge are valuable, providing them with the choice to work in environments that reflect their values and lifestyle. Just as their employers no longer offer secure employment, so they feel free to build their careers to suit themselves and to move at will. Loyalty between them and their organization has changed and it may only exist within a framework that implies a new contract of employment. To attract and retain bright people employers need to offer development opportunities and real participation in the business. To be attractive to these employers individuals need to demonstrate a commitment to learning and a willingness to take responsibility and initiative, and to be prepared to undertake a variety of roles and opportunities. The new generation of workers are minded to work where they want, work when they want, work how they want, and move often.

The changing face of the blue-collar worker

Flexibility is the climate of employment for those able to participate in the new organizational approach to competition. It is not the whole story. The social history of organizations in the past few decades is about change in work grouping and allegiances. The application of information technology to manufacturing and transport processes affected blue-collar workers. Labour, which at the beginning of the industrial era had been comparatively cheap, became, in the Western world, expensive. Machines could work more efficiently, make fewer mistakes and reduce costs by replacing people. Traditional skills were in less demand as processes changed and employers began to look for alternative and more technological skills. The production-line mentality gradually gave way to group manufacturing, quality circles and flexible manufacturing so that traditional blue-collar work became drawn into team and group working, interacting with a variety of skills and expertise. Being a skilled worker took on a wider meaning.

Although there are many elements contributing to this change, the 1970s and 80s saw the death of apprentice schemes in the UK, breaking the tradition of the student learning from the master to develop a specific craft. Just as the trade guilds of the 1880s and earlier had given way to the solidarity of trade unions, so the mixing of new and old skills in individuals and work teams began to change the nature of workplace relationships and representation. The craftsman of today is as likely to be a self-employed artisan or small businessman selling skills to organizations, much as the unskilled labourers of the 20th century sold their skills on a daily or project basis.

Changing management groups

Managers and the management structure have also been affected by ICT and organizational change. The responsibility of middle management was traditionally that of managing resources to achieve the outcomes that were generally set by senior management. In a hierarchical organization the senior level decides on what the organization is going to do and how they are going to do it, the middle level translates what is required of their section into tasks and actions, monitors and measures productivity and quality, and balance their budgets. The staff in their departments have specific tasks to perform and work within the procedures handed down to them. The interrelationship of the activities, their significance and relative importance, may not be well understood by most people undertaking them, or by those who manage them. Support activities fulfil roles that are based on 'the way we do things' rather than an understanding of what value they add. The approach is inward looking, designed for internal efficiency.

A range of management ideas have challenged this structure. Customers are the most valuable part of the organization, argue some, and the structures must focus the majority of the staff on interacting with and understanding the customer, on meeting their requirements for quality and service. Others attack what they view as the waste of management effort on activities which are not 'core to the business' and advocate the outsourcing of support services and concentration of management effort on the prime product and service. Other trends focus on pushing responsibility and decision making out to the staff throughout the organization, on enabling them to 'realize their full potential', to have more of a stake in the organization. Empowering individuals implies providing them with the information on which to base action and processes for feeding their experience back to business planning. Business process re-engineering challenged the management view of the organization by arguing that core processes can be identified and that they flow across departments and functions, taking no account of boundaries or power bases. Effective business processes are not based on managers directing the activities of their staff but are facilitated by people who understand the process, design the procedures and provide the resources.

The role of middle management is changing, leading to flatter structures, project-based and team work, and networked organizations, providing individuals with a number of leaders and reporting lines. The control role of the departmental manager is disappearing. Staff management still remains. People, it is argued, need to belong somewhere for 'pay and rations'. They need people who will facilitate their appraisal, encourage development and act as mentors, monitor their effectiveness and champion their requirements. Detailed direction is not required. As individuals, managers will have as many allegiances as the staff in the area. They will be members of a number of teams, will play different roles and may not have staff reporting to them. Managers as a group are becoming closer to a profession than an expression of organizational structure. However, it is worth reflecting that, according to the recent research by Cully, hierarchy is still the predominant form of business organization particularly, but by no means exclusively, in the public sector (Cully et al, 1999).

The changing face of professionalism

The role of professionals is also at a crossroads and the term 'professional' is one applied in many contexts. A professional employee can be interpreted as any employee engaged in work that is predominantly intellectual and varied, involving the exercise of discretion and judgment, and good knowledge of a specific field of activity or learning. A 'professional' is also someone who applies his particular skill for monetary reward, such as a professional golfer or boxer.

Being professional is applied to describe an approach. It implies quality work guided by an accepted set of ethics and standards, the ability to apply judgment and objectivity, the notion of contribution to a community or body of knowledge. The concept of professionalism is widely accepted and the description of an individual as 'professional' is a positive statement about their attitude to and execution of their work. Professional skills and approaches are, therefore, part of the desired organizational mix.

The term 'the professions', however, is much more specific, requiring evidence of the education and training in a specific area of learning or expertise, and demonstration of the ethics and standards required by that profession. These professions generally have high-level entrance requirements, including public examination and periods of guided application. They have professional bodies that set and maintain standards. Members of these professions, such as the medical, law, scientific and accountancy professions, recognize a hierarchy of expertise and experience and use their professional network to exchange ideas and research and to develop their body of knowledge. Their professional status can be crucial to the right to practise, as in the medical profession, and professional activity may be part of their career plan. Some professions have become essential to corporate activity, law and accountancy for example, while others, such as human relations and information science, have developed as professions in order to establish and maintain a standard of expertise recognizable as valuable.

A feature of the professions is the strong networks that underpin them, providing individuals with ready access to a peer group and validation of their activities. Many members of a profession identify with their profession rather than the organization with which they work. The application of their skill has been as the professional advisor rather than as part of the team that delivers services to the ultimate client. It is this area that is the last to be challenged by the emerging organizational structures. While professional skills and attitudes are increasingly valued, support functions are being incorporated into mainstream business. Professionals are now being challenged to become part of the delivery team, to move beyond their professional networks and familiar working groups.

Conclusions

How far the world of work will continue to change, and in what direction, cannot be predicted, and that is nothing new. What is certain is that change is happening, and what is new is the speed at which it is taking place. Organizational structures are changing, competitive platforms are being reassessed, and partnership and collaboration is becoming part of corporate life. Individuals are embarking on a variety of relationships with employers. Some take the route of permanent employment – but for a series of employers. Many work, through choice or circumstance, in a variety of temporary assignments: contract workers are employed for specific projects; temporary staff fill personnel gaps and service peaks in workload; self-employed consultants bring experience and expertise to assist with problems. Individuals have variety and flexibility, for which they exchange security and certainty. Virtual working provides the opportunity to work from home and manage a mix of lifestyle demands.

The underlying theme is mobility and change: working with new people and structures rather than an established network of colleagues, acquiring different skills and working with others willing and able to learn. Modern organizations are challenging – not a soft option. There appears to be increasing competition for the roles and opportunities that they provide. Just as organizations are learning that collaboration and partnership are the most fruitful way to develop and succeed, so are the individuals they employ. The ability to work with, and learn from, other people is the individual's competitive advantage.

References

Cully, M et al (1999) *Britain at work: as depicted by the 1998 Workplace Employee Relations Survey*, Routledge, 43 (Figure 3.4).

ETHOS (1999) ETHOS. 'Intermediaries in electronic commerce', ETHOS Technology Briefing Series 4: *Developments shaping procurement and electronic commerce*, TB 16.4.1, August 1998, prepared for the European Commission's Telematics Applied Programme, reissued 1999.

Modern markets: confident consumers (2000) The Stationery Office (Cmnd 4410). Also available at **www.dti.gov.uk/consumer/whitepaper**

Saint Onge, H (1999) *Cultivating corporate culture towards a knowledge environment*, European Business Information Conference, TFPL.

Schumpeter, J A (1943) *Capitalism, socialism and democracy*, Allen and Unwin.

2

Emerging knowledge environments

If the environments in which organizations live and work are changing then the challenge for those organizations is to keep up with, and, if possible, lead the change. Many management writers have influenced this process of change with views on adaptive cultures, stakeholders, business processes, knowledge sharing, learning organizations and other aspects of organizational change with common themes and elements. Culture and identity, involvement and commitment, process and flexibility, learning and sharing, creativity and innovation, trust and respect, are aspects of the changes advocated, the best practice rehearsed and the lessons demonstrated through case study. At the core sits the crucial interaction between the people of the organization; its customers, suppliers and partners; and the structures that underpin the organization.

Of the management themes developed and explored in the last quarter of the 20th century five have been particularly influential in changing the way that people and organizations work. These are:

- total quality management
- business process re-engineering
- intangible assets
- learning organizations
- knowledge management.

The themes are not exclusive or exhaustive, and their complimentarity has fed and expanded them. They have been responsible for a significant portion of business language. Their common thrust is away from using the balance sheet and financial accounting as the main tool of management to a broader understanding of what creates value and sustainable business success.

Total quality management

Quality became an issue for manufacturing firms in the 1970s and 1980s when quality assurance standards began to bite. Once government departments and large companies made possession of a quality assurance certificate, whether national or company-specific, a prerequisite of becoming a preferred supplier, then implementation of the procedures and processes required to obtain certification became a common hurdle for most manufacturing companies. For many, the initial stages of the process were felt to be mainly about documentation and its control, rather than any change in working practices, but as success stories demonstrated real benefits from a total quality approach so more fundamental changes occurred. The philosophy of quality being the delivery of goods and services suitable for the customers' purpose, and the result of the combined efforts of everyone in the organization may seem a very downbeat objective in the 1990s, but its implications were initially quite radical. It put the customers and their requirements before the operational requirements of the firm. It also related quality objectives to corporate strategy, moved the focus of quality away from control and inspection at the end of the production line to all functions and activities in the firm, and made explicit the contribution of people, their expertise and experience to the quality of the final product. The influential consultants and writers on quality, such as Deming, emphasized the motivation of people as an inherent success factor in improving quality.

> Deming fervently believes in the 'intrinsic motivation' of mankind, and that it is management's policies that often serve to demotivate employees. Instead of helping workers develop their potential, he asserts, management often prevents them from making a meaningful contribution to the improvement of their jobs, robs them of the self esteem they need to foster motivation, and blames them for systematic problems beyond their control.   (Gabor, 1990)

Deming was, with Juran, one of the most influential consultants and writers on quality, gaining a following in Japan and the USA, and his

14 points concerning the 'building of quality' reflect the importance he places on people and include education and training as core activities. As quality standards gained ground, the application for BS5700 and other national or corporate certification was often accompanied by the development of company learning centres, individual and team training programmes and the setting of group quality targets. The emergence of networks and groups, such as quality circles, were mechanisms to enable everyone involved in the delivery of the product, from marketing to distribution, to contribute to problem solving and quality improvements. Within a very short time the concept of TQM had spread to all sectors, being equally applicable to the service sector, education and government as to manufacturing. TQM directors and managers appeared, quickly followed by quality manuals outlining processes and procedures, measuring and monitoring.

The initiative had its enthusiastic followers and its detractors, but elements of TQM have become part of the life of every organization, and part of the structure of business in the developed world. Professional bodies and industry networks have developed, such as the British Quality Foundation, the European Foundation for Quality Management (EFQM), and the American Quality and Productivity Federation (AQPF). The development and current activities of the EFQM, founded in 1988 by the presidents of 14 major European companies, with the endorsement of the European Commission, illustrates how far the approach has become established and how it relates to the emergence of knowledge environments.

EFQM's mission is:

- to stimulate and assist organisations throughout Europe to participate in improvement activities leading ultimately to excellence in customer satisfaction, employee satisfaction, impact on society and business results; and
- to support the managers of European organisations in accelerating the process of making Total Quality Management a decisive factor for achieving global competitive advantage.

(EFQM, 2000)

With its emphasis on meeting the needs of customers, employees, financial and other stakeholders and the community at large, it echoes, or is echoed by, other initiatives such as the RSA's Tomorrow's Company. The establishment of the EFQM Excellence Model (formerly the Business Excellence Model) reflects the belief that the TQM approach is about the management of the organization, not an activity undertaken by a few people responsible for quality:

> Regardless of sector, size, structure or maturity, to be successful, organisations need to establish an appropriate management system. The EFQM Excellence Model is a practical tool to help organisations do this by measuring where they are on the path to Excellence; helping them understand the gaps; and then stimulating solutions.
>
> (EFQM, 2000)

The following concepts underpinning the model, taken from the EQFM website in January 2000, will be familiar to those who have followed the development of the KM philosophy.

- Excellence is dependent upon balancing and satisfying the needs of all relevant stakeholders (including people employed, customers, suppliers and society in general as well as those with financial interest in the organisation).
- The customer is the final arbiter of product and service quality and customer loyalty, retention and market share gain are best optimised through a clear focus on the needs of current and potential customers.
- The behaviour of an organisation's leaders creates a clarity and unity of purpose within the organisation and an environment in which the organisation and its people can excel.
- Organisations perform more effectively when all inter-related activities are understood and systematically managed and decisions concerning current operations and planned improvements are made using reliable information that includes stakeholder perceptions.
- The full potential of an organisation's people is best released through shared values and a culture of trust and empowerment, which encourages the involvement of everyone.
- Organisational performance is maximised when it is based on the management and sharing of knowledge within a culture of continuous learning, innovation and improvement.
- An organisation works more effectively when it has mutually beneficial relationships, built on trust, sharing of knowledge, and integration with its partners.
- The long-term interests of the organisation and its people are best

served by adopting an ethical approach and exceeding the expectations and regulations of the community at large.

The EFQM Excellence Model is based on the premise that 'Excellent results with respect to performance, Customers, People and Society are achieved through Partnerships and Resources, and Processes' (EFQM, 2000). The diagrammatic form of the EFQM Model shown in Figure 2.1 includes nine boxes representing the criteria against which organizations can measure themselves, with each criterion supported by a number of sub-criteria.

It is worth noting that:

- Criterion 2, Policy and Strategy, includes the sub-criterion:
  - Policy and Strategy are based on information from performance measurement, research, learning and creativity related activities.
- Criterion 3, People, includes the sub-criteria:
  - People's knowledge and competencies are identified, developed, sustained.
  - People are rewarded, recognized and cared for.
- Criterion 4, Partnerships and Resources, includes the sub-criteria:
  - Technology is managed.
  - Information and knowledge are managed.

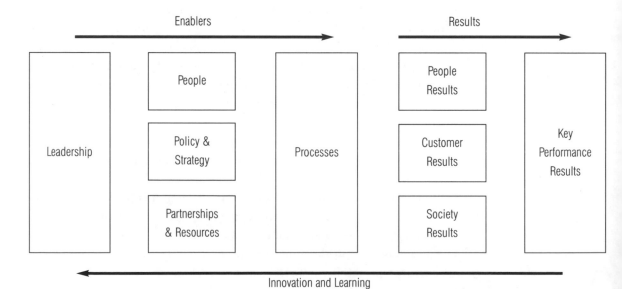

Fig. 2.1 *EFQM Excellence Model*

- Criterion 5, Processes, includes the sub-criterion:
  - Processes are systematically managed.

Within the EFQM Excellence Model framework, people, processes and knowledge play a significant part in the continuous business improvement package, and the activities of the EFQM have been important in raising awareness of knowledge management as a concept among its members.

Business process re-engineering

Business process re-engineering (BPR) is among the list of management fads that people will quickly point to as those that failed. The goals of the authors of the concept, James Champy and Michael Hammer, as set out in their book (Hammer & Champy, 1993):

> 70% decreases in cycle time, 40% decreases in costs; 40% increases in customer satisfaction, quality and revenue; and 2.5% in market share

were not realized by 'as much as 30%' (Champy, 1995). The reasons for this apparent lack of success are varied, with James Champy arguing in his later book (Champy, 1995) that the earlier focus on re-engineering *work* – 'the operational processes performed by salespeople, clerks, factory and warehouse hands, repair people, engineers, technicians, customer-service folks, field representatives – anyone and everyone on the value-adding chain' (Champy, 1995) – did not address the need to rethink management approaches and processes. It has also been argued that the approach was translated by too many companies as a formula for cutting costs by cutting people, which is to misunderstand the concept.

Whatever the failures of BPR, the Hammer and Champy approach did much to popularize the concept of business processes. To manage key processes the initial step is identification and understanding, and the acknowledgment by many organizations that the processes were not in place to be re-engineered. BPR created a challenge to the view of an organization as a series of departments and functions, each controlled by a hierarchical suite of managers setting target outcomes for their staff and fighting for resources for their department. Business processes flow through the organization and it is the process that is designed and managed, not the organization. Marketing, for example, becomes as much a process as production, and is not primarily the name of a department. The marketing process has sub-processes which reside throughout the organization: in selling and accounts, in research and development, in strategic planning and finance. In a BPR environment it is the role of the manager to facilitate the design of the process, ensure the resources are available and act as coach and mentor for those carrying out the process. The enterprise becomes a collection of explicitly interconnecting processes and sub-processes which are developed and maintained by teams mixing expertise and skills. Control at a senior level becomes less visible and responsibility is spread throughout the organization.

In his later book Champy suggests that the apparent failures of 're-engineering' reflected its popularity as a concept coupled with a lack of commitment to the application of the whole concept. He identifies the issues that

the actual practice (successful and otherwise) has kicked up, all of which must be addressed for reengineering to succeed.

There are four issues:

- Issue of purpose. Insistently, persistently, relentlessly, the new manager must ask, 'What for? What is it that we're in business for? What is this process for? This product? This task? This team? This job? What are we doing here anyway?'
- Issues of culture. If successful reengineering requires a change in a company's whole culture, as seems to be the case in many instances, how is it to be accomplished? . . . If it is true (and it is) that reengineering is unlikely to succeed where the corporate atmosphere is charged with fear (and its twin, mistrust), how do we generate another, better environment – one, say of willingness and mutual confidence.
- Issues of process and performance. How do we get the kind of processes we want? How do we get the performances we want from our people? How do we set norms and standards, or measure results – for worker performance, management performance and the performance of the whole enterprise? Reengineering demands radical objectives, leadership and political skills to realise. But do we know whether we have the right stuff? What does it take to be a good manager today?
- Issues of people. Who do we want to work with? How can we find them from both inside and outside the company? How do we want them to work with us? How do we know whether they're the kind of people we want?

(Champy, 1995)

Champy, Hammer and many BPR experts and exponents argue that the approach has to involve everyone in the organization, not just those directly involved in the re-engineering transformation. The real issues are about people, culture and processes in customer-driven organizations.

The Business Processes Resource Centre at Warwick University, funded by the Economic and Social Research Council, reflects the issues in the three major themes on which they base their work: complexity, knowledge management and professional development, and business restructuring. Management of knowledge is seen as part of an overall management approach to business improvement, sitting alongside culture, people, learning and the re-structuring of business to cope with a complex and changing marketplace.

Intangible assets: the value of intellectual capital

During the second half of the 20th century the basis of business success moved inexorably from reliance on financial and physical assets to the management of intangible assets – such as customer and partnership relationships, people, processes, infrastructure and intellectual capital. However the financial markets have been slow to reflect intangible assets in their valuation of a company. Their preference for assessing the worth of the company by its financial performance and physical assets has made it difficult for management to demonstrate the value of its intellectual capital such as knowledge, people, brand and relationships. The problem of assessing the value of a company is not new. Business groups have been lobbying for several decades to have the value of brands and goodwill included on the balance sheet. The difference between book price (the worth of a company expressed by financial measurement of its tangible assets) and its market value (the value of the company expressed by the amount that the market, or potential purchasers, think it is worth) has received increased attention. The owners of Body Shop and Virgin demonstrated their frustration with the stock market valuation of their companies by buying back their shares and returning their companies to private ownership, thus retaining their ability to build on the assets that they, rather than the financial analysts, judged as valuable.

In his book on intellectual capital Patrick Sullivan traces the history of intellectual capital as a means for assessing the worth of a company in other than financial terms. He describes intellectual capital management as a discipline with three distinctly different origins:

> The first was in Japan with the ground breaking work of Hiroyuki Itrani, who studied the effect of *invisible assets* on the management of Japanese corporations. The second was the work of a disparate set of economists seeking a different view of the firm . . . Finally, the work of Karl-Erik Sveiby in Sweden, published originally in Swedish, addressed the human capital dimension of intellectual capital and, in so doing, provided a rich and tantalising view of the potential for valuing the enterprise based upon the competencies and knowledge of its employees.
>
> (Sullivan, 2000)

His timeline, starting at 1980, illustrates the diversity of people contributing to the field and includes Itami (publishing from 1980); Sveiby (publishing from 1986); Treece (publishing from 1986); Stewart (publishing from 1991) and Saint Onge, who established the concept of 'customer capital' in 1993.

Leif Edvinsson of Skandia, appointed as the world's first Director of Intellectual Capital, at Skandia AFS, a Swedish insurance company, built on the work of Sveiby to develop ways of reporting intellectual capital in the company's annual report. The concept of 'Intellectual Capital' as 'Human Capital' + 'Structural Capital' gained recognition in the corporate world and became part of business language. Human capital includes the people within the organization, its customers and partners, the way they work together and the expertise and knowledge they employ; although those who follow the Hubert Saint Onge approach separate out human capital (internal staff and relationships) from customer capital (external relationships). 'Structural capital' represents the processes and infrastructure that supports the work of those people – what is left behind when people go home. Skandia developed a 'Navigator' as the model around which to base their reporting:

> The Skandia Navigator is a new business management model. The Navigator helps provide a more balanced, truer picture of operations – a balance between the past, the present, and the future.
>
> (*Skandia Annual Report*, 1998)

The Skandia model develops measures for intangibles; for example, measures for customer relations, for human resource development, for future growth, for management quality, etc – measures that reflect the potential of the company, and its market standing, over and above the financial returns. Skandia was, arguably, the first company to report intangible assets in its annual reports, and has since taken the premise of its dependence on these assets further. In 1999 Edvinsson created an intellectual laboratory, Skandia Futures Centre, for Skandia's future work. Based in a renovated villa, furnished with modern IT equipment, future-oriented literature and networking stations, the centre is being developed to 'reach the future faster'. The laboratory is populated with a carefully selected, generationally diverse group of knowledge pioneers, a handpicked team of approximately 30 people from around the world.

Authors, academics and consultants have continued to develop the concept of identifying and using critical success factors as a means of managing and monitoring business performance. Sveiby's Intangible Assets Monitor has been developed to help an organization assess its overall health through 'indicators that indicate change, i.e. growth and renewal as well as efficiency and stability measures' (Sveiby, 1999) arising from three categories of organizational focus. The examples in Table 2.1 demonstrate his approach to managing a company through monitoring intangibles and their alignment with corporate strategy.

Table 2.1 *Intangible Assets Monitor*

	External structure indicators	Internal structure indicators	Competence indicators
Indicators of growth/renewal	Profitability per customer	Investment in IT	Level of education of staff
	Image enhancing customers	Structure enhancing customers	Training and education budget
			Competence turnover
			Competence enhancing customers
Indicators of efficiency	Sales per customer	Proportion of support staff	Value added per employee
	Win/loss index	Values/attitudes index	Value added per professional
			Profit per employee
Indicators of stability	Proportion of large customers	Age of the organization	Professional staff turnover
	Loyal customers ratio	Rookie ratio	Pay structures
	Frequency of repeat orders	Support staff turnover	

Adapted from Sveiby's website with permission

Using this model, Sveiby argues, it is possible to assess strategy and make tactical and operational decisions on the basis of the value they might add to the business. For example, would work with a particular client enhance the desired client profile and track record? If repeat business and close client relationships are important to the business, are the processes in place to sustain them? Does the work undertaken contribute to the knowledge and learning of the organization? Does it contribute to the development of the organization's people?

These notions reflect the balanced scorecard approach – a set of performance measures that are identified as key for judging the health and progress of organizations and which have become part of the business vocabulary of the 1990s. Monsanto is one company that identifies the creating of a balance scorecard as part of the development of a knowledge environment (Junnarkar, 1998).

The focus on intangible assets has also contributed to an increasing valuation of intellectual property: of patents and processes, of reports and the outcomes of projects, the tangible record of the organization's knowledge and experience. It also reflects the work undertaken by the Hawley Committee (1995) to draw to the attention of the boards of companies their responsibility to ensure the use of information in the decision-making processes of their organizations.

The initiatives to bring intangible assets and intellectual capital into the mainstream of organizational concern focuses on issues of people, processes and culture, and emphasizes the crucial role of information content within a knowledge environment.

The learning organization

A focus on knowledge and learning makes sense: knowledge is increasingly an important source of competitive advantage, the vision of the learning organisation is seductive and several prominent companies have achieved spectacular results.

This was the view of Lucier and Torsilieri of Booz-Allen and Hamilton when assessing the business impact of knowledge and learning organization programmes in 1997 (Lucier & Torsilieri, 1997). Their phrase 'managed learning' reflects their belief that 'effective management of learning simultaneously builds a learning organisation and creates and uses knowledge', and reflects the synergy between the two philosophies.

One of the exponents of the philosophy is Arie de Geus whose remit as Head of Planning for Shell in the 1980s was 'to stimulate thinking by bringing Shell's planning process closer to line management' (de Geus, 1995). In a lecture delivered to the Royal Society for the encouragement of Arts and Manufactures and Commerce he described the research undertaken by Shell to identify the characteristics of long-established organizations – those which were in existence in the last quarter of the 19th century and which were still 'alive today with their corporate identity intact'. The conclusions were that the companies that survived and thrived were those that were good at 'management for change'. They were able to alter and change their internal structures in order to adapt to the changes in the external environment. 'The internal changes in these successful survivors appeared to have occurred gradually, incrementally and in response to opportunity, or rather, in anticipation of demand. This can only mean one thing: these companies reacted earlier rather than later, by foresight rather than by crisis.' He identified the characteristics of these companies as:

- conservatism in financing
- sensitivity to the environment
- sense of cohesion and company identity amongst employees
- tolerance of new ideas, circumstances and change.

and argued that the most successful companies will be those that are best at learning. He also argued that successful organizations are living communities which nurture trust and development among their members and which operate to community rather than economic rules. At TFPL's European Business Information Conference in 1999 de Geus elaborated on his theme, referring to the hypothesis of Alan Wilson, a microbiologist at the University of Berkeley. Wilson's thesis is that, within generations, certain species learn to develop skills to exploit the environment in a new way. De Geus suggested that was the definition of competitive advantage – learning to develop a new skill to exploit the environment in a new way, or to exploit changes in the environment in a new way. For this learning to happen three conditions are necessary:

- The community (the species) has to have numerous mobile individuals.
- Some of these must have the capacity for innovation.

- The community (species) has to have an effective capacity for the development of those innovations.

  'In other words innovation doesn't take place and then stay in one place, it spreads through the community.'

His illustration of his thesis – the Blue Tits and Robins example – is a memorable explanation of a learning organization:

The practice, in the United Kingdom, of delivering milk in bottles to the doorstep began in the 19th century, and until the 1930s the tops of these bottles were open. Two British garden birds, Blue Tits and Robins, learned and developed the physical skill to exploit this opportunity in their environment and became adept at drinking the cream from the top of the milk. In the 1930s the Dairy Board put aluminium seals on top of these bottles. It is well documented that by the early 1950s the whole Blue Tit population had learned how to pierce the aluminium seals. Robins, as a species, have still not developed the skill.

Wilson's explanation, used by de Geus to demonstrate community learning, reflects the different social behaviour of the two species, the conditions he proposed for community learning. Both robin and blue tit species have numerous mobile individuals, and both have innovative individuals that learn. Individual robins succeed in penetrating the seals but the skill hasn't spread through the robin population, whereas it has through the blue tit population. The blue tit species has been more effective in propagating the innovations of the few individuals. This, it is suggested, is because blue tits live and operate in cooperating flocks whereas robins are not only solitary but defend their 'patch' against other robins. Individual blue tits move between flocks and geographical locations, spreading new skills. Robins protect their individual skills, new and old.

The de Geus theory is that birds that flock learn, therefore companies should be organized for intense flocking. Developing individuals is not enough, the organization needs a social propagation system. For example, if the planning process is organized as 'flocking', ensuring that generations sit around the same table, that will be part of the learning process and contribute to successful, long-term community development, producing higher profitability, if that is the measure.

Arie de Geus has not been the only champion of the learning organization philosophy. Other authors and disciples have explored the theme, including Peter Senge whose 1990 book was to prove influential in developing the concept (Senge, 1990). A learning organization is, according to Senge:

> where people continually expand their capacity to create results they truly desire, where new and expansive patterns of thinking are nurtured, where aspiration is set free, and where people are continually learning how to learn together.

The key is in the 'learn together'. The learning organization moves on from training individuals for new skills – it is an environment that maximizes collective experience and learning, where collaborative learning benefits individual, group and organization. Its focus is not only on people and their development, but also on culture and processes, and on communities and networks.

Knowledge management

The article by Nonaka (1991) and the later book by Nonaka and Takeuchi (1995), both entitled 'The knowledge creating company', arguably gave an identity to a framework of processes that were already happening or were in the pipeline. As Skyrme (1999) notes, the interest in knowledge is not new. Greek philosophers 'set out key principles that have stood the test of time' and Francis Bacon's observation in the 16th century that 'knowledge is power' is often quoted.

Knowledge management (KM) is like beauty – in the eye of the beholder. There is no universally accepted definition of the term, perhaps reflecting its essential character, its unique interpretation by the organization that adopts the philosophy.

Marc Auckland, Chief Knowledge Manager at BT, says:

> Knowledge Management is a discipline that promotes an integrated approach to the creation, capture, organisation, access and use of an enterprise's Intellectual Capital on customers, markets, products, services and internal processes.

The Business Processes Resource Centre at Warwick sees KM practices as a 'crucial element of the global business process' within organizations and a major source of competitive advantage. Their definition reads:

> Knowledge Management practice can be broadly defined as 'the acquisition, sharing and use of knowledge with organisations, including learning processes and information systems'. The emerging field of Knowledge Management seems to reflect a constellation of changes – some profound, some more cosmetic – in the business environment.
>
> (BPRC, 2000)

These changes, they suggest, include:

- the increasingly widespread perception of knowledge as an important asset
- the rise of occupations based on the creation and use of knowledge
- the convergence of information and communications technologies
- theoretical developments that emphasize the importance of unique assets such as tacit knowledge.

This helps to explain both the wide ranging interest in the concept across many different business sectors and the diversity of practices that have been labelled as KM. 'Although such practices share a common interest in targeting knowledge rather than information or data, they tend to perform distinctively different functions depending on the business context' (BPRC, 2000).

Warwick University's BPRC goes on to identify four 'different types of knowledge management' although they do not suggest that these are exclusive:

- Valuing knowledge: knowledge viewed as intellectual capital, the Skandia approach
- Exploiting intellectual property: particularly in research-based organizations such as pharmaceutical firms
- Capturing project-based learning: 'Consultancies, professional firms, aerospace companies, etc, are in the vanguard of developing systems to codify and communicate such knowledge'
- Managing knowledge workers: reflecting 'managers' desire to increase the productivity of knowledge workers, breaking down some of the barriers to knowledge sharing which are associated with "professionalism" '.

The explosion of conferences, media coverage and consultancy offerings that emerged in the last three or four years of the 20th century has led some to dismiss KM as yet another expensive management fad. Closer examination does suggest that it is a way of describing a management response to a fast-moving, customer-led marketplace where knowledge is the basis of competition. The need to integrate the expertise and knowledge of people from different backgrounds and cultures with the strategic aims of the organization drives the KM approach in global organizations. At a professional meeting in 1999 Tony Rubin, Programme Manager of Mobility Leaders, BT Group Strategy and Development, asked, 'How can global companies create a culture that allows its people located in different countries, culture and time-zones to exchange knowledge and information in a timely, efficient and economical manner?'

As a manager in another global company put it, 'Knowledge management is about trying to make an organisation of 46,000 people feel like an organisation of eight.'

The need to implement government policies and interact effectively while remaining responsive to customers drives KM in the public sector. The need to innovate and bring new products to the market more rapidly than competitors drives private organizations. All need to integrate the knowledge of their staff in order to gain and retain customer confidence and loyalty. KM is part of a continuous business improvement model.

Research undertaken by TFPL in 1998/9 showed that, despite the hype and exposure, very few organizations were undertaking corporate-wide KM programmes (TFPL, 1999a). Those that were are the KM pioneers, some of whom had remarkable success stories to tell. Buckman Laboratories, for example, one of the earliest to develop the approach, demonstrated that they have been able to build a global workforce which:

• operates as a global community
• identifies strongly with Buckman aims and values
• shares problem solving and expertise
• is continuing to develop the concept.

Bob Buckman had a particular vision and, as the owner of the company, has been able to implement it. He was able to authorize investment, insist on carrot and stick mechanisms to change corporate

culture, and provide the strong leadership that a major change programme needs. He was also clear about the objectives of the programme, setting out a number of targets, the primary one being to
change the percentage of people working with clients from 40% to
80% by 2001. While this is part of the KM programme, the main business objective is to remain a successful supplier of speciality chemicals. The CEO's analysis of what would provide success in their
marketplace was their ability to help customers solve problems and to
identify products that would contribute to the success of their clients.
This required 'smart' people working with the clients and the combined experience of Buckman people round the globe. This philosophy drove the KM approach.

When the UK public utility, Anglian Water, became a privatized
company, their first challenge was the strongly embedded culture of
a public sector organization. Their aim was to become the most successful UK water company and included expansion to overseas markets. They needed a flexible, competitive workforce. Their approach
was to include everyone in the company in a learning 'journey', to
teach new skills and to demonstrate that everyone had the potential
to work successfully in a commercial company. The programme
focused on individual and corporate learning and on the development of structures and procedures to support this learning. They
measure the success of this approach by their penetration of the UK
and overseas market.

Despite examples of successful corporate programmes, KM is a
label that is losing its capital letters. It is a philosophy, not a standard
approach. TFPL's research showed that while many companies were
investigating the ideas and applying those that fitted their circumstances. relatively few were adopting the KM label.

> You can't manage knowledge – nobody can. What you can do, what a
> company does, is to manage the environment that optimises knowledge.

And the optimization of knowledge is the objective of whatever 'KM'
programme is adopted, with people at the core of this optimization.

> The idea is not to create an encyclopaedia of everything that everyone
> knows, but to keep track of people who 'know the recipe', and nurture
> the technology and culture that will get them talking.
>
> (Arian Howard, Hughes Space and Communications)

Organizations are taking a cautious and targeted approach to creating knowledge environments, reflecting their own cultures and needs. KM is not a 'one size fits all' approach, it is a philosophy that needs interpretation within the organizational context. Many organizations are avoiding the term. The KM label may be a convenient label for authors, journalists and those wishing to influence, but corporate environments have their own language and few feel that the KM label fits. A pragmatic approach to making the change has emerged. TFPL discovered that few organizations take the major change programme but many undertake activities that are influenced by KM philosophies. The KM leaders attending the second CKO Summit in 1999 (TFPL, 1999b) all agreed that the implementation of a corporate KM approach is best done through target activities that have beneficial results and demonstrate the approach. 'Quick Wins' and 'low-hanging fruit' are phrases that have become part of the business vocabulary for organizations building a knowledge management environment, indicating projects that help build the KM culture: projects with objectives that are achievable within a timeframe that people can visualize, that have identifiable business benefits and benefits for individuals, and whose implementation with the changes they bring takes into account the horizons and concerns of the people they affect.

A knowledge-based philosophy

What is the knowledge management philosophy? At its simplest, it is managing the balance of people, processes and technology that determines the organization and its relationship with its market. Beneath this there are layers of values and attitudes that determine whether the organization is a knowledge environment. It is about creating an environment where knowledge is valued and where the difference between information and knowledge, and their interdependence, is understood, an environment that values creativity and innovation, encourages a variety of working patterns and facilitates communication between people in different locations and from different departments. A knowledge management philosophy creates an organization that encourages ideas, rewards success, allows people to fail and learn from failure, enables people to admit problems, reflect on and share failure, success, problems and solutions, and encourages people to ask for help. It creates an organization that is aware of its environment, developing a corporate instinct that allows it to react quickly and make informed decisions. Employees are valued for their knowledge and skill and it is an attractive environment for creative people and risk-takers. It is, in fact, Utopia.

The knowledge management approach reflects methods and criteria to be found within many other business improvement models and programmes, such as the Business Excellence Model, Investors in People and the European Foundation for Quality. Many of the organizations taking a close interest in KM have also shown interest in, and adopted, other business improvement ideas: total quality management programmes, the balanced business scorecard, the learning organization approach, and many others. All reflect the desire to increase organizational capability and flexibility – to develop an environment that gives the best chance of gaining competitive advantage.

The objectives of KM programmes are many, some common to all organizations, others reflecting particular industry or organizational drivers. The overall aims are business driven and are common to all organizations:

- Competitive advantage
- Increased effectiveness and competitiveness
- Increased innovation and creativity
- Reduced risk and cost control.

Specific objectives reflect the organization's particular view of what is required to achieve these aims. The following are some examples of knowledge management objectives:

- World-class customer intimacy and satisfaction
- Products and services that add value for the customer
- Increased knowledge of the market, clients and competition
- Improved decision making and developed corporate instinct
- Better allocation of investment funding
- Improved utilization of new ideas
- Reduction in development time and time to market for new products
- Creative and insightful solutions
- Support for a virtual organization
- Effective global operations
- Leverage of intangible assets
- Attraction, maximization and retention of a skilled workforce
- Effective use of expertise and best practice

- Avoidance of
  - duplication of effort and waste
  - mistakes and their repetition
  - time wasting
  - missed opportunities.

The above aims and objectives could be accredited to many management initiatives and projects. The difference with KM is in its integrated approach to achieving them. The aims and objectives of KM, as expressed by its champions and disciples, are expressed in terms of processes and people.

From their viewpoint the aims of KM should be to:

- know what you know
- learn what you need to know
- use knowledge effectively

and the essence of KM is:

- connecting people with people
- connecting people with information
- enabling conversion of information into knowledge
- encouraging innovation and creativity through the nurturing of a knowledge environment.

The integration of corporate and individual values, people and their skills and competencies, processes and market knowledge builds the corporate capability.

Issues and barriers

A knowledge environment is Utopia. A place where we all want to work, and concepts we have probably heard before. We all know the organizations who value their staff so highly that no-one really likes working there – but the bonuses are good. The development of knowledge environments exposes many problem issues that few companies claim to have solved completely. The main issues are related to business benefit, people and culture, technology and processes. These issues reflect all the main areas of concern in a knowledge environment and can produce the barriers or road blocks to achieving the corporate environments that most of us would claim we wish to inhabit.

People issues

People issues are closely aligned to corporate culture. The way individuals respond to change reflects their past experience. The questions people ask when requested to cooperate with change include:

- What's in it for me? How does it make my job easier?
- What recognition will I get for sharing my knowledge?
- If I share it will others abuse it?
- Can I trust the knowledge that others make available?
- Will I lose control/power?

The people issues that the organization may consider are a mixture of strategic and tactical issues and include:

- Identification of the knowledge/information that people need
- Identification of the knowledge/information that people already possess
- How to make the right knowledge available at the right time
- How to link people and knowledge processes.

Process issues

The process issues will include:

- How to integrate knowledge creation and utilization into business processes
- How to ensure knowledge access where it will have the most impact
- People make processes work, often through informal steps – how can these be formalized?
- How to build communities around business processes
- Processes must 'learn' – how to achieve the commitment of people to the learning process
- Development of performance and benefit measures
- Processes need technology support – how to integrate business benefit and technological capability
- Linking knowledge process to business benefit.

Technology issues

Information and communications is a key component of a modern organization, and a key enabler of a knowledge-based environment. It is the last element that really modern 'knowledge' organizations can admit to worrying about for fear of being accused of being too technology focused: today's knowledge business is about people, culture and processes. More down-to-earth observers issue a challenge: try running a knowledge based enterprise of any size without addressing the technology issues and see what happens.

The technology issues to be dealt with include:

- compatibility of technology platforms and tools across sites and applications
- incorporation of legacy business systems
- integration of workflow and people with software applications
- IT applications and business benefit
- user training and motivation.

Other barriers

In addition to the issues noted above, there are other barriers to the development of knowledge environments which reflect problems in the implementation of any change programme.

Primarily there is the ongoing commitment of senior management. The difference between a novel idea that seems attractive if it provides swift benefits and senior management commitment to a major long-term programme is significant. The former can produce the feel-good factor quickly, the latter requires longer-term investment before achieving tangible results and thus needs faith in the approach.

Other barriers include:

- Confusion over the focus of the initiative: information or knowledge management; knowledge management or learning organization; which should lead – human resources or information technology.
- A misunderstanding of the differences between tacit and explicit knowledge resulting in their being treated in the same way.
- A focus on collection, not connection – on an attempt to capture all organizational knowledge in repositories, often creating elec-

tronic buckets in place of physical filing cabinets.
- An over- or under-reliance on technology.

Conclusions

Change does not happen overnight, and perfection may never be within our grasp. That does not mean that the journey is not worth making, both for the organization and the individual. Anglian Water does not claim to have completed the transformation and uses the metaphor of a journey to illustrate their approach. The knowledge-based environment is formed and nurtured by people in all parts of the organization: managers of all types, stakeholders of all varieties, anyone with a commitment to the organization – it is their journey that will make the difference.

References

BPRC (2000) *Business Processes Resources Centre*
   http://bprc.warwick.ac.uk/KMweb.html
Champy, J (1995) *Reengineering management*, HarperCollins.
de Geus, A (1995) Companies: What are they?, *RSA Journal* (June), 26–7.
EFQM (2000) *European Federation of Quality Management*
   http://www.efqm.org/history.htm
Gabor, A (1990) *The man who discovered quality*, Times Books.
Hammer, M (1998) *Beyond re-engineering*, HarperCollins.
Hammer, M and Champy, J (1993) *Reengineering the corporation: a manifesto for the business revolution*, Nicholas Brealey.
Hawley Committee (1995) *Information as an asset: the board agenda*, a consultative document for chairmen, chief executives and boards of directors developed on behalf of the KPMG IMPACT Programme by a committee under the chairmanship of Dr Robert Hawley, KPMG.
Junnarkar, B (1998) *Creating fertile ground for knowledge at Monsanto. Perspectives on Innovation Issue 1: Managing organizational knowledge*, available at
   http://www.businessinnovation.ey.com
Lucier, C E and Torsilieri, J D (1998) *Why knowledge programs fail: a CEO's guide to managing learning*, available at
   http://www.strategy-business.com/strategy
Nonaka, I (1991) The knowledge-creating company, *Harvard Business Review* (November–December).

Nonaka, I and Takeuchi, H (1995) *The knowledge creating company*, Oxford University Press.

Senge, P (1990) *The fourth discipline*, Doubleday.

Skandia Annual Report (1998).

Skyrme, D J (1999) *Knowledge networking: creating the collaborative enterprise*, Butterworth-Heinemann.

Sullivan, P (2000) *Value-driven intellectual capital: how to convert intangible assets into market value*, Wiley.

Sveiby, K-E (1999) *Intangible Assets Monitor*, available at **http://www.sveiby.com.au/IntangAss/CompanyMonitor.html**

TFPL (1999a) *Skills for knowledge management: building a knowledge economy*, TFPL.

TFPL (1999b) *TFPL CKO Summit Dublin 1999*, TFPL.

3

Approaches and features

> Organizational knowledge creation should be understood as a process that 'organizationally' amplifies the knowledge created by individuals and crystallizes it as part of the knowledge network of the organization.
>
> (Nonaka and Takeuchi, 1995)

The objective of a knowledge-based organization is to improve the creation and use of collective knowledge by facilitating the exchange, sharing and utilization of knowledge and information. It is an environment that recognizes the inter-relationship between information acquisition and the expertise of the people who create knowledge. Information technology is an important enabler but is only part of the infrastructure underpinning the business, work and operational processes that enable knowledge building and sharing to be embedded in the way that people work. Equally important are the organizational structure and ethos that enable the individual and the organization to learn and develop (or hinder them from doing so), and the processes that embed knowledge sharing and use into everyday activities.

The approaches to creating this environment differ, reflecting the unique character of each organization. Hansen and his colleagues (1999) suggest that organizations take one of two very different KM strategies: one a 'codification strategy' which sets out to collect, code and make knowledge available for re-use – the person-to-document approach; the other a 'personalization strategy' which bases the sharing of knowledge primarily on person-to-person contact. The selection of approach is very dependent on the products and services of the organization. Organizations that offer standardized or mature products, for example, take an approach that depends on stores of re-usable knowledge; those that have customized or innovative products and services take an approach that builds relationships and links between people. Whilst each strategy cannot stand alone, they argue, it is vital that an organization selects to follow primarily one route or another. In practice many organizations do take a mixed approach, although often one will dominate. But despite the variations there are nevertheless common elements and features that are characteristic of the environments that are being developed to compete with knowledge.

Approaches
Tacit and explicit knowledge

In their book Nonaka and Takcuchi (1995) described four processes for the conversion of tacit and explicit knowledge which they believe are crucial to creating value.

- tacit-to-tacit (socialization): where individuals directly share and test knowledge
- tacit-to-explicit (externalization): the transformation of knowledge into a tangible form through documentation or discussion
- explicit-to-explicit (combination): combining different forms of explicit knowledge such as documents or databases
- explicit-to-tacit (internalization): where individuals internalize knowledge from documents, discussion or learning into their own body of knowledge.

This idea is used widely by authors and presenters and is generally shown graphically in quadrants such as those in Figure 3.1.

This illustration has influenced many organizations in their development of approaches to KM. Subsequent writers and organizations have adopted other ways of describing the focus of the approach but all reflect:

- people and culture
- customers, partners and markets
- technology, space and organizational structures
- content and intellectual capital.

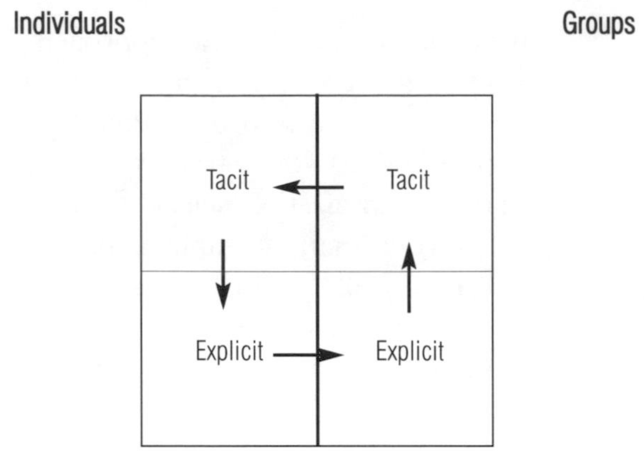

Individuals   Groups

Fig. 3.1 *Exchanging and capturing tacit and explicit knowledge*

Organizations take different approaches to the business improvement process, building corporate capability in ways that reflect their particular priorities and concerns. The approaches are not exclusive but the primary focus will dictate the features that emerge. As Nonaka and Takeuchi point out, there is no correct or systematic way to create a knowledge environment. Activities can be stimulated by a need, recognized in any part of an organization, or proposed to address problems in any one of the quadrants. Such activities, once introduced, will trigger others.

Michael Earl of London Business School suggests that the approaches can be classified under the main headings of Technocratic or Behavioural with associated foci, aims and breadth. His thesis is being developed more fully in an article to be published in 2001.

An alternative analysis of types of approach is to plot them on to the quadrant suggested by Nonaka and Takeuchi, thus reflecting the relative emphasis placed on mechanism for improving the interaction between tacit and explicit knowledge. See Figure 3.2.

Tacit to explicit

In this model activities on the left – those that focus on converting tacit knowledge into explicit knowledge – include processes for:

- building databases that share best practice
- directories (Yellow Pages) of skills and expertise
- the formal gathering and integration of knowledge about customers, competitors, market environments, product development

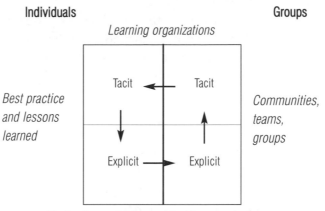

Fig. 3.2 *Exchanging and capturing tacit and explicit knowledge*

- intellectual assets management
- mapping and signposting knowledge.

Consultancy firms such as PricewaterhouseCoopers (PwC) focus many of their KM activities on building explicit knowledge bases, together with cultural change activities oriented towards improving consultants' ability and willingness to record and re-use what they have learnt on assignments. The challenge of enabling project staff to record experience gained has led organizations, such as ICL and KPMG, to employ journalists to interview project staff and summarize key points.

Explicit to explicit

The technology axis focuses on access to explicit knowledge and the facilitation of communication between individuals, resulting in the development of intranets, portals and communications platforms to facilitate the exchange of knowledge with sophisticated functionality. BG Technology, for example, have developed an intranet that enables access to team and group documentation at a variety of levels and facilitates the identification of experience and expertise.

Explicit to tacit

Dow Chemicals started its approach to KM by taking stock of its patents – its intellectual assets – designing processes that identified what assets they owned, whether they were being used, which had potential for additional exploitation, and how that could be realized. The initiative increased revenue by millions of dollars a year.

Explicit to tacit and tacit to tacit

Approaches on the right and at the top of this model focus on sharing, nurturing and building tacit knowledge and are primarily concerned with facilitating interaction between people and the development of partnerships, networks and communities of interest. They include spaces and facilities designed to encourage both formal and informal conversations; ways of sharing best practice and lessons learned through discussion, master classes and stories; and also individual development and learning. They are also very focused on changing organization cultures and individual behaviours. The activities on the learning organization axis, on the other hand, place learning and development within the framework of the whole organization as a learning environment.

Whatever the theories, the practical approaches taken by organizations reflect the areas that they judge will produce most business benefit. They tend to start with a focus on one of four themes:

- people: including the development of sharing behaviours, and the skills required for people to operate effectively in a knowledge-based environment.
- organizational culture: dealing with the way in which the organization is structured and operates, its value system and cohesion, and the development of common purpose and objectives.
- processes: creating business processes that embed knowledge building and utilization into everyday working practices
- corporate physical and technical infrastructure: starting with the premise that physical and technological facilities enable or inhibit the knowledge environment.

The earliest approaches favoured the infrastructure focus, in particular the utilization of information technology as the major driver of knowledge capture and sharing. Initially, knowledge management became synonymous with capturing and collecting, with building databases of 'knowledge', with using web technology to provide access to silos of information throughout the organization, and with the installation of groupware and communications technology to encourage communication and sharing. This focus was relatively short lived. Attempts to utilize technology for knowledge sharing highlighted issues of organizational culture and people development. The focus shifted to these latter issues which remain firmly at the centre of many knowledge management programmes.

The importance of processes has been an underlying theme, reflecting other initiatives that place the understanding of key business processes at the core of organizational success. The creation of knowledge-building processes aligned to business objectives is the objective of many KM initiatives.

> Whatever we choose to call it, the main thing is that we have to manage the knowledge processes and we have to have access to the knowledge.
> (Jaakko Ihamuotila, Chairman and CEO, Neste Corporation)

The focus on people reflects the need to build organizational capability, including the ability to build processes and know-how unique to the organization, based on the expertise and skills of its staff. The 'learning organization' approach seeks not only to identify and build on best practice and good methodology, but also to build and develop teams who continue to learn and develop, and have the confidence to contribute to, and challenge, corporate knowledge.

Learning organizations and corporate universities

The learning organization is an approach connected to the purpose and strategy of the organization which seeks to identify and learn from its corporate experience. The objectives are to create a flexible, agile organization able to handle uncertainty, using learning to generate new ways of working, to build on success and learn by mistakes. It is, in some organizations, their explicit approach to building a knowledge environment, but even where this is not the case the aspects of organizational learning, creating an environment for personal and team learning and effectiveness, are very evident. British Airways (Rapley, 1999) identified culture as the biggest barrier to learning and sharing and set out to create an environment where learning and sharing was easy. This included providing time and space for learning, with public areas conducive to meeting and informal interaction, together with facilities to access repositories of knowledge, training facilities and libraries. Internal experience is enhanced by exposure to external expertise and the process is underpinned by processes that reinforce the benefits of participating in learning and development. The facilitation of personal contacts and networks and the enhanced role of training and development as a core activity become part of the new culture. British Airways developed a network of information and learning access points, Quest Centres, to facilitate access to self-development and training programmes complementing courses designed for individuals, teams and communities.

British Aerospace views its entire organization as a university, devising integrated frameworks for learning and research: 'A coherent strategy to share and leverage knowledge and best practice and linking business needs to learning and research' (Kenney-Wallace, 1999). Its 'academic' body includes employees and contractors, company partners and members of its supply chain. This Virtual University, a strategic partnership between academe and enterprise, is a 'business strategy towards international competitiveness', based upon British Aerospace plc becoming 'the Benchmark' through individual and corporate learning, research and technology. It is an approach based on partnerships: 'a learning strategy for all employees, twining academic and business excellence, aligned to business strategy'.

As mentioned earlier, Anglian Water became a private company in 1989 and began to develop a global strategy in 1990. It used the learning organization approach as the primary mechanism to change the culture of the organization from that of a public utility to one of a company needing to respond to a new commercial environment with shareholders. It needed to increase the level of service and become essentially customer focused, improve cost effectiveness and grow the business. In 1993 it began its 'transformation journey', which included the development of its University of Water, reflecting its belief in learning as the major foundation of change.

Corporate memory – Knowledge is the only renewable resource

The corporate memory resides in the heads of the people who work with and for the organization, the information they create and the records they make or acquire. Knowledge management processes set out to make the corporate memory effective and robust, enabling the whole organization to learn from previous corporate experience. Corporate instinct is developed through a healthy and active corporate memory – collective knowledge and organizational 'know-how'. The recognition of this fact has been a long time coming but the KM philosophy, and authors such as Kransdorff (1998), have emphasized the point that staff mobility and new contracts of work mean that organizations are losing valuable knowledge and corporate 'insight' whenever their staff walk out the door.

Corporate memory is a complex mix of who knows what, who has been where, who understands through analysis, who understands through intuition and the information collected and recorded throughout the organization. Corporate memory is the natural product of a knowledge-based approach, but some organizations have concentrated their KM efforts on 'collection and storage' as an end in itself. Far from building a corporate memory they have built electronic filing cabinets which are no more likely to be consulted than the physical ones.

Although 'KM software' covers a range of products that may or may not assist in the building of a dynamic and living corporate memory, the concept is generating a great deal of thought about how information is used and accessed and what can be recorded and codified, and the imaginative use of packages such as Insight, Excalibur and Autonomy.

Technology

Information and communications technology is a key enabler of a knowledge environment. The message from all organizations is that it should be harnessed to support knowledge, it should not be the driver. Neither should it be a barrier. Despite rapid developments, many fundamental KM concepts and principles are not dependent on employing the latest release or the next generation of software. Increasingly it is recognized that it is effective implementation of IT that can help change behaviour for the benefit of knowledge sharing, while poorly managed implementation can be detrimental.

The most common and visible development has been the use of web technology to build knowledge-sharing environments although one of the early KM pioneers, Buckman Laboratories, based their

K'Netix™, the backbone of their global knowledge sharing forums, on e-mail systems, Compuserve initially, with a recent migration to Outlook Express. The intranet lies at the heart of most knowledge systems, allowing access to diverse data sources, discussion groups and signposting. BG Technology, for example, use their intranet to provide a document library, discussion forums and databases for teams and groups, with connecting areas for sharing appropriate material throughout the company. It is highly structured and carefully managed and provides the core of their KM initiative.

Software for CSCW (Computer Supported Co-operative Working), groupware such as Lotus Notes (and collaborative software such as BT Presence) also feature in enabling shared working. The use of ICT enables virtual working that is almost akin to sitting round a table together, but online working needs careful facilitating and leadership. It requires new skills and mindsets, and while it allows more inclusion for some it presents barriers for others. Paradoxically, collaborative software enables people in one room to work creatively together by providing the opportunity to contribute to discussions, present and challenge ideas, and vote on outcomes, *anonymously*, thus allowing the group to have a frank discussion without individuals feeling inhibited by their lack of confidence, or status. This approach also needs careful facilitation, as do discussion groups, bulletin boards and online training. Use of IT in knowledge sharing demands that the team has skills available other than technical ones. These are dealt with in more detail elsewhere in this book.

Features

At the Strategic Planning Society Conference in 1999, Michael Earl spoke of the '5 Cs of knowledge management': Communities, Communication, Connectivity, Codification and Confidence. The outcomes of the TFPL Chief Knowledge Officers' Summits suggest that there are two primary aims – Connection as well as Collection. Whatever the semantics, there are a number of distinguishable features within organizations that are developing knowledge environments. They are not mutually exclusive. Nor do they fit neatly with the particular approaches that an organization takes to build its knowledge community. Many features are common to all approaches.

In the third volume of his work *Knowledge management methods* (1995) Karl Wiig deals with the building blocks of KM. In his detailed discussion of the development of activities to management knowledge he identifies and puts into context many activities that have become features of knowledge environments, and provides the following illustrations.

Building blocks to create knowledge

1 Experts build knowledge tacitly and hold it personally within their own minds

Innovative individuals who discover or invent new approaches through their work or through research become the (recognized) experts and knowledge resources.

2 'Lessons-Learned' systems

Formal systems whereby, after each 'episode' worthy of remembering, those involved sit down and discuss and document the nature of the situation and what has been learned. Results are assembled and kept in a repository to be:

- referred to whenever a user determines a need to consult them
- used as training material
- used as input to knowledge professionals for extraction, codification, and other means of dissemination.

3 Individuals 'self-elicit' and encode their own knowledge

Individuals are equipped with knowledge-elicitation tools to explain what they know so others can use it.

4 Knowledge Professionals (KPs) elicit and encode knowledge from experts

A designated team of highly competent KPs work with experts (perhaps on a periodic or 'roving' basis) to model their knowledge for inclusion in a knowledge deployment mechanism.

Building blocks to disseminate knowledge

1 Reassignment of personnel to new functions

Experts in one area are assigned (often temporarily) to work in a different function to transfer their knowledge.

2 Expert networks

Formal referral paths to experts to provide backup and support within areas of expertise

Informal (often unwanted – considered unwelcome interruptions) access to experts — often based on who knows whom and how much goodwill requesters have in the eyes of experts.

3 Roving 'emissary'

A person who is usually knowledgeable in many non routine areas travels between field offices to work there, and to communicate new practices and lessons learned.

4 Distribution of 'lessons learned' documents

Periodic distribution to all locations of a printed document.

5 Training or educational programs

Periodic training seminars to communicate 'what has been learned'
Multimedia formalized training programs.

6 Passive or active knowledge base on the network

Knowledge expressed in the form of natural language in computer-based 'knowledge base' available for querying when problems arise
Codified knowledge in computer-based 'knowledge base' available for querying when problems arise.

7 Active Knowledge Based System (KBS) on knowledge worker's workstation

Advisory KBS that responds with suggestions
- the user presents a situation or
- when the KBS determines the presence of a situation for which it has advice.

(Wiig, 1995)

Leadership

The knowledge environment is enabled by top management and there is one issue on which all academics, writers and practitioners agree – the need for strong leadership. Understanding of leadership has changed dramatically in the last decade. It is a topic that has attracted almost as much research and media interest as knowledge management. In a lecture for the RSA Amin Rajan presented some of the findings of a research study in which he interviewed 120 business and community leaders and over 500 professionals who have the substantive responsibility for developing leaders inside their own organizations (Rajan, 1996). The results suggest that the knowledge age has created a need for more leadership but of a style very different to that of the authoritarian leaders of the past. Management of organizations in the knowledge age is about managing tacit knowledge to increase the speed of innovation, but 'tacit knowledge walks on two feet' and management of talented people is different from the old style of management. It is a style that motivates and inspires, nurtures a healthy corporate culture and attracts followers. The keywords associated with leadership that emerged from this study included 'vision', 'passion' and 'persistence'. Among the high level of required leadership skills identified are included the ability to inspire trust and to motivate, and a willingness to listen.

Tacit knowledge is about insights and instincts. An organization can live within walls or via communication networks. Structures are changing, there is a move away from control and command hierarchies to the facilitation of creative groups of people. The leadership of such organizations is dynamic, creating and communicating a vision and making available resources to enable individuals and groups to achieve that vision. Leadership cannot be confined to one inspirational individual. Leadership is distributed throughout the organization and is as important to successful outcomes in teams, communities, departments and on projects as in the Board Room. A successful corporate leader can inspire, but needs other leaders to deliver the vision. Leadership becomes a skill that is nurtured in many people, and an area where a diverse range of people are encouraged to explore and develop their potential.

Partnership

Partnership is a key KM concept in the outward-facing knowledge environment. The customer-orientated approach builds relationships with clients and suppliers and alliances with other organizations, and seeks to become part of a number of market, geographical and social communities. It is an environment where customers and suppliers work together to develop what is required for the marketplace by the preferred route, rather than playing one supplier off against another. It is also an environment where the stakeholders not only include the suppliers of finance, the staff, suppliers and customers, but also the local, national and international community. It is based on a recognition of mutual dependency and respect.

Partners may also include potential competitors. The emerging world of communications brings together the telecom, computer and media industries with end products that encompass publishing, entertainment and communication. Within just one area, that of mobile telecommunications, industry relationships are complex and face many challenges in a fast-moving arena where swiftly developing technology and applications are creating new allies and competitors across industry sectors. Two of British Telecom's KM initiatives reflect the complexity of those partnerships and the extent to which the development of the area is dependent on the effective leveraging of knowledge and experience. 'Mobility Leaders' and 'Netconnexions' provide a platform and portal of knowledge sharing for their external alliance partners and strategic business partners. The fact that some of these partners in the mobile area may also be competitors in other arenas is acknowledged and illustrates the extent to which knowledge sharing can be seen as more strategically valuable than hoarding. Similarly, the pharmaceutical sector is increasingly one of growing alliances, a complex supply chain and cooperative networks, where competitors may be among the cooperating organizations.

External partnerships raise many issues around knowledge sharing, issues such as intellectual property, matters of trust and respect, the practical problems of managing the knowledge exchange process. Similar issues arise when attempting to create partnerships – close working relationships – between individuals and groups from different parts of a business or organization.

Team working, communities and networking

Corporate knowledge is a mix of tacit and explicit – that has become a KM truism. Tacit knowledge is the unique mix of a person's expertise, experience and knowledge of their world that enables them to understand and see significance in information or to undertake tasks, build solutions or contribute to problem solving. Explicit knowledge is that which can be articulated and communicated, and perhaps recorded. The mix is complicated and its management has become the focus of many KM activities. The emphasis on converting tacit to recorded explicit – downloading the brain – misses part of the point. The process by which an individual:

• makes a particular decision
• arrives at a particular conclusion
• places a particular interpretation on a piece of information
• decides to undertake a task in a particular way
• decides what is 'best practice' while something else needs improving

is all part of their understanding and skill, experience and expertise which enables them to act – which makes them knowledgeable. The sharing of such knowledge helps others to learn and enriches the individual who shares. The act of trying to visualize and explain the knowledge they have moves that knowledge on. Others contribute – knowledge grows. Working on problems together, recognizing expertise wherever it resides in the organization and the sharing of expertise and problem solving is key to building knowledge.

Mechanisms to improve this exchange of knowledge, which requires a mutual trust on the part of the participants and some aspect of reward and recognition, focus on the building of teams, communities and networks.

Team working is certainly not new; what has developed significantly is the building of teams of people with different backgrounds, experience, locations and concerns. Skandia's Futures Centre purposely includes mixed ages, younger people to bring new ideas, older people to bring experience. Cross-functional and multidiscipline teams with a common purpose are more likely to result in creative solutions. Virtual teams with a common goal and infrastructure support can share experience and expertise to solve problems or develop ideas. The example of British Petroleum's (BP) work with virtual teams is a valuable indication of what an organization can achieve through an imaginative approach to team building. First they identified a specific issue – that of problem solving on oil platforms. BP was, and is, a performance-orientated company: managers on oil platforms have individual targets to meet. They also work in environments where many technical problems and challenges can arise. Obviously the quicker the solution, the less downtime or impact on production. BP is also a company that has technical expertise dispersed throughout the world – on oil platforms, refineries and elsewhere. People working on any problem can benefit from the past experience of anyone who has encountered the same problem or who has relevant expertise. A group of experienced people working together on the problem is even more effective. BP's problem was to bring expertise together, as required and quickly, from dispersed locations, without disrupting the smooth running of their individual operations. Modern communications and information technology provide the platform for a virtual meeting place, but the key lay in their investment in training and developing the potential team members, in building trust and the willingness to help each other. The cultural development was as important as the technological one (Collison, 1999).

Communities are fundamental to a knowledge environment. They provide a mechanism for informal knowledge exchange, personal and group learning and for the development of ideas and best practice. Communities are based on groups of people with a common sense of purpose and common interests, who share work-related knowledge and experience. They operate through relationships built on trust, respect, loyalty and friendship, as well as for mutual advantage. To operate successfully within an organization communities need recognition and support – people need to feel that it is a valued activity. Meeting and communication is important. There is some debate as to whether 'formal' communities can be successful but many organizations encourage formal or informal communities and in some cases both. Typically, communities of interest are created or facilitated in order that people who may not work together can discuss their areas of interest and create an informal development and learning group. These tend to be informal, while communities of practice support people with roles that have common professional concerns. The latter are essentially networks that people may join and where their participation is a question of personal responsibility.

Community activity is often focused on the intranet with support for individual home pages and community sites, such as AstraZeneca's Concert community (Brown, 1999). Shell's view of 'communities' is that people like to connect with others with similar issues or problems and are willing to listen to their peers. Shell's view is that communities work when a business imperative exists to improve performance, although they may be geographically or organizationally dispersed.

Sharing

ICL is a people business, and is about giving people the right toolkits. With knowledge management I want to get into a position where the individuals have at their finger tips all of the knowledge that I have and all of the access to knowledge that I have.

(Keith Todd, then Chief Executive, ICL)

The objectives of networking, communities and teams is to encourage the sharing of information and knowledge and one of the most common goals of many KM activities is to encourage knowledge sharing. It is also one of the areas that is felt to be most difficult. While most organizations will admit that knowledge sharing requires a change in corporate culture, from 'information is power' to 'knowledge sharing builds power', many also look at the application of rewards and incentives to encourage knowledge-sharing behaviours. There have been some experiments with financial incentives, paying salesmen for contributing their contacts to a common pool, for example, but these have not been considered effective enough for others to follow. In a previously referred-to example, Bob Buckman of Buckman Laboratories speaks of his 'carrot and stick' approach in the early days of building his technology-based knowledge-sharing culture as being a way of demonstrating that he was committed to the approach. His visible monitoring of who was participating, with ad hoc rewards, helped prepare the ground and build the culture.

The most effective way of encouraging individual sharing appears to be through appraisal systems where individuals are asked to assess their own knowledge-sharing behaviours and consider their colleagues' view of their sharing performance. The results of appraisals may affect promotion and salary, but their use is part of the development of a culture that includes knowledge sharing as a core competence. There is an increasing trend to identify and agree core competencies that include sharing.

But it is generally accepted that 'intrinsic motivation' is the only real motivator of knowledge sharing. An individual, group or community sympathetic to each other's goals and those of the organization work for collective goals – and if these are best achieved through sharing knowledge, that is what happens. This is the philosophy held by those KM exponents who emphasize the importance of 'modern' leadership and the development of corporate values that reflect the values and aspirations of those that make up the organization. Intrinsic motivation is the business of management, and is more about ensuring that reward and recognition systems are those that make individuals want to feel part of the business, than devising either carrots or sticks.

Knowledge mapping

Sooner, rather than later, any organization looking to improve its knowledge infrastructure starts to undertake, or discuss, a knowledge-mapping exercise. If the organization is fundamentally about creating and exploiting knowledge then it needs to understand the key knowledge flows. Who knows what? What do they need to know? How do they find out? What knowledge does the company have? What knowledge is created and what happens to it? What supports and what hinders knowledge flow? These are the questions that knowledge mapping seeks to answer.

Patricia Seeman at Hoffman LaRoche was one of the early pioneers of applying knowledge mapping in a business critical area. Focusing on new drug development she mapped the knowledge flow around this crucial area where 'every day gained in the market availability of a new drug, Roche had determined, the company stood to gain a million dollars' (Seeman, 1998).

A knowledge map is a representation of the knowledge assets of the company, tacit (experts, groups, organizations) and explicit (records in documents and databases, on tape or video, etc). It will cover internal and external assets and show how these flow into and out of the business process. Figure 3.3 is an example of a top-level knowledge map, and Figure 3.4 is an example of an outcomes flow diagram.

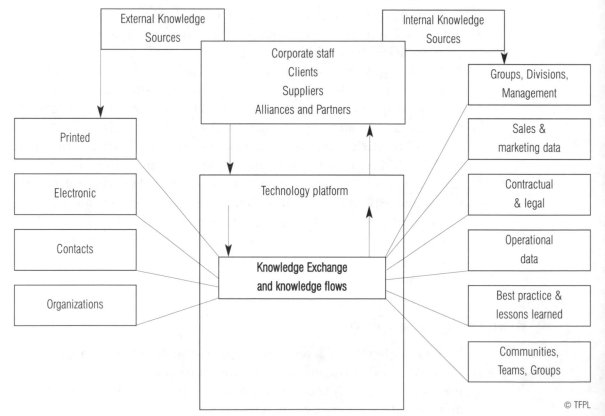

Fig. 3.3 *A top-level knowledge map. Source TFPL*

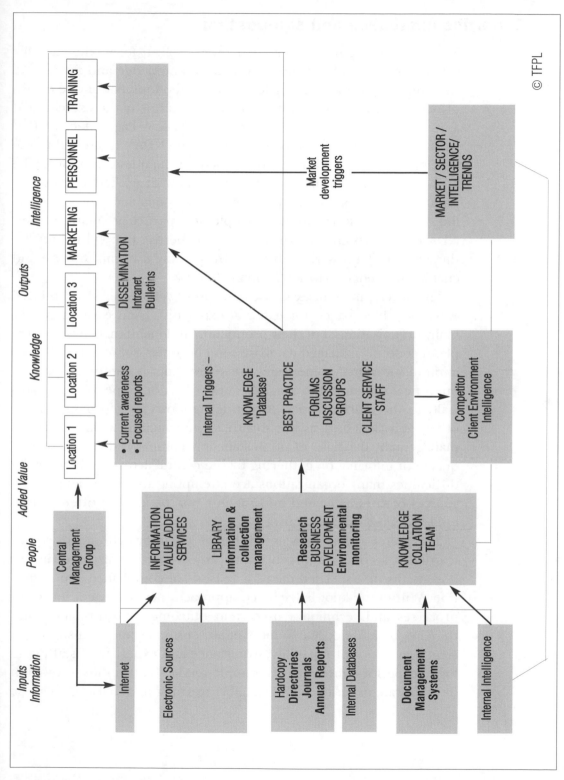

Fig. 3.4 *Outcomes flow diagram. Source TFPL*

Expertise databases and signposting

Knowledge mapping is not an activity in itself. It forms the basis for the development of a strategy to manage knowledge and for tactical decisions. Typically, mapping leads to the development of one or two primary activities. In the case of Hoffman LaRoche the exercise had a very specific objective and led to a 'Yellow Pages' facility that pointed to experts in new drug applications (NDA). It also led to the development of a 'Question Tree' based on the questions that Roche knew it needed to answer about every new drug. These questions pointed to the source of the answer. It also enabled more dynamic links to be developed to alert people at a particular phase in their NDA to the existence of knowledge or expertise that exists but that they may not necessarily hunt out. In this way it began to drive and enable knowledge sharing (Seeman, 1998).

The development of expertise databases ('yellow pages' for internal expertise, 'blue pages' for external expertise), is an early target for many organizations, but their production and maintenance is not simple. A centrally managed database soon becomes out of date. The creation of individual home pages on the intranet is another approach, but it needs to appeal to a significant proportion of people and especially to the reticent expert. Creating signposts to information from other activities, such as the wealth of information within a project management database of a construction company, depends on the quality of information gathering by the central activity. Whatever the difficulties many organizations are attempting to create signposts to sources of knowledge and information, and people are often considered the most valuable source.

The use of project files as sources of key information and lessons learned is a common target. Many project-based firms have files of documents of associated data for reasons of compliance and regulation. Within the knowledge-based approach they become a source of processes and techniques used, and outcomes; interpretation and thinking by knowledgeable individuals; customer and industry experience; evidence of capability; experience and expertise of staff; costing and performance records; sample tenders and results – a wealth of corporate experience and valuable learning materials.

The value of intellectual capital

Some organizations argue that identifying and building the value of their intellectual capital is the main feature of their KM programme. Skandia's view, as stated earlier, is that the non-financial aspects of a company are as crucial in determining its worth as its financial worth or shareholder value. In their model, human capital and the people who work for the organization – their quality, their management, and their ability to learn and adapt – determine the future of the organization. Customer capital is the relationship with the marketplace. Customers are the future of any organization, private or public. Determining and organizing intellectual assets is a significant part of knowledge mapping. For some exponents the management of intellectual capital equates with knowledge management. In an environment where the business scorecard, EFQM'S Excellence Model, or something similar is used as a basis for defining a set of performance measures, knowledge about intellectual assets will be critical.

Lessons learned, best practice and storytelling

Transferring good and bad experience, what worked and what didn't, becomes an important aspect of the knowledge environment. Asking people to record their learning from a project or bid process, asking them to admit what went wrong, and why, and what can be learned from it, or to record 'best practice', has a number of culture challenges. Developing an environment where people feel it is permissible to make mistakes and ask for help has been part of the KM focus. Examples have been taken from military practices of debriefing, and the Israeli airforce approach of filming fighter crews in action to enable frank discussion round the video. Processes to enable the discussion and capture of lessons learned are becoming a feature of knowledge environments.

Mechanisms are being developed to enable the organization to trap and replicate successful practices. Shell International uses web-enabled technology to support Practice Excellence through Accelerated Replication (PEARL), which is designed quickly and simply to share successful practices, tailored to the Shell/Texaco refining environment, among those who can benefit. The purpose of PEARL is to increase the return on assets of refineries by sharing learning, assisting in managing knowledge, capturing potential synergies, and to increase community pride (see Figure 3.5) (Charalambous, 1999).

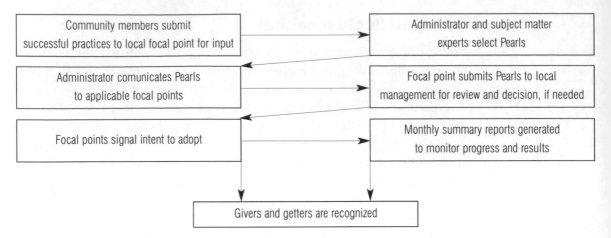

Fig. 3.5 *PEARL. Source Charalambous (1999)*

There are many practical issues involved in capturing lessons learned and best practice. PEARL technology is tailored to the business process and addresses to an extent the issue of finding the time to undertake the additional effort required for recording and sharing. PEARL is an approach to embedding the knowledge creation and utilization process in the business process, although such an approach cannot take for granted the ability to identify and describe key points from successful practices.

The quality of submissions to any lessons learned/best practice system needs management. As already noted, ICL and KPMG are examples of two organizations which have employed professional journalists to help capture post-project experience and coach people in writing relevant and accessible summaries. Other organizations, for example Booz, Allen and Hamilton, have mixed teams of subject experts and content specialists to review and monitor submissions.

Content

In creating KM initiatives it has become apparent to many organizations that they are dealing with 'content'. Content is not only the information and data that resides in databases and printed documents. It is the messages that are contained in e-mails and group discussions, the newsfeeds from external and internal sources, the outcomes of discussions and presentations: any knowledge that is recorded for use by a number of people. Once exchange of information and knowledge is encouraged and facilitated the need to be able to assess and manage the content becomes crucial. Knowledge initiatives have given rise to an interest in codification of information and a means of assessing its quality and currency.

While 'content management' is not a specific focus of a knowledge management initiative it is fast becoming a fundamental prerequisite of success. The Knowledge Café of ICL, an innovative use of an intranet, is an example of an early adoption of the principle that knowledge posted should have both an owner, giving validity to the information and a contact for expertise, and also a review date, to ensure currency and accuracy. 'Content', explicit knowledge recorded in appropriate vehicles, and with structures and codification that allow ease of access and use, is becoming the added value of knowledge management. The need for structure and codification – classification and indexing – has fuelled the interest in a raft of information management skills and tools, such as corporate taxonomies, which facilitate the delivery of 'the right information to the right person at the right time'. Information management is not a focus for building a knowledge environment, but it is an enabler that is rapidly gaining recognition.

From KM to quick wins

Despite the early KM hype, knowledge management, as mentioned earlier, is fast losing its capital letters. As an increasing number of organizations asscss what benefits the KM philosophy offers, there is more emphasis on the identification of activities with real business potential through a KM approach. This is achieved through stimulating the evolution of a corporate knowledge base and creative environment rather than through major corporate 'big bang' change. It is a change of management approach based on a senior management commitment to activities that are grown and led through the workforce. 'Quick wins' is a term used to describe mechanisms to deliver a benefit within a timeframe that allows the approach to demonstrate a real (short-term) benefit to the organization and the people involved. In some organizations this will be aimed at facilitating communication between people with common interests and problems, in others it will have an operational target, such as saving costs in purchasing. The quick win is achievable, has business benefit and answers the question 'what is in it for me?'. It also begins to identify and address the organizational, cultural and practical issues that are inherent in changing working practices.

A number of KM practitioners argue that caution is needed with this approach. Bipin Junnarkar says of the KM developments in Monsanto that 'If Monsanto's efforts at knowledge management are succeeding, it is probably due most to our holistic approach. Rather than relying on a single bullet, such as knowledge sharing incentives, or groupware, Monsanto is drawing on a whole arsenal of people, process, and technology related changes' (Junnarkar, 1998). While accepting that argument, many 'quick wins' address the people, process and technology issues within a cross-functional, corporate-wide approach.

Conclusions

While there are many paths to the development of a learning organization or knowledge management environment there is no single 'best' way. There are certain challenging fundamentals, centred around the people and the culture of the organization, that are critical to success and it is clear that KM, however it is implemented or whatever approach is used, is not something that is handed down as a management edict. KM implementation is a participative activity which has to be led from the top but driven from throughout the organization.

References:

Brown, F (1999)   *Project Concert: effective external investment for AstraZeneca Pharmaceuticals Amoco*, SPS Knowledge Management Conference 99, October 1999.

Charalambous, I A (1999) *Knowledge and best practice sharing*, SPS Knowledge Management Conference 99, October 1999.

Collison, C (1999) *Knowledge capture and sharing and BP Amoco*, SPS Knowledge Management Conference 99, October 1999.

Earl, M (1999) *Emerging strategies or knowledge management*, SPS Knowledge Management Conference 99, October 1999.

Hansen, Morten T et al (1999) What's your strategy for managing knowledge?, *Harvard Business Review* (March–April), 106–116.

Junnarkar, B (1998) *Creating fertile ground for knowledge at Monsanto*, available at
www.businessinnovation.ey.com/journal/issue1/features/creati/ body/html

Kenney-Wallace, G (1999) *Positioning knowledge management to the top of the strategic agenda*, SPS Knowledge Management Conference 99, October 1999.

Kransdorff, A (1998) *Corporate amnesia: keeping know-how in the company*, Butterworth-Heinemann.

Nonaka, I and Takeuchi, H (1995) *The knowledge creating company*, Oxford University Press.

Rajan, A (1996) *Leading people*. CREATE.

Rapley, K (1999) *Stimulating a learning culture in British Airways*, SPS Knowledge Management Conference 99, October 1999.

Seeman, P (1998) A prescription for knowledge management: What the Hoffman LaRoche case can teach others, Business Innovation 1, available at **www.businessinnovation.ey.com/journal/issue**

Wiig, K M (1995) *Knowledge management methods: Practical approaches to managing knowledge*, Schema Press.

Part 2

Creating knowledge-
based environments

4

Integrating information and knowledge

Knowledge or information

The previous chapters have concentrated on knowledge and corporate approaches to improving the creation, flow and use thereof. As we hope that we have demonstrated, the building of a knowledge environment is dependent on dynamic interaction; it is the interaction between people and information that creates knowledge, and it is the ability to express and share that knowledge that creates a 'knowledgeable environment'. Information is exchanged between people within an organization, and between them and the people who represent their marketplace – customers, suppliers, partners, regulators, government and many other stakeholders. Information in many formats flows around, in and out of the organization. It may be the outcome of 'knowledge work' or the by-product of daily operations; it may be complete in itself – providing the definitive answer to specific questions; it may be a signposting/road map to expertise or a collection of information; or just part of a bigger picture.

The most common of the many definitions of the difference between knowledge and information is the pyramid illustrating a progression from data, through information with knowledge at the apex. In some versions this is capped by wisdom. This hierarchical approach, while simple to deal with, does not allow for subtleties or complexities, for the data that is one man's information and for the information that is knowledge when transferred to another. The difference is essentially that knowledge is about the ability to understand context, see connections and spot significance when dealing with information. Individual and organizational learning and experience convert information into knowledge and a knowledge-based environment is founded on an understanding of the dynamics of that process. It understands

- what information there is, and where it is
- what people do with it and why
- if people don't use it, why they don't
- the end result of its use.

In addition it can map where skill and experience reside, how they impact on the business and the effects of organizational change and development.

The discussion of the difference between knowledge and information is absorbing and it is worth considering the concepts and language used when discussing their interaction. The KM approach has, if nothing else, begun to re-awaken an interest in the power of language as the vehicle through which we express ideas and concepts, as the means by which we exclude or include people groups, and its use as a defence mechanism. Information technologists have become as notorious as doctors once were for using a language that is difficult for a layperson to penetrate with confidence and accuracy. Other professions use their own vocabulary as a means to communicate precisely and easily with each other, and at the same time to assess the expertise of new acquaintances through their understanding and use of this language. The information profession has been as guilty as all the others in this respect and is now seeing their professional concepts being 'reinvented' and represented by a new language. Taxonomies, for example, have become an accepted feature of a KM environment, together with codified information. In such environments the terms thesaurus, classification and cataloguing are not much used, although in practice they are much in evidence. Tacit and explicit knowledge have become part of business vocabulary – but not structured and unstructured information. The point, however, is that information and knowledge meet, converge and overlap. They are not the same but it is difficult to see how one exists without the other. Information is not of itself valuable. Its value is in its use and its effective use depends on the ability of an individual to see meaning and significance in that information and thus to create new knowledge. Knowledge, on the other hand, is equally lacking in value unless used. Richard Branson's insight and flair, enabling him to provide novel services to the market, is knowledge – a mix of the information he gleans from a variety of sources and activities, his ability to spot meaning and opportunity from that information, and his expertise and experience which enable him to decide on a course of action. This only has value if he can communicate the ideas and the information needed to support the solution. At some point in the process knowledge produces information in order that actions can take place. The data/information/knowledge relationship is more of a circle than a pyramid (see Figure 4.1).

In summary, knowledge is the expertise, experience and capability of staff, integrated with processes and corporate memory; information is the raw material that knowledge work requires and is made up of a variety of forms and types. It may be ephemeral or part of the information assets of the organization. Tom Stewart, a prominent journalist, editorial board member of *Fortune Magazine* and author of 'Intellectual Capital', differentiates between intellectual capital (that which the organization needs to retain and manage for future use) and working intellectual capital (that which flows through the organization and relates only to day-to-day operations). The challenge for any organization is to manage and link the two.

Perhaps the simplest definition, however, is that knowledge is what people know; information is how they communicate it.

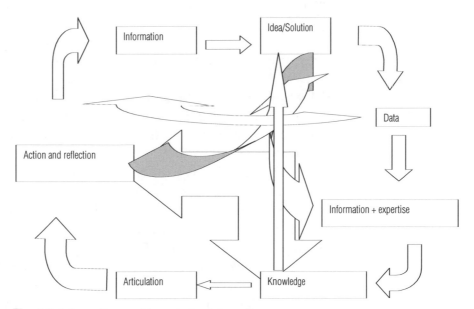

Fig. 4.1 *Information and knowledge interaction*

Mapping the integration

If the success of a knowledge-based organization depends on understanding these differences and managing the integration process, then the challenge is to understand the knowledge and information flows. Any organization that begins to consider a KM approach sooner or later wants to clarify what exactly is the knowledge and information they seek to manage. Knowledge mapping and information auditing are becoming a popular approach to 'first steps in KM', which is not surprising considering the complexity of information and knowledge that underpins most organizations.

The information component of an organization itself is very complex and there are a number of people from different disciplines involved in the process. Considering that all organizations rely for their success on effective information flows, it is surprising that there is no one cohesive information management discipline. Figure 4.2 illustrates some of the complexity of organizational information flow and Figure 4.3 demonstrates the variety and breadth of functions and departments that have an information management component.

It is this complexity that appears to be responsible for the apparent lack of involvement, at a senior level, of members of the information professions in the understanding, planning and sustaining of KM activities. The organization's most valuable resource is managed by a 'rag bag' of skills, experience and expertise. Each is valid and valuable, but not managed as a cohesive whole. The example that leaps most readily to mind for many is the management of IT as a separate function with no responsibility for content or the use of content. The history of the problems these departments have had in delivering perceived benefit to business units has been well documented, but less well understood is the drag effect of having the infrastructure department at odds with the departments who deliver information.

Operational data is generated by day-to-day activities, and enterprise information systems deliver reports and monitoring data. Document management packages control the creation and lifecycle of business critical documents, sometimes creating new workflow cycles. Datamining resides with IT but records managers are becoming increasingly involved with the content of the records and wrestle with issues around electronic documents. Competitive intelligence departments look for meaning in the information that flows into the organi-

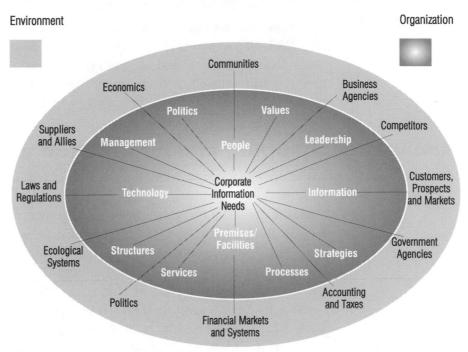

Fig. 4.2 *Complex information*

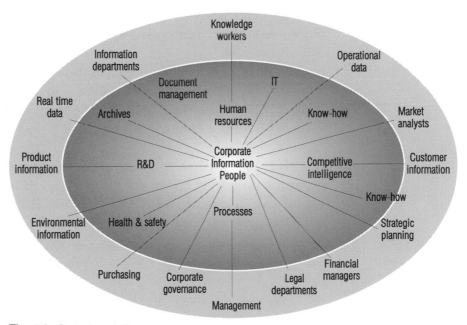

Fig. 4.3 *Complex skills*

zation and market research functions commission and create information. R&D departments produce their own levels of information, often commercially sensitive and increasingly in need of control for regulatory requirements. It is no wonder that senior management is perplexed by the term 'information professional'. What, or who, is it?

Knowledge mapping and information auditing

Knowledge mapping and information auditing are business processes and, as do all business processes, require clear objectives and outcomes. Unless the objectives are clear, the process is unlikely to yield a result that has true value to the organization. In the context of this chapter the objective would be to enable integration of knowledge and information assets, but even that begs the question as to whether the mapping exercise is to enable integration or to investigate the desirability of integration. The whole area of information use and knowledge sharing is sensitive and assumptions about the best course of action to create a KM environment can create unnecessary barriers. Careful definition of the objectives of a mapping or audit process ensures that preconceived ideas are examined. It will also determine the scope and mapping process.

The scope of a mapping exercise, both in terms of its functional coverage and the numbers of people involved, will depend on the objectives and practicality. It will reflect:

- the knowledge and information flows to be covered, whether group, department, site, or organization wide
- the key people affected by any subsequent change or integration
- the stage of the mapping process.

At BNFL Ltd, for example, the process was piloted in a particular department in order to test the process and to demonstrate benefits. In this case the design of the process was department specific and although principles stayed the same, modifications would be made for other departments.

The information audit of the UK's Department of Trade and Industry, on the other hand, was designed from the outset to cover the complete organization. Once the process had been piloted and tested it was standardized across the organization.

The scope may also be determined by the focus of the mapping exercise; whether it is built round individuals, decisions, products or business processes.

Focus on individuals

Although not the most common of approaches, mapping the knowledge and information flows of key individuals can be very illuminating. Such individuals may be identified as 'key' because of their seniority, their 'ownership' of a process or key activity, their role as unofficial knowledge gatekeeper, or their position within as 'information handler'. Provided that their selection does reflect their individual impact on the organization, and not just their seniority and time served, this approach identifies key flows and interaction in a time-efficient way. It also allows an assessment to be made of how far those flows and interactions would be damaged if the individual were to leave and how robust the system would be without them. Take, for example, an individual providing technical support to customers. Although the advent of call centres has made trouble shooting and customer support a heavily process-controlled activity, there are still many individuals who become invaluable within an organization for their ability to deal with the customer interface. Tracking the information use and knowledge applied by these individuals is often the first step in developing an enquiry handling process to deal with the 80% of predictable enquiries in order that the individual can focus their expertise on the remaining 20%. It is also an exercise that enables the organization to identify what can be learnt and shared by integrating one individual's work more closely with that of the people responsible for the product (see Figure 4.4).

Focusing on the individual, however, shows up very readily those exchanges and knowledge flows that take place outside the individual's jurisdiction.

Focus on decisions

Decisions are taken every day by all organizations. Some are operational, some tactical, others strategic. Some are based on closely defined information, often governed by quality standards or other forms of compliance. At the other extreme others are based on instinct. Most are based on the knowledgeable interpretation of information and, in the case of strategic decisions, the ability to assess and

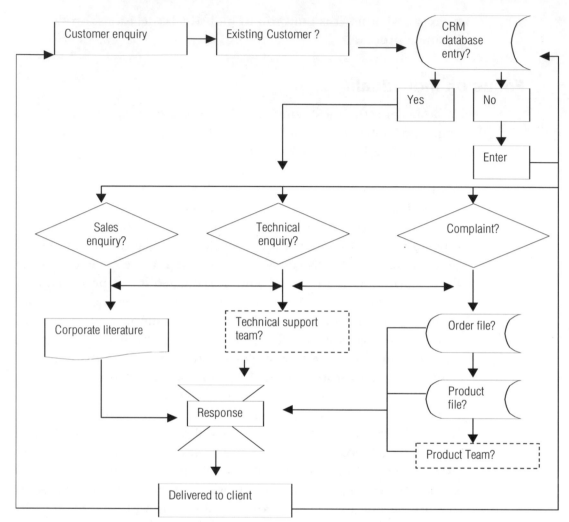

Fig. 4.4 *Mapping operational decisions and information flow – customer support*

manage risk. Some decisions are obviously time critical, but most have an optimum time, and perhaps the first step in decision making is to identify at what time the decision has to be made and the information needed in order to make it. Identifying business critical decisions, and mapping the information and knowledge required by the people who make them, is becoming a valuable approach to building decision-making support systems. For example, the choice of which lead compound to take through to the research phase in a pharmaceutical company is crucial. The costs and the long lead-time needed to take a potential drug through the research and development stage mean that every wrong or delayed decision has a knock-on effect on profitability and competitive position. Integrating the information and knowledge from across the organization to support those decisions has become the aim of every pharmaceutical company.

Focus on products

An alternative is to work backwards from the product or service itself – a sort of reverse engineering. Although this approach has probably been superseded in a formal sense by that based on business processes, it is reflected in the product workshops that became associated with Unilever's knowledge management approach. The Unilever approach is to bring people together from different sites to talk about all aspects of a product – the most well-known example being tomato paste. Through focus workshops every aspect of that product is examined – from the agriculture to the marketing – sharing knowledge across geographies and functions, and between people. The object of this exercise is not necessarily knowledge and information mapping, but the process can be used to identify the integration of information that takes place. Figure 4.5 illustrates at top level the types of information involved and it is possible to drill down in different elements to achieve the level of detail required.

Focus on processes

An understanding of key processes, and the ability to improve or change them as appropriate, has become the ambition of most organizations. This change has not only been brought about by fashionable management approaches. The implementation of enterprise information technology applications required that these processes were well understood if the organization was to achieve return on its investment. Following the early days of IT implementation where the processes were expected to fit the application, process mapping became associated with the development of information systems.

Processes also play an important role in the implementation of KM. They not only cut across functional and departmental silos but are also the means by which KM activities and work processes can be embedded into organizations. Mapping the flow of information and knowledge through, into and out of key processes therefore allows the interaction to be identified across sites and departments and

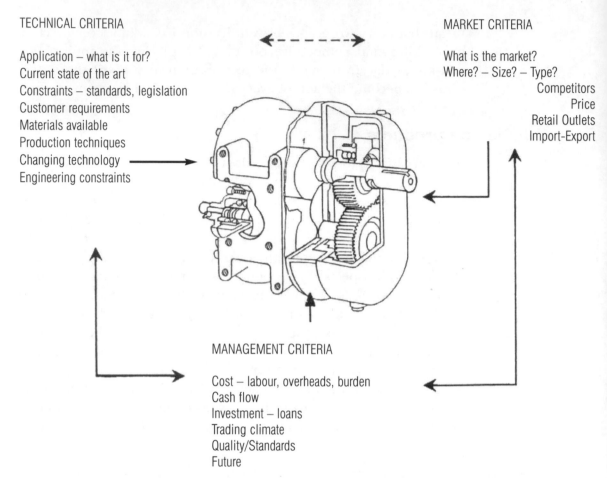

TECHNICAL CRITERIA

Application – what is it for?
Current state of the art
Constraints – standards, legislation
Customer requirements
Materials available
Production techniques
Changing technology
Engineering constraints

MARKET CRITERIA

What is the market?
Where? – Size? – Type?
Competitors
Price
Retail Outlets
Import-Export

MANAGEMENT CRITERIA

Cost – labour, overheads, burden
Cash flow
Investment – loans
Trading climate
Quality/Standards
Future

Fig. 4.5 *Information and knowledge integration in a product*

between processes. It also enables maps to be drawn that relate to current ways of visualizing workflow in many organizations. Figures 4.6 and 4.7 are examples.

Techniques for mapping

Whatever the approach and scope, the techniques for mapping developed will, although tailored to each organization and its culture, have common elements. This book does not set out to cover information audit or knowledge-mapping methodology, and there are several books and articles on the subject. Woody Horton, for example, set out a technique for information mapping in 1988 (Horton and Burke, 1988); Karl Wiig set out sophisticated knowledge mapping, and knowledge use and

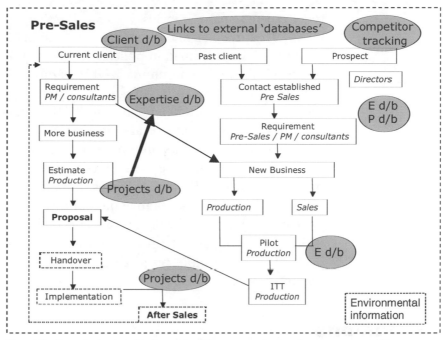

Fig. 4.6 *Knowledge and information flow around a business process (1)*

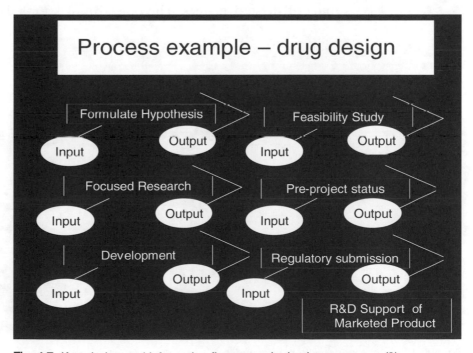

Fig. 4.7 *Knowledge and information flow around a business process (2)*

requirements analysis, in his 1995 work (Wiig, 1995); while Elizabeth Orna talked in detail about information auditing in the second edition of her book on information policies (Orna, 1999).

The TFPL approach, summarized in Figure 4.8, is based on a series of steps that involve those affected by the mapping exercise at every stage. Interviews with key people in the first stage ensure that objectives and business purpose are understood, and that key issues are identified. Group discussions enable information gathering plus sharing of ideas and problems, while face-to-face interviews allow specific problems to be discussed. Questionnaires (if appropriate) are designed to collect quantitative data and their design is informed by the earlier discussions. Conclusions and recommendations are tested with focus groups and presented to the management with action plans. This is a simple project management approach but one that requires a mix of skills.

Conclusions

This chapter set out to demonstrate the complexity of knowledge and information flows in organizations and ways of approaching the mapping of these dynamics. The objective of knowledge management is

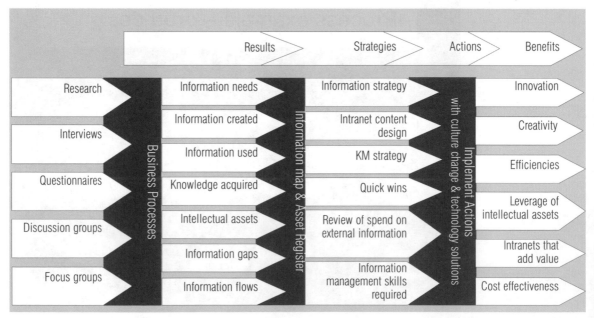

Fig. 4.8 *TFPL approach to information audits*

to build an understanding of and maximize these relationships. The skills of the people who do this are discussed in the following chapters.

References

Horton, W and Burke, C F (1988) *InfoMap: a complete guide to discovering corporate information resources*, Prentice Hall.

Orna, E (1999) *Practical information policies*, Gower.

Wiig, K M (1995) *Knowledge management methods: practical approaches to managing knowledge*, Schema Press.

5

Roles in the knowledge environment

The development of a knowledge environment depends on the ability to create knowledge processes and to convince people to value and to use them, and to develop a knowledge exploitation attitude. Figure 5.1 summarizes the breadth of the task and the areas of influence that need to be addressed. Within this framework sits a range of activities and issues that need to be addressed. The question is, by whom? KM strategies cover Context, Content, Competence, Connectivity, Technology, Process, Culture and Values in order to yield knowledge-based differentiation. This mix dictates the adoption of team approaches from the outset and the roles that emerge create changes in existing structures.

Developing roles and structures

In his 'building blocks of knowledge management' Karl Wiig (1995) includes the reassignment of personnel to new functions and the building of expert networks for formal and informal referral paths under the heading 'building blocks for dissemination'. In reality, the creation of a knowledge environment has an impact on everyone. New roles are created and other tasks assimilated into existing roles, to design and maintain knowledge-related processes and procedures. There is no blueprint for the ideal knowledge mobilization team, knowledge management unit or knowledge transformation department. Each organization's approach is specific and is not transferable as a 'one size fits all'. The diversity of unit names and job titles reflect not only differences in approach and focus, but also the search for

Organizational development
- leadership and vision
- allowing knowledge 'space'
- processes that encourage the creation, storage and use of knowledge
- redefining employment contracts
- managing and facilitating change
- focus on leveraging intangible assets

Infrastructure
- technology
- applications
- environment – physical
- TQM, best practices, procedures
- keep infrastructure in perspective, it's just the railroad

Culture
- redefining core values
- learning, coaching, mentoring
- sharing
- trust and security
- empowering
- encouraging and rewarding curiosity, creativity and innovation

Content
- differentiating between Intellectual Capital and Intellectual Working Capital
- identifying and recording Intellectual Capital
- creating connectivity (eg people to experts, people to content)
- building tools to acquire, organize, integrate, distribute and retrieve

Fig. 5.1 *KM development activities*

descriptive and meaningful designations. KM has increased the understanding of the importance of language in the business context and the meaning attached to words.

Some of the emerging roles are explicitly labelled KM, others not. Some are full-time roles, others part time and some are re-alignments or extensions of existing roles. Existing roles may be considered to be within the KM environment. For example, some organizations now consider the HR or IT director posts as full-time KM roles. Another scenario is where a new role, such as Learning and Development Director, will be the 'new' KM role, with the traditional training or HR functions remaining outside the 'official' KM structure but contributing as appropriate.

KM is essentially an organization-specific activity in its infancy. Consequently, developing a picture of generic roles must be overlaid with caveats. The assignment of roles within a KM framework suffers greatly from the lack of a common language. Despite the differences in approach and the wide disparity in scale, a pattern of structures, roles and activities is discernible, and there are some common features.

Even in the largest organizations there are relatively few people assigned to the task of developing the knowledge environment. Designing and embedding processes and effecting changes in behaviour to maximize knowledge creation and transfer do not result in large numbers of new specialist knowledge directors or managers. Existing roles are assessed in terms of their contribution to the knowledge process. Many of the people currently holding senior KM posts, especially the 'Chief Knowledge Officers' (CKOs), do not expect their roles to be permanent. They are viewed as project or change management roles, whose main objective is to bring about a way of working that is knowledge based. Their aim is to create an organization that is knowledge centric, and their roles then disappear, in the same way that organizations lose their Total Quality Management Director but remain quality driven.

The variety of job titles that has emerged during the last two or three years is both confusing and invigorating. There has been some relabelling and rebadging, but the processes of deciding what they want to achieve requires organizations to reconsider the posts they have and the ones they want. In some cases the problem of job title has been set aside – no job title or a temporary one. In other cases the title has been intentionally vague. There has been a reluctance to allow job titles to dictate the post, or even the job or person specification. The creators of knowledge environments focus primarily on what they want to achieve and less on how individuals should engineer that achievement. Knowledge environments are 'strong on strategy, weak on control'. It isn't certain how these senior posts will develop or for how long they will be in evidence, but it is likely that the CKO, the leader of the change management programme, will remain in evidence until a knowledge-based way of working is the best practice norm. It is also likely, and certainly desirable, that the role will be replaced by a Board-level responsibility for corporate information and knowledge. Future Directors of Information and Knowledge or Chief Knowledge and Information Officers will be less concerned with changing attitudes and processes than with ensuring that corporate strategy is based on, and develops a strategy for maintaining and exploiting, its corporate knowledge base.

A generic approach to developing knowledge environments

Figure 5.2 illustrates a structure that typically evolves during implementation of KM approaches. Not many organizations have all aspects of the structure, but it is one that will be recognized by representatives of KM environments of all sizes and from all sectors. Whatever parts of this structure are implemented, or whatever the

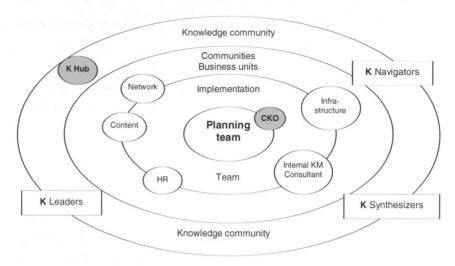

Fig. 5.2 *Generic KM structures and roles*

configuration of KM roles and networks, it is noticeable that knowledge communities become a feature of KM environments with champions and enthusiastic practitioners and users forming their own support, information and knowledge exchanges.

The figure is generic in nature; the actual roles and functions in a KM implementation would not be described in this way.

Table 5.1 provides a top-level overview of KM activities and where responsibility for these is likely to fall within the organization. In the rest of the chapter some of the roles and structures are developed in more detail.

Table 5.1 *KM activities and responsibility*

Level	Activity
Board/Top management	Vision, championship, leadership
Top/Senior management	Strategy and leadership
Senior management	Planning/implementation team
Senior/Middle management	Management of day-to-day activities; knowledge centres/hubs
Middle management/practitioners	Day-to-day KM activities
Organization-wide	Communities of practice/knowledge centres/hubs
Organization-wide	Knowledge communities
Organization-wide	IT infrastructure (including web)
Organization-wide	Information/content infrastructure
Organization-wide/Business units	Knowledge centres and information services
Business units	Knowledge hubs

Management roles – vision, championship, leadership

Commitment to the concept at top level is crucial, CEO for corporate-wide programmes, top management for regional, targeted or departmental activities. The experience of organizations where KM activities have been 'authorized', rather than led, by top management has been that the initiatives are likely to flounder through lack of Board-level attention and direction of resources. The vision for the KM programme should be set by top management, even though the initial 'visionary' may well have come from senior or middle management.

There are a number of approaches to the implementation of KM. A common initiator is a mixture of CEO and/or Board expectation leading to proposals for change from senior managers. New ideas are adopted if a reasonable business case can be made. In a small number of cases the initiative arises when a CEO goes to a conference, sees an article, has a conversation with someone he respects, and wants to try out the new idea. The problem with this approach is not initial lack of vision or commitment, but the potential difficulty of delivering some real results within an acceptable (short) timeframe. A third version is where the organization is going through a major change, privatization for example, or a merger or acquisition, and new approaches are deemed to be essential. In the first two examples change and new approaches are part of the culture, and it is part of the Board's role to back this. In the third case the Board or the management in situ have to find ways of engineering the most effective means of dealing with change; if KM is part of that solution the backing will be there.

Where managers have not convinced the Board, do not think that it is worth trying to convince top management, or feel that it is a concept that would bring a groan of resistance from many, 'KM by stealth' has emerged as a method. Here the champion, visionary or leader, or group of individuals, may come from less exalted levels but will instigate small projects that have benefits and demonstrate a change: the 'quick wins' mentioned in Chapter 3.

The ability to sell the concept to all levels is essential from the outset. The missionary, catalyst and champion appear throughout KM structures.

Implementation roles

Implementation roles are represented in Figure 5.3 as a series of related functions which reflect a common approach to the development of KM.

Planning team – Benefits and strategy/Leadership and resources

Strategy will be developed and set by a team drawn from top or senior management, ideally representing different facets of the KM approach. It could be a one-man team, but its essence is in the ability of senior personnel to become committed to a multidisciplinary (multifunctional) way of working. This will be part of management responsibility. The team will set the approach for the development of the KM programme. It is their commitment to breaking down the

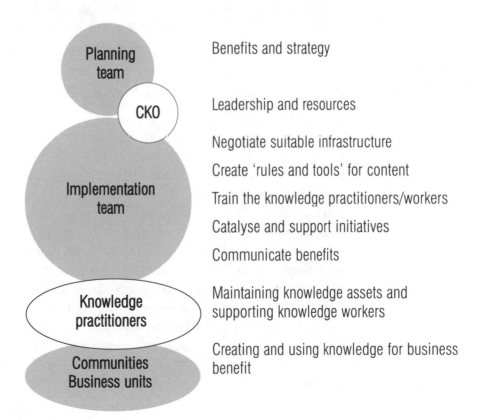

Fig. 5.3 *KM implementation roles*

boundaries between functional silos and business units that sets the strategy and encourages the development of KM ideas.

The CKO

What does a CKO do?

- 'Cartographer': mapping expertise and making connections
- 'Geologist': drilling into specific areas and applying tools
- 'Spark plug': igniting an awareness of the need to change
- 'Architect': designing the physical and cultural environment.

This shorthand view of the role of a CKO, first suggested by Victoria Ward when CKO of NatWest Markets, may appear flippant but reflects well the actual tasks performed. The essential attribute is an ability to assess the most appropriate methods to apply and when to apply them. As mentioned earlier, the specific role is not always created to avoid 'cultural' problems or to avoid creating any new 'supremo' structures.

Implementation team – Infrastructure/Rules and tools/Training/Catalysis

Planning, implementation and support are undertaken by a small, multidisciplinary team representing different aspects of the organization and its approach to KM. They will work with business units or work groups in order to tie the activities into the organization and will facilitate KM committees and planning groups. In smaller organizations the implementation team may comprise people who have taken on this role in addition to their main responsibilities. In larger organizations the implementation team is likely to be full time, although relatively small. Even in the largest consultancies and global companies, with well-developed KM programmes and teams of significant size, they are small relative to the number of fee earners or employees. The size of supporting infrastructures, which may already exist even if re-aligned under KM, reflects the size and nature of the organization.

Catalysts

Members of the implementation team are catalysts. Their role is to design activities, devise policies and standards, create and support organization – or department-wide KM networks and act as the KM project management team. They also coordinate and monitor KM projects and initiatives across the organization and promote success and lessons learnt. Primarily their role is to understand where and how a KM approach can add value and then convince the business units involved. They are the practical arm of change management.

Knowledge centres

These centres may be the only 'physical' evidence of a knowledge initiative and include cafés, discussion areas or informal meeting rooms to encourage knowledge creation and sharing, as well as physical and electronic information resources and services. As Figures 5.4 and 5.5 illustrate, information services may be embedded within KM centres, or have a separate identity and work in partnership with knowledge practitioners, using the ICT infrastructure.

Knowledge hubs within business units act as the focal point for that unit taking responsibility for the collection and maintenance of internal information and knowledge bases and for sourcing internal and external information. In some cases they will also provide the research analyst roles. They will often be linked either formally or informally as 'knowledge communities'. In the model shown in Figure 5.5 one knowledge hub acts as the central knowledge centre, providing information services and often leading the central knowledge management team.

Information technology

IT infrastructure is an underpinning requirement. The KM team needs someone who is familiar with the present software and IT platforms, the requirements of KM programmes and the communication needs. The development of a knowledge environment requires the integration of ICT with all activities. In early KM development IT was central, the sole manifestation being the computer network and the intranet. Later developments have seen the need to factor in IT strategy, particularly KM-enabling software and associated networking capabilities.

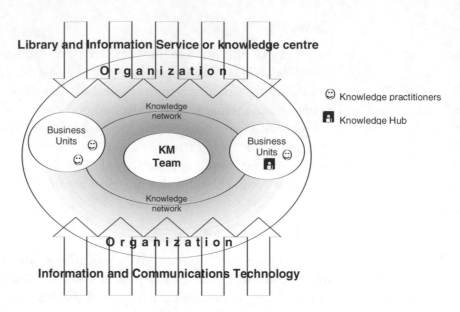

Fig. 5.4 *KM structure with separate LIS function*

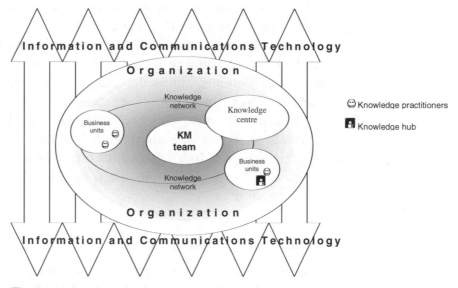

Fig. 5.5 *KM structure with embedded knowledge centre*

Content

Content infrastructure is key to success. Roles such as 'Knowledge Architects' are emerging with responsibilities for developing corporate taxonomies (classifications), codes, templates, etc, to give structure to captured knowledge and information, and to give direction to knowledge flows and sharing. In order to implement KM environments across organizations a certain number of 'rules and tools' are required. These may be as mundane as document templates for common appearance or as sophisticated as a dynamic taxonomy which suggests appropriate sources of knowledge to seekers. The level of sophistication will be a function of the complexity of the data as well as a function of the amount of central control which is required and/or acceptable.

In the early days of development of the Knowledge Galaxy, Cap Gemini set out prescriptive standards such as common IT platforms and common software, and then provided the 'rules and tools' for its global development. Offices in individual countries could decide how they would develop the concept, allowing for their culture and priorities. It may have produced some interesting variations but it did achieve a global commitment to the system.

Elisabeth Lank, among others, suggests that the evolving KM environments call for a new set of roles. One view of the many roles that are suggested is to align to the publication and distribution process as shown in Table 5.2.

Table 5.2 *Content creation and distribution roles*

Sponsor	Commissioning – responsible for providing the reason and funding for the generation of knowledge
Author	The creator and, generally, 'owner' of the knowledge assets
Contributor	Owner of knowledge or information feeding into the knowledge asset
Editor	Responsible for the quality and relevance of the knowledge asset, including navigability
Owner	Responsible for the maintenance of the knowledge assets, who may be the author or, as in the case of a contacts database, for example, the person responsible for its upkeep and access control
Designer and publisher	Responsible for standards and tools to enable publication and distribution
Distributor	Responsible for the infrastructure and delivery tools – Webmaster or information service provider

Human resources

Human resource expertise is crucial to the core KM implementation team. Changes to job descriptions, the inclusion of knowledge sharing and exploitation in appraisal schemes, the development of members of the knowledge network and everyone affected by the knowledge-based way of working, are key HR concerns. Their expertise in staff reward systems and staff development plays a crucial role. HR is generally regarded as part of the corporate infrastructure and can feel threatened by the impact of KM implementation on its work. Aligning HR to KM is a key challenge.

KM development roles

Generic KM development roles are emerging which can be grouped in four areas. The names assigned here are not generally used in organizations implementing KM; they are intended as generic descriptors.

KM champions and strategists

Generally drawn from top/senior management who consider the development as part of their management responsibility. Within this group there is likely to be a 'visionary' who will be particularly interested in change management.

KM planners and facilitators

A multidisciplinary team responsible for developing policy, standards and tools. The team could contain any or all of the following depending on the size and approach of the organization:

- Directors and/or managers to oversee and champion KM activities.
- Content architects, responsible for structuring content.
- IT developers and infrastructure specialists to handle the IT infrastructure, web development and IT tools.
- Knowledge network specialists, responsible for developing expertise and processes within communities and business units; this role may include HR responsibilities.
- Knowledge process developers.
- Project managers to facilitate and monitor agreed KM activities; this role may also sit within the strategy team.
- External content managers.
- Help desk staff to provide assistance to communities or groups; could be call centre model able to deal with standard and frequent enquiries, or a signposting function.
- KM trainers – likely to link to the help desk.

KM practitioners

A range of full- and part-time roles supporting business units or communities:

- Knowledge leaders, responsible for championing the KM approach, the quality of knowledge activities, the arbiter for confidentiality, etc. The role is generally that of validating and facilitating the work of those assigned to KM roles within their group or business unit. Like the CKO they will be someone well respected as knowledgeable in their field and as a business-focused leader.
- Knowledge managers, responsible for the acquisition and management of internal and external knowledge.
- Knowledge navigators, responsible for knowing where knowledge can be located.
- Knowledge synthesizers, responsible for facilitating the recording of significant project or unit knowledge.
- Content editors, responsible for codifying and structuring.
- Publishing facilitators, responsible for internal publishing functions, usually on an intranet.

Information and/or knowledge generators

These are groups of people who are the creators of the corporate knowledge. The most information-intensive roles identified by respondents to the questionnaire distributed as part of the TFPL KM skills research (TFPL, 1999) were (ranked in order of importance): Research and Development, Marketing, Strategic Planning, and Competitive Intelligence. Board members came fifth in the ranking with less than 50% of the sample identifying their roles as information or knowledge intensive. The breakdown is given in Figure 5.6. Although individual responses reflected the nature of the organization, the aggregate results suggest that a range of roles are recognized as being based on the acquisition, interpretation and management of information. The full list of knowledge- or information-intensive roles identified in the questionnaire is as follows:

- IT
- human resources
- administration

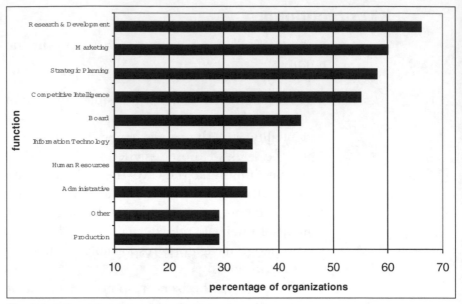

Fig. 5.6 *Information-intensive roles*

- consultancy
- design
- education
- financial management/planning
- legal functions/practices
- sales/after sales support
- business units
- production
- military operational planning
- product management
- professional services to members
- public affairs
- policy advice/development.

KM has accentuated a debate that has existed for some time on the differences, if any, between knowledge workers and information workers. Various definitions have been put forward; they may assist the understanding of how information is created and used and demonstrate the different perceptions of the terms 'information' and 'knowledge'.

Information workers

Qualities of information workers include the following (McGovern, 1999):

- Highly adaptable and eager to learn new things
- Good at searching for, evaluating and managing information
- Computer literate
- Self-motivated
- Creative and innovative
- Excellent communication skills
- Good at working in teams
- Good networking skills
- Mobile and independent-minded.

This valuable employee is also, he argues, scarce.

There are many definitions of knowledge workers that seek to differentiate them from information workers. For example:

> Knowledge work is the intellectual activity that is performed by people upon data, information and knowledge in order to discover business options. Knowledge work produces mature content. Knowledge work differs from automated work, wherein the human element does not significantly contribute to the output of the process.
>
> (Fourth Wave Group Inc)

Many organizations claim that all workers are 'knowledge workers' and the criteria for the knowledge worker such as those below suggest that the claim could be made for most of the workforce in a KM environment. Knowledge workers:

- work in a team – either local or virtual (a characteristic throughout KM environments)
- work with information that provides a competitive or beneficial advantage (a KM environment is based on the premise that all information has potential for competitive advantage)
- typically use IT for day-to-day activities (a typical KM approach for the whole workforce)
- work in an area that has direct impact on the bottom line (the KM philosophy argues that everyone has impact on the bottom line).

These criteria emphasize the context in which information is used, rather than the ability to manage information as in the McGovern definition. Kit Sims Taylor of Bellevue Community College (Taylor, 1998) argues that the essence of knowledge workers is that they divide their time between the elements of knowledge work:

* *Finding* the data needed to produce the knowledge.
* *Creating* knowledge out of data.
* *Communicating* what has been produced or learned.
* *Networking*, promoting, socializing.
* *Routine work* that is hard to separate from knowledge work. Formatting an article, for example, is work that might be done by a typist, but would be done by the knowledge worker when that takes less time than preparing the document and giving formatting instructions.

Whether or not it is possible to differentiate between the two groups, information and knowledge workers, it is among people with these characteristics and job functions that the implementation teams seek to establish the knowledge practitioners and network.

KM posts and their holders

Despite variations in the structure of the approach it may be possible to identify key roles that would be recognized by many KM-based organizations. Appendices 1 and 2 to this chapter provide a chart of roles and their responsibilities, and some of the job titles that relate to KM activities, based on the TFPL KM skills research (TFPL, 1999).

Where do the new knowledge strategists, planners and facilitators come from? In Chapter 6 we discuss whether there is, or could be, a knowledge management profession but while some of us may debate this point, organizations are recruiting people to undertake change assignments and the design of knowledge-based activities.

The most common feature of the people moving into these activities is that there is no single pre-determined route or background. No one profession is truly dominating, and no particular form of education appears to have been associated with success in this area. The key features that KM post holders have are their ability to work across boundaries and cope with ambiguity, be solution rather than task focused, creative, good team leaders and members, passionate and restless.

What sort of CEO or director for example, is likely to take the KM idea forward? Those organizations with the most developed programmes have CEOs with a style of leadership that determines the direction and then encourages the organization to find various paths to the goals agreed.

The role of CKO has evolved as a senior management responsibility, often as part of another role, and comprises leadership and change management. It is generally time limited and provides the focus and drive required to steer KM programmes through critical stages and facilitates planning and development. The key criteria for CKOs are their knowledge of the business and the organization, and the respect they have from people at all levels of the organization. It is a role, therefore, that is almost always assigned to a well-established member of the organization who has often already worked in a number of key customer-facing positions.

The backgrounds of people filling roles in KM planning and implementation are less consistent. As the roles within the KM environment become clearer some new posts emerge that require a new set of skills, while other roles are in effect new applications of existing skills. A steady demand for 'knowledge management' practitioners and for people who contribute to KM development is arising, but there remains a preference for the 'grow our own' approach, particularly in the initial planning and early implementation stage. This probably reflects the view that the main requirement for people working in this area is to 'know the business', allowing practitioners to identify and develop 'quick wins' and sustained approaches in the particular organizational culture, but increasing their chances of succeeding in implementing changes. This approach also reflects the early stage of the concept when most organizations do not have a well-developed idea of the roles they may wish to fill or the most appropriate person to recruit to them. There are very few experienced KM practitioners to select from, and even fewer well-established job and person specifications to consult.

Conclusions

The range of knowledge management roles that have emerged, and are still emerging, reflects the recognition that the creation of environments supporting the development and creative use of knowledge requires diverse experience and skills. One feature is clear and consistent. People in KM positions represent a wide variety of educational experiences and backgrounds, and arts graduates are as successful in this area as scientists and technologists. The understanding of sociology, anthropology, linguistics and organizational behaviour is an essential part of KM, providing opportunities for a broad mix of skills in a KM team. More significant is that the team members bring a wide variety of experience to the job. Some are from relevant functional backgrounds, such as HR, IT or Information Management, but a whole range of organization-wide roles are represented. Interest in the bigger picture is a characteristic of a KM practitioner. The skills required to join the emerging ranks of the KM profession – if that is what it is – are discussed in Chapters 6 and 7.

Perhaps more significantly the focus of roles is consolidating. The core team looks as if it will remain as the enabling KM hit squad, sometimes centralized, often not. Their role will remain that of providing tools and processes, support and advice. Similarly, the role of top level KM leader and champion – making KM issues visible at Board level – is becoming increasingly evident. But the real growth is happening in business units, functions and departments. As the client-facing units recognize the potential of KM approaches, so they are increasingly identifying the areas where it can have most business impact for them – and creating KM posts to implement and support the solutions they identify. It is clear that the growth of KM roles is as much within business units as within KM teams.

References

McGovern, G (1999) *The caring economy: business principles for the new digital age*, Blackhall Publishing.

Taylor, K S (1998) *The brief reign of the knowledge worker: information technology and technological unemployment*, paper presented at The International Conference on the Social Impact of Information Technology, St Louis, MO, 12–14 October, 1998, available at **http://online.bcc.ctc.edu/econ/kst/Kstpage.htm**

TFPL (1999) *Skills for knowledge management: building a knowledge economy*, TFPL.

Appendix 1: KM roles and functions

Key:
A = Application of existing knowledge – new role – new mix of skills
B = New role – mix of new and existing skills
C = New applications for existing skills
D = Rebadge skills – new mix of skills

Generic roles – core KM	Type	Responsibilities
Chief Knowledge Officer	A	Strategy, leadership, coordination
Global CKO	A	
National CKO	A	
Business unit practice CKO	A	
*(Chief Knowledge Team) – Planning Team		Leadership, catalysis
Development and training	A	HR processes; structural and development implications; learning and training implications; reward, motivation, support for team working, etc.
Information systems and technology	A	IT infrastructure implications
Information content	A	Policy issues re inclusion, purpose, etc
Process Manager	A	Development of business processes with KM integration; change management
Strategy	A	Alignment of KM strategy to corporate and departmental strategies
Implementation Team		
Knowledge Director	B	Overseeing development of processes, infrastructure and information resources
Knowledge Manager/Project Manager	B	Overseeing implementation of agreed knowledge activities
Network Coordinator	B	Development of knowledge community and knowledge roles and responsibilities
Content Coordinator	C	Development of standards and policies for content inclusion, structure, coding, etc; database structure and design
Infrastructure development	C	Development of appropriate common platforms and software
Internal KM consultants	B	Selling KM activities into business units etc
KM help desk	C	Assistance with KM tools and facilities
KM training	B	Introduction to tools, processes and resources

Project Manager	C	Management of resources and project in order to deliver agreed results
Knowledge Practitioners		
Knowledge Centre/Hub Manager/Knowledge Navigator	C	Facilitation of access to internal and external information
Knowledge Coordinator Broker	C	Acquisition of internal and external information and knowledge in specific areas
Content Editor	D	Structure and codifying of information
Synthesizer	B	Debriefing and synthesis of project material
Researcher	D	Identification of new material
Analyst	D	Interpretation of knowledge/information for a specific purpose
Infrastructure roles		
Intranet Developer	B	
Database/Notes designer	C	
Knowledge Workers		
Knowledge Leader	A	Subject/practice leader, fostering KM practice

* In some organizations the CKO role is undertaken by a team rather than one person. In this case the team may also be the planning team.

Appendix 2:
Job titles in 1999

Core KM roles	Job titles examples
Chief Knowledge Officer	CKO
	Head of Knowledge Management and Education
	Consumer Market Knowledge Manager
	Global Knowledge Manager
(Chief Knowledge Team) – Planning Team	
Development and training	Group Internal Communications Manager
	Internal Communications Advisor/Manager
	Head of Training
Information systems and technology	Director of I&T
	Regional Director of Communications
	Senior Communications Executive
Information content	Head of Know-How
Process Manager	Process Knowledge Specialist
Strategy	Knowledge Architect
Implementation Team	
Knowledge Director	Knowledge Policy Advisor
Knowledge Manager/Project Manager	Head of Internal Communications
	Internal Communications Manager
Network Coordinator	Network coordinator
Content Coordinator	Knowledge Architect
Infrastructure development	Intranet Developer
	Webmaster
	Database/Notes Designer
	Producer
Internal KM consultants	
KM help desk	Knowledge Assistant
KM training	Career Developer
Project Manager	Project Manager

Knowledge Practitioners

Knowledge Leader	Subject Leader
	Community Facilitator
Knowledge Centre/Hub	Knowledge Centre Leader
Manager/Knowledge Navigator	Knowledge Centre Manager with specific responsibility
	Information Specialist
	Process Competency KM Analyst
	Senior Legal Information Officer
	Information/Knowledge Manager
Knowledge Coordinator/Broker	Knowledge Administrator
	Knowledge Scout
Content Editor	Knowledge Steward
Synthesizer	Knowledge Analyst
	Subject Specialist
Researcher	Knowledge Broker
	Knowledge Scout
Analyst	Knowledge Analysts
	Business Analyst

6

KM skills and competencies

A knowledge environment is about the development of a corporate capability – a unique mix of skills, expertise, processes, management and intellectual capital that enables an organization to respond to and develop its markets. The development of appropriate skills and expertise is an essential element in building this capability. It is also dependent on people enjoying working together and the structures that allow them to do so, but people's real potential is realized by processes and facilities that allow them to develop individually and collectively. This is core. 'KM recognizes that the ability of individuals to contribute to knowledge environments is dependent on more than professional and technical skills.

KM environments are demanding. They require people who are competitive and ambitious for the organization and their peer groups as much as for themselves. They require initiative and a willingness to share ideas, however raw. Such behaviour carries an element of personal risk – confidence and trust are required. KM environments need reflective and thoughtful people as well as those who seize the opportunity. They need completers and finishers as well as visionaries, mavericks and facilitators; people with an eye for detail as well as those with their vision on the grand design. It is the mix of skills and personalities, and the ability to manage that mix well, that provides the potential creativity required. In KM organizations sharing behaviours are positively encouraged, people are not constrained by functional boxes and everyone's contribution is valued. But for many individuals there is a personal challenge in working comfortably in an environment where jobs and roles are less well defined than in more traditional structures and where a key skill is working in multidisciplined teams or with internal and external partners.

Competencies

This focus on the mix of skills, attitudes and behaviours that should be characteristic of a KM environment has led to the increasing acceptance of 'competence' as a concept. A definition is hard to pin down. The Public Service Commission of Canada, for example, says that

> Competencies are general descriptions of the abilities necessary to perform successfully in areas specified. Competency profiles synthesise skills, knowledge, attributes and values, and express performance requirements in behavioural terms.
>
> (Public Service Commission of Canada, 1998)

In their survey of organizations with competency initiatives (carried out in the Spring of 1998) 25 of the organizations defined competencies as

> components of a job which are reflected in behaviours that are observable in the workplace. The common elements most frequently mentioned are knowledge, skills, abilities, aptitudes, personal suitability, behaviour, and impact on performance at work. We can conclude that there is little difference in the definitions of the concept of competency in the organizations consulted. Without question, the common denominator is 'observable behaviour' in the workplace.
>
> (Public Service Commission of Canada, 1998)

At is simplest a competency is the mix of skills, experience and behaviour that allows an individual to execute their work successfully.

Resulting from this acceptance of 'competence' competency profiles, or frameworks, are beginning to appear in large organizations and are being used as an aid for recruitment, as a personal and organizational tool for assessing training and development requirements, and as a basis for appraisal. Such profiles take different approaches, reflecting organizational choice and style, and there are examples of different approaches available on the web. Essentially they seek to identify the competencies core to the organization, or to specific roles, and describe these in terms of the behaviours demonstrated by the competency in question. Very often a level of competence will also be described. See Table 6.1 for an example:

Table 6.1 *Levels of competency – based on that developed by PricewaterhouseCoopers (UK)*

Level 1 (Awareness)	Applies the competency in routine situations
Level 2 (Practitioner)	Applies the competency in demanding situations
Level 3 (Expert)	Applies the competency in challenging, unusual or highly sensitive situations
Level 4 (Guru)	Acts as a point of reference within the firm, people go out of their way to seek their advice

The competencies identified will also have a range of aspects or sub-competencies, as the example taken from a set of development competencies illustrates (see Table 6.2, pages 108–9).

The 'competence' approach clearly fits the KM environment well where development is seen to be as much about changing behaviours and attitudes as it is about acquiring hard skills.

Matching roles and competencies

In Figure 6.1 Karl Wiig illustrates with a spider diagram and seven levels of proficiency how an understanding of the competencies required for each role can be used to profile the role and identify matches and gaps between role requirements and the post holder (Wiig, 1995).

Identifying the competencies required for any role requires an understanding of the outcomes of that role. We have addressed the four clusters of KM roles in Chapter 5, typifying these as:

- KM strategy teams
  - leading and championing the KM approach at senior level
- KM implementation teams
  - providing KM tools and processes; working with business units to identify KM applications and approaches; championing the concept and acting as a catalyst
- KM practitioners
  - maintaining knowledge assets, supporting knowledge workers and acting as a focus for KM activities in business units and teams
- Business units, communities, functions – mainline business
  - people who create and use knowledge.

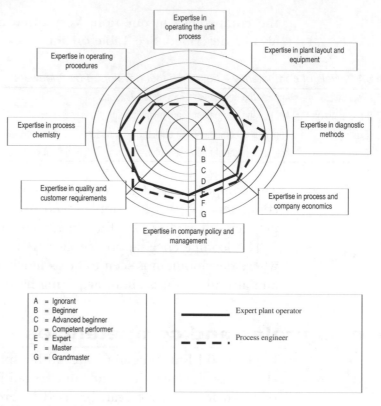

Fig. 6.1 *Examples of knowledge profiles from the process industry*

1999 research (TFPL, 1999), subsequent research in 2000 and the results of discussions at the TFPL Chief Knowledge Officers Summit in October 2000 (TFPL, 2000), indicate that there are core competencies required for each cluster of KM roles. Many of these overlap and the emphasis changes to reflect the focus of the role. However, there are a number of competencies that are emerging as core to all KM organizations – and desirable for all members of staff whether in KM roles or otherwise.

Core KM competencies for the organization

The early KM adopters focused on the exploitation of technology: KM was an IT solution. This phase has been superseded by the view that KM is principally about people and processes. Those organizations which take this approach seriously are also leading the way in identifying the skills and competencies that are required throughout the organization in order to create and maintain a KM culture.

Table 6.2 *Interpersonal competencies from a set of leadership development competencies*

Interpersonal skills	Level 1 behaviours	Level 2 behaviours	Level 3 behaviours	Level 4 behaviours
Uses communication approaches that are effective, appropriate and influence others.	Plain language presentations or written communications are completed with accurate spelling, grammar and content.	Consciously uses direct, open, two-way communication that is effective. Assesses the needs of audience in order to deliver appropriate message and content	Communication shows conviction and enthusiasm. Personal impact is clear, positive, and succinct. Communication demonstrates an understanding of stakeholder interests.	Communications have maximum impact, drive action and enhance image of individual organization. Content demonstrates a comprehensive understanding of issues and varying perspectives.
Displays excellent listening skills.	Hears other people and discusses how their ideas fit with own personal viewpoint. Listeners may not always be certain that their idea or question has been accurately interpreted.	Takes notes and feeds back key items, issues, and decisions to ensure understanding.	Accurately integrates and builds on comments and ideas: level of contribution of others is high.	Team members feel at ease and he/she provides full attention during discussion. Body language and verbal cues indicate he/she is internalizing what is being said.
Gives feedback to achieve continuous improvement of performance.	Gives feedback to identify gaps between general performance and expectations. Employee is expected to develop strategies for improvement.	Feedback is timely and linked to specific performance outcomes based on customer expectations and departmental objectives.	Performance is assessed and feedback given within each situational context. Employee is encouraged to conduct self-analysis and seek coaching or training where needed.	Employee and supervisor develop continuous improvement objectives in line with strategies, business plan and personal goals. Strategies for new opportunities and directions are initialized by employee and supervisor.
Resolves conflict.	Is aware of conflict situations and understands a variety of responses can be used. Is comfortable with conflict but tends to use one approach regularly in addressing it.	Recognizes reasons for disagreement. Seeks to suggest the appropriate approach to dealing with the conflict.	Confronts conflict in a non-judgmental fashion. Understanding of 'positions' and 'interests' is built and the different frames-of-reference are used to achieve trade-off/agreement.	Can leverage conflict by building 'common interests'. Able to partner to produce new, creative, win–win solutions. Effectively uses a variety of conflict/dispute resolution approaches as required.

(continued)

Table 6.2 *(continued)*

Interpersonal skills	Level 1 behaviours	Level 2 behaviours	Level 3 behaviours	Level 4 behaviours
Uses formal and informal mechanisms to stay in tune with internal and external clients.	Stays in regular personal contact with key clients. Knows what it is like to be a client of own organization.	Ensures that team members stay in regular contact with clients and knows what it is like to be client of own organization. Discussion of key findings and action ideas is facilitated.	Builds/leads appropriate customer feedback gathering processes (eg focus groups, questionnaires, complaint analysis, etc). Task team and individual ideas are supported.	Ensures information from customer feedback is shared, discussed and acted upon. Understands how the customer adds value within the customers' environment. Takes action to add value to the customer's customer. Builds and maintains a 'partnership' with customers.
Builds and motivates teams.	Helps individuals form a team by providing clear expectations for individual contributors.	Ensures that team members understand each other's roles and the benefits of communicating and working cooperatively toward planned outcomes.	Ensures that the team and individuals succeed by engaging in proactive activities that promote team goals. Recognizes self and others as adding value.	Creates vision and action where all members of the team have a sense of ownership and mission aligned to the overall organizational goals. Team members motivate and support each other. Team may extend to external partners, customers and suppliers.

Eighteen chief knowledge officers (CKOs) participated in the two-day discussion Summit hosted by TFPL in October 2000. There were no presentations, just round table discussions of selected topics. 'Skills and competencies for knowledge environments' was one of the topics, and the group considered: 'the skills required by a core (central) KM team', 'a KM implementation team', and 'the skills required throughout a KM culture'. The CKOs identified, in all, 32 competencies for a KM culture and selected the following as the core competencies:

Core competencies for knowledge cultures
- Ability to learn – curious, seeks new knowledge
- Self initiation – acts like a business of one, doesn't wait to be told
- Collaborative – a team player, positive regard for other people, not status driven
- Intellectual linking – sees the big picture, makes connections
- Humility – recognizes that other people know things, learns from mistakes
- Ability to think and do – with a focus on outcome
- An appreciation of information management techniques.

This vision of the worker in a KM environment is similar to the core competencies expressed in competency frameworks by some of the early adopters of KM, learning organization or similar initiatives. Knowledge sharing behaviours, although expressed in different ways, are becoming regular features. Sometimes these are explicitly expressed, other times they are integrated into team working or interpersonal skills. Typical examples of core competencies in KM environments are:

Working with others
Works well with others internal and external to the organization, in a variety of capacities.

Interpersonal skills
Ability to understand feelings, motivations and behaviours of others. Communicates well orally, in writing and through listening.

IT skills
Use of software products and electronic media to enhance work processes and ensure the efficient transfer of information.

Planning and organization
The ability to effectively prioritize activities and approach tasks in

a structured and organized manner.

Business understanding

Understands the nature of the business, including its organizational structure, key processes, services, markets and business strategy.

Contributes to the knowledge base

Shares learning and information with immediate and extended work groups. Contributes to appropriate knowledge-sharing activities and processes.

Skills and competencies for KM teams and communities

The emerging communities of knowledge strategists, facilitators and practitioners require the core competencies outlined above to thrive and have impact. TFPL research for 'Skills for KM' explored, through questionnaires, interviews and in-depth case studies of 500 employers and practitioners in Europe and the USA, the optimum mix of competencies for KM teams. By aggregating the results and plotting them using the 'novice, expert, guru' ranking similar to Wiig, it is possible to identify the skills mix required and assess how the skills mix changes with the roles (Figures 6.2 and 6.3).

This 1999 research also identified the top skills and attributes that employers looked for in KM teams shown in Table 6.3.

Table 6.3 *Top skills and attributes for KM teams*

Top skills for KM teams	Top attributes for KM teams
Business awareness/experience/understanding	Creativity
Communication	Vision
IT skills/literacy	Team player
KM awareness/experience/understanding	Enthusiasm
Strategic awareness/management planning	Determination
Information management skills	Entrepreneurial ability
Leadership	Persuasion
Change management	Ability to see the big picture
Content awareness/organization	Confidence
People management	Flexibility
Project management	Lateral thinker
	Tenacity
	Credibility

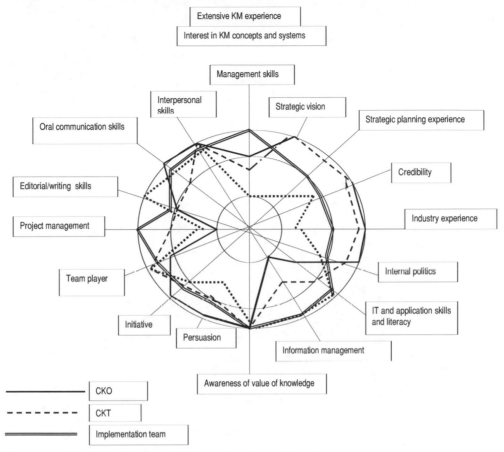

Fig. 6.2 *Skills required by CKO, Planning (CKT) and Implementation teams*

Skill sets

Our 1999 research led us to identify three sets of skills and competencies that underpin the KM approach (as in Figure 6.4, page 114):

- Professional and technical core competencies
- Organizational skills
- KM enabling skills.

Two of these sets relate to individuals and reflect the competence approach which has since become more firmly established. The third relates to the skills set of KM teams, communities or networks. The three skill sets together represent the competency building blocks that an individual, group or organization requires in order to build KM capability.

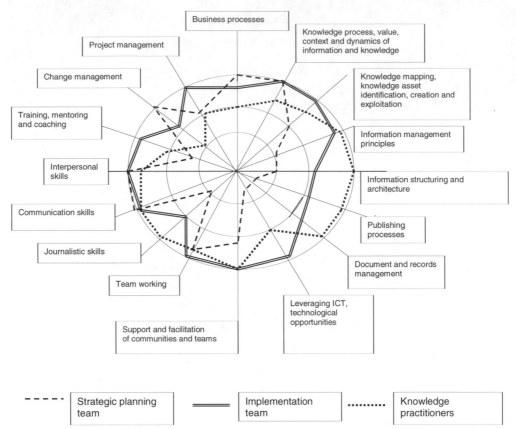

Fig. 6.3 *Aggregated competencies for knowledge practitioners*

1 Professional and technical core competencies

This is the core set of skills and competencies that make up the 'offer' that an employee makes to the employer. These will be acquired through education, professional or technical qualifications, training and experience. They will reflect personal attributes, preferences and experience, and will normally continue to develop. The understanding of one's core competencies and the ability to develop and extend them is becoming a key factor in employability.

The development of individual core competencies – those which are required by the profession or occupation – are not, generally, the primary focus of KM approaches, although such environments do set high expectations of performance and responsibility, requiring all staff to maintain and develop their occupational competence. KM based organizations are more likely to invest in training and development programmes to enable and encourage staff to develop their individual competence.

Core competency building	KM enabling skills and competencies	Organizational skills and competencies
Core competency building Continuing professional and technical education and training Business, sector and work experience	**KM enabling skills and competencies**	**Organizational skills and competencies**
	Business process identification and analysis	
	Understanding the knowledge process within the business process	
	Understanding the value, context and dynamics of knowledge and information	
	Knowledge asset identification, creation, maintenance and exploitation	
	Knowledge mapping and flows	
	Change management	
	Leveraging ICT to create KM enablers	
	An understanding of support and facilitation of communities and teams	Communication Team working Negotiation Persuasion Facilitation Coaching Mentoring Understanding business processes
	Project management	
	Information structuring and architecture	
	Document and information management and work flows	
	An understanding of information management principles	
	An understanding of publishing processes	
	An understanding of technological opportunities	

Professional, technical and craft skills and education
The occupational competence of individuals

Fig. 6.4 *Skills profile for KM practitioners*

2 Organizational competencies

Organizational skills – those required to survive and thrive in a modern organization – were the set of skills most frequently cited as key skills for KM teams. They are the skills that everyone requires in a modern organization in order to apply their professional or technical competencies effectively. They have also been identified in the RSA report *Opening minds: education for the 21st century* as core competencies for the next generation (Bayliss, 1999).

These skills are the essence of many specifications for people required for KM posts. They are interpersonal, and increasingly essential for people who want to contribute effectively and make their mark in any community. Communication skills are key. The ability to express oneself clearly, to explain complex situations or thoughts, to get one's point across, are needed by anyone in any activity. Communication can be verbal or written, graphic or textual, active or passive. It is also about listening and understanding, and about being aware of the needs of one's audience and of the objective of the communication.

Negotiation and persuasion, the ability to influence, are also skills that determine the ability to act effectively; it can be argued that they are a combination of communication and political skills. The ability to be sensitive to situations and environments is also required. Facilitation, mentoring and coaching may not be recognized as core organizational skills, but in a KM environment most people are in a post where they are required to help develop understanding, knowledge, skills and expertise in others. In a knowledge environment much of the exchange and sharing of knowledge depends on individual capability to pass on experience and understanding, and thus to contribute to team working. Effective team working requires individuals to play different roles at different times, and facilitation, whether of a formal meeting, of a group problem-solving event or of a social interaction, can be needed by any member of the team.

The understanding of business processes emerged in TFPL research as a key skill. Its interpretation can range from a working knowledge of specific processes to an understanding of the core business drivers and an overview of the processes involved.

A knowledge environment requires all its members to engage with the business of the organization, ie to understand it. They need to see where their contribution fits, where they add value, and where they can increase that value. It assumes that those working for the organization want it to achieve its goals as passionately as those who set them. That does not mean that individuals become locked into one sector, let alone one organization. What is required is a capacity to learn and absorb the business of the organization very quickly and effectively.

3 KM enabling competencies

The third skill set relates to the mix of skills required to plan and implement KM approaches. The emphasis on these skills may well change as KM becomes embedded in the organization and its processes. The initial years will, for example, place emphasis on developing corporate KM behaviours and processes, requiring human resources management, the establishment of business processes and the development of management skills. As the organization matures in KM terms, the need for these skills at a core level is likely to diminish. On the other hand, the requirement at top management level for a KM leader well grounded in KM strategic skills is likely to be maintained or even to grow.

KM enabling competencies encompass a diverse range of activities and experience. They are found in people from equally diverse backgrounds and with a variety of professional and educational circumstances, and include functional, managerial and business skills, some of which have not been widely considered outside their functional area. Information management, human resource management and organizational development are among the areas of expertise which have created interest in KM environments, but which are not widely understood.

Two key areas of enabling competence were identified in the original TFPL research. The first is the ability to understand the knowledge process, and the second is associated with change management.

Understanding the knowledge process

In defining KM skills and development requirements Arthur Andersen (UK) Assurance and Business Advice assigns responsibilities for different parts of the knowledge process (Table 6.4). This approach enables an assessment of the skills and competencies required by everyone involved in the process.

Table 6.4 *Organizational responsibilities for KM*

Define context for knowledge	Use/User
Define what is required	Use/User
Identify the options	Use/User
Select/use appropriate options	Use/User
Integrate knowledge obtained	Use/User
Share knowledge	Contributor
Develop/maintain knowledge content	Knowledge developer
Develop knowledge options	Knowledge manager

Source: Arthur Andersen UK Assurance and Business Advice (reproduced with permission)

Change management

One message that came through consistently in the research was that key skills are those associated with change management. These include the ability to:

- identify the benefits of change for the organization and for individuals
- involve people in the development of ideas and thinking about direction
- identify barriers and roadblocks and ways around them
- understand the art of achieving the possible before tackling the impossible
- influence crucial organizational and infrastructure developments
- retain a missionary zeal for the process.

Passion may not be a change management competence but it is a word frequently used by current KM practitioners. Those pushing the ideas forward and implementing new procedures tend to feel passionately about what they are trying to achieve.

Clusters of KM enabling skills

As a result of the original 'Skills for KM' research the KM enabling skills were organized into three clusters which were described as:

- Experience and diversity
- Information complexity
- Management skills.

1 Experience and diversity

These competencies reflect the experience of the organization or sector that is brought to the role. Knowledge of the business of the organization, and how it works, is crucial. The more senior the post the more highly this ability will be rated. It does not mean that KM practitioners cannot change from one organization or sector to another. It does mean that they need to demonstrate the ability to understand and absorb the fundamentals of an organization quickly. The ability to perceive the differences between organizations and sectors, and to bring knowledge of best practice and lessons learned to a new post, is immensely valuable. Maintaining a close hold on 'the way we did things there' is not. A feature of many people in KM implementation teams is the variety of roles they have undertaken. In the case of UK Ernst and Young for example, one member of the team had a track record which included human resources and change management. 'KM people' recognize options for their skills in different contexts, and opportunities to expand and develop those skills. They take a chance, but a considered one. They do not define themselves entirely by their profession or function.

They are also flexible. This has long been a quality seen as desirable by employers, but regarded with some suspicion by employees. From the employer's point of view flexibility means the ability to change roles, ways of working, plans and aspirations. To the employee it can hint at being required to go in directions they don't enjoy, accept working conditions they don't like and lose control of their career plans. A knowledge environment has to assume a flexible workforce. It needs people who are willing to:

* look at and accept ideas
* discard and 'unlearn' ways of doing things and previous perceptions
* work within teams which may be multidisciplinary, cross-functional and without regard to hierarchical situation
* tolerate ambiguity and enjoy diversity.

It also requires people who have integrity and loyalty, neither of which can be maintained in an environment where the employer does not offer the same loyalty and integrity to staff. Flexibility is a two-way process:

* The organization supplies a framework which creates trust, supports individual development, provides opportunities, recognizes achievement and allows people to fail occasionally.
* The individual understands their contribution to the organization and is willing to take, or create, opportunities to increase this, even if that means trying new directions and learning new skills.

2 Information complexity

An organization is underpinned by complex information flows, and a diverse range of people manage that information. KM practitioners need a fundamental understanding of the flow, impact and value of information and its interaction with the people who will use it in order to create business opportunities, deliver products and services, and improve market share, cost/price ratio, etc. The focus is on 'information' and not 'knowledge' – on the content that feeds daily operations and strategic decisions, that provides the raw material for people to do their work. It is the interaction of information management with organizational structure, management, experience and expertise that enables knowledge creation.

The value that KM practitioners add to the management of the information process depends on their understanding of key business processes. This is the basis for the skills and activities included under the information complexity heading. Not surprisingly, business process analysis heads the list.

3 Management skills

The development of a knowledge environment is a change management exercise, and the management skills required are related to this. Interpersonal skills come high on the list, but core management skills are as important. The ability to design reward and recognition systems, that motivate and support people through the process, is a typical example. Business acumen ensures the selection of projects with the most likely chance of success and significant impact. Aptitude in design monitoring and feedback loops, in order to assess realistically the value of what has been achieved – and the confidence to stop a project if it is not meeting its objectives – are other key management requirements.

Many of the practitioners interviewed in TFPL's research likened their role to that of a consultant. In some cases they work explicitly or implicitly as internal consultants. The set of skills required includes the ability to:

- identify value and sell the project
- set objectives that have a business purpose
- scope accurately and identify resource requirements
- set targets and milestones
- plan and monitor
- sell to everyone involved
- listen and provide feedback.

In fact, a typical list from a project management textbook. In the context of KM many people have described their role as having responsibility without authority – of having goals but no resources. The key skills are to be able to deliver through negotiation and persuasion, through demonstration and commitment, and through leadership and credibility.

Further sets of competencies, particular to knowledge environments, are concerned with the support and facilitation of communities and teams. The skills required are essentially those associated with human resource management, organizational development and the application of ICT. Also required is an understanding of how people work together, and of how space, time and attitudes affect the success or otherwise of group working or of community building. A KM practitioner may not be able to address all the problems that may arise, but a good understanding of the issues involved will help considerably.

The emerging skills mix

As a knowledge environment matures, the focus of skills development changes. In the initial stages the concern is with selling the KM philosophy and concepts, changing behaviours to engender knowledge sharing and build communities, leveraging ICT to enable the sharing of communication, and developing a range of skills to enable the knowledge management process.

With implementation comes the need for a mix of practical skills to develop and maintain the processes and systems which will help members of the organization to exploit their own and organizational knowledge. The key to success at this stage is a thorough understanding of the skills required and an ability to build appropriate teams to undertake the work. Table 6.5 is an example of the skills and competencies required by knowledge practitioners in order to undertake some specific KM activities. In this case they are focused on information handling, but a similar assessment can be applied to any KM activity.

Table 6.5 *KM information related activities and associated competencies*

Activity	Skill
Business process understanding	Business process analysis
Knowledge processes	An appreciation of the context and dynamics of knowledge and information
Knowledge mapping and flows	Knowledge asset identification, creation, maintenance and exploitation
	Identification of flow facilitators and inhibitors
	An ability to estimate information value and quality
	A broad knowledge of sources of information supply – internal and external
Information structuring and architectures	An appreciation of information management principles
	An understanding of how people work and absorb information
	An understanding of 'organization of knowledge tools' eg indexing, classification, metadata, etc
	An appreciation and knowledge of information technology platforms and applications
Document and records management	Workflow understanding
	A knowledge of the document life cycle
	An acquaintance with governance and legislation
Leveraging ICT	An understanding of the application and use of ICT to gain business value
Knowledge and information sharing	An appreciation of the publishing process
	Journalistic skills
	An understanding of team and community information use and processes

TFPL's understanding of the mix of skills required by different KM teams was refined through work to update the KM skills research in the Summer of 2000, and this progress was continued at the discussions at the CKO summit in October 2000. The CKO summit participants identified two 'dream teams' which illustrate the differences between a more central strategic team, and a broader team of practitioners who have to make things happen (Table 6.6).

The lists of skills and competencies, which are a result of the last two years' research, have been clustered into seven groups. The skills profile of a typical chief knowledge officer, a central strategic planning and implementation team, and KM practitioners out in the business, have been plotted against these groups to provide an overview of the requirements and where they fit – a KM skills map (see Figure 6.5 on pages 124–5).

Table 6.6 *KM dream teams*

KM dream team – central enabling		KM dream team – practitioners	
Skills	Attributes	Skills	Attributes
Communication	Pragmatic evangelists	Project management	Inclination for implementation
Leadership	Persistent but humble	Business process analysis	Attention to detail
KM methodology	Organization aware	Interviewing	Persistent jugglers
Knowledge processes	Connected to the top	Content management	Enthusiastic champions
KM tools	Systems view	Networking	Natural connectors
Negotiation	Intuitive	Marketing	Willing to judge and be judged
Strategic planning	Risk taker	Metrics	
		Business planning	

Conclusions

The creation of a KM environment requires a mix of skills, behaviours and attitudes – appropriate competencies throughout the organization. Many organizations are developing competency profiles/frameworks which reflect the need for interpersonal skills, and the development of learned experience throughout the organization.

The competencies required in KM teams are a mix of hard and soft skills, of personality and expertise, of diverse and complementary backgrounds. KM roles and teams present good opportunities for many professions – not least information professionals – whose skills are among the most crucial KM enabling skills. The key to applying such skills successfully depends on:

- the recognition of the complex mix that is required
- the ability to work and thrive in ambiguous roles
- an understanding of empathy with the organization and the people in it
- the ability to change roles and behaviours as KM approaches maturity
- the ability to make KM become the concern of everyone in the organization and to encourage its development by business-based people.

Skills sets: Knowledge Management awareness includes:
- an understanding of the KM concept – the philosophy and theory – and an awareness of the experience of other organizations in developing KM solutions and approaches.
- an understanding of, and the ability to identify, the business value of KM activities to the organization.
- an appreciation of the range of activities, initiatives and labels which are employed to create an environment in which knowledge is effectively created, shared and used to increase competitive advantage and customer satisfaction.

CKO

Strategic Planning Team

Strategic and business
Business awareness/experience
Business processes
Business planning
Change management
Entrepreneurial
Forward thinking
Globalization issues
Industry/sector knowledge
Leadership
Organizational design
Organizational skills
Prioritization
Process understanding
Risk management
Strategic thinking
Strategic planning
Understanding value chain
Visioning

Management
Administration
Business processes
Change management
Coordination
Cost control
Financial management
Leadership
Measurement
    performance
    impact
    value
People management
Process mapping
Project management
Persuasion
Prioritization
Quality assurance
Relationship management
Team building
Time management
Training and development
    skills mapping
    needs analysis

Thinking and learning
Ability to deal with ambiguity
Analytical
Bigger picture view
Conceptual thinking
Emotional intelligence
(Self-awareness, self motivation, persistence, read emotion in others, rein in emotions, zeal)
Innovation
Lateral thinking
Learning techniques
Mentoring
Organizational skills
Original thinking
Perspective
Problem solving
Positive thinking
Personal accountability
Self motivation

Communication and interpersonal

Client/customer service
Coaching
Communication
oral and written
Community building
Consulting
Counselling
Diplomacy
Facilitation
Influencing
Listening
ability, willingness and self
discipline to listen
Marketing
Mentoring
Negotiation
Networking
Partnering
Political
Presentation
Teamworking
Training

Information management

Abstracting
Analysis
Archives management
Bibliometrics
Cataloguing
Codification
Content management
Document management
Editing/writing
External sources
Indexing
Informatics
Information architecture
Information auditing/mapping
Information design
Information/document life cycle
Information processes
Information analysis tools
Intranet/extranet management
IT applications
Metadata
Problem formulation
Research skills
Records management
Search and retrieval
Synthesis
Taxonomies
Text analysis
Thesauri
Understanding user needs
Vendor management

IT literacy

Database design
Database management
Data warehousing
Distributed publishing
E-business minded
Hardware
Information architecture
Internal and external sources
Integration
Intranet/extranet design
Programming
Software applications
Workflow

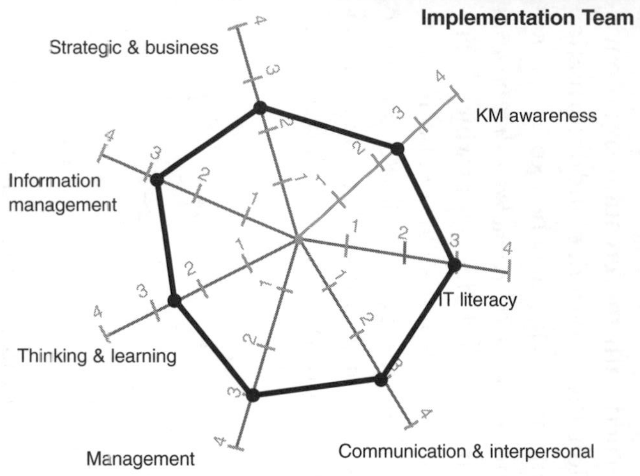

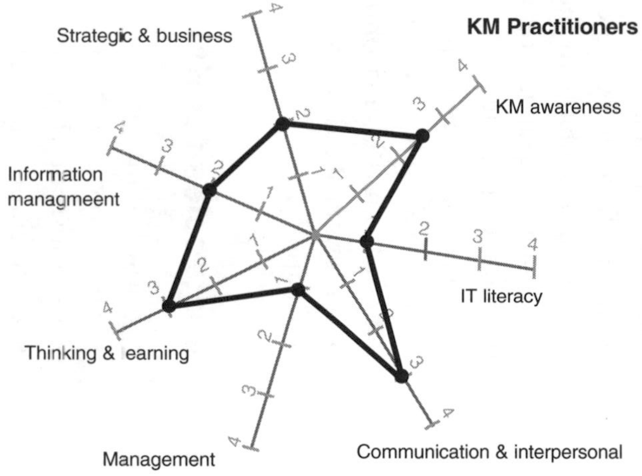

Implementation Team

KM awareness
IT literacy
Communication & interpersonal
Management
Thinking & learning
Information management
Strategic & business

KM Practitioners

KM awareness
IT literacy
Communication & interpersonal
Management
Thinking & learning
Information managment
Strategic & business

Fig. 6.5 *KM skills map*

Knowledge management is concerned with the creation of an environment where everyone can exploit the knowledge and information created and available in the organization. This may be explicit knowledge, tacit knowledge or what the authors of *Knowledge-driven work* (Cutcher-Gershenfeld, 1998) call virtual knowledge – that which is created when a group of people pool their expertise and experience to address a problem or issue. Whatever the activity, for everyone to benefit from this environment the organization needs to be information literate. We discuss the implication of this for skills development in Chapter 7.

Key competencies for KM

- Know the business
- Know how to apply core competencies
- Demonstrate flexibility
- Understand enterprise-wide information – internal and external
- Appreciate information integration and structuring
- Understand business processes and information flows
- Apply change management
- Apply project management
- Apply people skills
- Apply consultancy skills.

References

Bayliss, V (1999) How to determine a curriculum, *RSA Journal*, 3–4, 39–143.

Cutcher-Gershenfeld, J et al (1998) *Knowledge-driven work: Unexpected lessons from Japanese and United States work practices*, Oxford University Press, 1998.

Japan Business and Economics Series.

Public Service Commission of Canada (1998) *Competencies in the public sector* **http://www.psc-cfp.gc.ca/prcb/comp-e.htm**

TFPL (1999) *Skills for knowledge management: building a knowledge economy*, TFPL.

TFPL (2000) *Executive summary of the CKO Summit*, Dublin 2000. Available from TFPL.

Wiig, K M (1995) *Knowledge management methods: Practical approaches to managing knowledge*, Vol 3, Schema Press.

7

Information literacy – a core competence

Our success depends on how we exploit our most valuable assets: our knowledge, skills and creativity. These are the key to designing high-value goods and services and advanced business practices. They are at the heart of a modern, knowledge driven economy.

(Rt Hon Tony Blair MP, Prime Minister, from the foreword to the Competitiveness White Paper, December 1998)

Twenty years ago a seminal publication made recommendations for core information skills to be included in the secondary school curriculum (Marland, 1981). They would provide a foundation for students to study effectively and would become one of the core competencies required by everyone for success in future life. Such skills would train students to take a logical path in their search for and application of information by posing the following questions:

- What (information) do I need?
- Where could I go (for it)?
- How do I get the information?
- Which resources do I use?
- How shall I use the resources?
- What should I make a record of?
- Have I got the information I need?
- How should I present it?
- What have I achieved?

It has taken the information age – with its reliance on digital information – to bring the significance of those skills home to employers, and the turn of the millennium saw organizations from all sectors expressing a need to increase their capability to define information requirements, find, analyse, use, share, store and create information. This capability needs an information-literate workforce.

This argument for everyone to have a basic competence in managing information reflects a view that every worker is a knowledge worker. Although there are specifically information-intensive roles, increasing numbers of people handle information, need to apply their judgment and expertise to it and need the skill to act on it. In order to develop its organizational capability, a KM environment needs people who are able to make decisions and act on their own initiative, think laterally, have and communicate ideas, work in teams and communities and are able to build networks They need skills to enable them to utilize information in day-to-day activities and for problem solving.

> Over the next twenty years, companies, government and individuals will face increasing difficulties in an environment of increasing complexity . . . we have enormous positive potential, including technology, improvements in communications, availability of capital, and great increases in the quantity and availability of information.
>
> (*Open Horizons: three scenarios for 2020*
> 1998 report from the Chatham House Forum)

In June 1999 the RSA published its report *Opening minds: education for the 21st century* (RSA, 1999) which is based on a programme of seminars and consultations that form part of their Redefining the Curriculum project. The objective of the programme is to stimulate debate:

> on what education must achieve in the 21st century: what will it mean to be well educated? How do we deliver the skills, knowledge and understanding to equip everyone for success? How can we make the reality of the 'lifelong learner'?
>
> (Lesley, 1999)

In her lecture the Project Director stated that: 'high standards of education and skills are now necessary for the mass of the working population, not just for a privileged aristocracy of society or of labour'. She went on to argue that it was necessary to define a competence framework to underpin the education curriculum and that: 'Defining the competence framework would effectively redefine what we mean by a well-educated person' (Bayliss, 1999)

In the light of this premise it is interesting to note that within the framework under discussion 'managing information' sits alongside 'managing learning' and 'managing situations' (see Figure 7.1).

The argument for the inclusion of information management as an essential part of the education curriculum is being increasingly voiced. Gerry McGovern of Nua says in his recent book (1999):

> Even if information was extremely well organised, there is simply too much information to make finding exactly what you want a simple process. While in the early days, we all learned as we went along with regard to searching the Internet, more formal training procedures will have to be set in place in the future. Ideally, information management should become part of the core curriculum of schools and education establishments.
>
> (McGovern, 1999b)

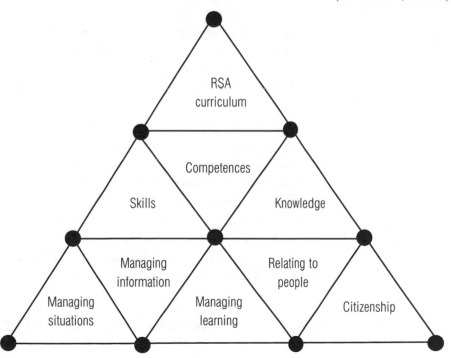

Fig. 7.1 *Defining the competence framework*
Reproduced with permission of the RSA from the Opening Minds report

A project similar to the RSA's was undertaken in the USA. The Commission on Achieving Necessary Skills (SCANS) was appointed by the Secretary of Labor to determine the skills young people need to succeed in the world of work. The Commission's fundamental purpose was to encourage a high-performance economy characterized by high-skill, high-wage employment.

'The primary objective was to help teachers understand how curriculum and instruction must change to enable students to develop those high performance skills needed to succeed in the high performance workplace' (Secretary's Commission on Achieving Necessary Skills, 2000). SCANS has focused on one important aspect of schooling: what they called the 'learning a living' system. In 1991, they issued their initial report, *What work requires of schools*. As outlined in that report, a high-performance workplace requires workers who have a solid foundation in the basic literacy and computational skills, in the thinking skills necessary to put knowledge to work, and in the personal qualities that make workers dedicated and trustworthy.

High-performance workplaces also require other competencies: the ability to manage resources, to work amicably and productively with others, to acquire and use information, to master complex systems, and to work with a variety of technologies (SCANS, 2000).

Information literacy was recognized as a term by the Association of Supervision and Curriculum Development (ASCD) in the USA in 1991, when they adopted the following statements:

> Information literacy . . . equips individuals to take advantage of the opportunities inherent in the global information society. Information literacy should be a part of every student's educational experience. ASCD urges schools, colleges and universities to integrate information literacy programs into learning programs for all students.
>
> (American Association of School Librarians, *Information literacy*, n.d.)

ASCD is one of 60 educational associations that have formed the National Forum on Information Literacy (NFIL).

Information/knowledge-centric organizations

However an organization defines its workforce, the past decade has seen increasing recognition of their reliance on information and knowledge. In 1995 researchers investigating the correlation between information and business performance conducted in-depth interviews in 12 firms from different industry sectors. The firms were selected on the basis of being successful, indeed on financial criteria and peer review. All defined themselves as information- or knowledge-based companies (Owens, et al, 1996). One of the outcomes of the work was an indication that activities undertaken by those who are not in (conventional) information-intensive roles increasingly rely on information. For example Xerox service engineers are recording and sharing solutions to technical problems, and oil platform engineers are forming virtual teams to solve problems at BP Amoco.

Despite growing reliance on the use of information, and the complexity of corporate information, little attention has been paid to developing core information skills throughout organizations. The emergence of personal computers and IT networking has led to widespread use of desktop computing. As a result a great deal of attention has been paid to the development of 'computer literacy', and computer literacy is now a core skill for many posts. The focus is on the ability to use computers and standard software applications, but stops short of being able to structure, find, evaluate and use the information to which a computer provides access. In some organizations staff may be required, or allowed, to acquire the ability to search the Internet; many others are developing intranets to provide access to an array of information sources, and online corporate universities are providing access to self-development programmes. Few, however, are giving thought to the skills required for the effective use of information systems, or to the creation and integration of information into work processes.

In Anglian Water the developers of the corporate university ensured that everyone had access to the same systems and the ability to use the same base tools. However, once the system rolled out they realized that they also needed to ensure that everyone also needed to know how to evaluate and assess information.

A long tradition of studying information-seeking behaviours within the information science academic arena/was brought together in the *ASIS Bulletin* of February/March 1999 with a review of relevant work (Yung-Rng Cheng and Shaw, 1999). The review points out that studies have also taken place in fields as diverse as business, public administration, market research, management, consumer research, medical informatics, health sciences, communication and psychology of personality. Carol Kahlthau (1999) has undertaken studies of students and individual information seekers and proposes a model of the information search process based on stages from task initiation to starting to write. She argues that the individual goes through a range of feelings from uncertainty to optimism, from confusion, frustration and doubt to clarity, from gaining a sense of direction to satisfaction (or dissatisfaction). During the process the focus changes from one of ambiguity to specificity, information seeking moves from searching for relevant information to seeking pertinent information. Other researchers have identified the complexity of information searching and the skill in recognizing when enough information has been acquired. Karl Wiig suggests that an understanding of the conceptual mapping process and critical thinking are crucial survival skills for everyone (Wiig, 1999).

Corporate information literacy

> Information Literacy combines an awareness of the value of information and knowledge to the organisation with the skills and competencies that enable an individual to play a full, effective and rewarding role in knowledge environments.
>
> (TFPL, unpublished, 1999)

The ability to create, store, access and use information is essential to everyone working in a knowledge-based environment. The concepts of information sharing, utilization and creation imply a level of information-handling skill. Xerox service engineers, for example, are required not only to be computer literate, but also to be able to record their experiences concisely, and to understand the concepts of storage and retrieval. Buckman Laboratories has a mobile workforce connecting to a virtual knowledge bank which has required the development of navigation and interpretation skills across that workforce. The universally acknowledged problem of information overload illustrates how poorly information management is understood or applied. A competence framework for these skills has not been developed although a number of corporate organizations and academics have begun work on the requirement.

The development of evidence-based medicine within the health-care sector has demonstrated the requirement for a wide range of people to be able to find, evaluate and apply research evidence

(Palmer, 2000). This is achieved by making research findings readily accessible and educating all members of healthcare teams to find, appraise and apply such findings. It is re-use of knowledge on a large and significant scale. Identifying the training requirements of health teams for these activities uncovered key areas of concern:

- problem definition and the identification of information requirements
- finding and identifying relevant information
- recognizing the difference between too little and too much information and being able to evaluate information.

These concerns were echoed consistently throughout the case studies, consultation and interviews undertaken for the TFPL research project on skills for knowledge management. Designers and champions of knowledge management activities are concerned about how they achieve knowledge-sharing behaviours while employers recognize that it is the *use* of knowledge that will bring business benefit. Sharing is an issue, but there are other essential skills that make up the picture. These include the ability to:

- understand what information is required
- formulate questions and think laterally
- find and access relevant information
- evaluate and assimilate the information accessed
- apply it creatively for business purposes.

The degree of need and focus varies between organizations but even in technical R&D environments where scientists and technologists are accustomed to searching for information, there is a lack of information management skills.

There are a number of ways to identify information-literate organizations. One approach is to consider whether the members of the organization:

- understand the processes they are engaged in and the information supporting those processes
- use the applications or systems that will enable them to navigate their way to the required information

- evaluate the information they are presented with and its relevance to the context in which they are working
- filter and discard information
- synthesize a range of information from diverse sources
- make decisions on the basis of validated information.

Understanding information flow in problem solving (see Figure 7.2) and the key business decisions and processes (see Figure 7.3) is the first step to a commitment to developing information literacy skills.

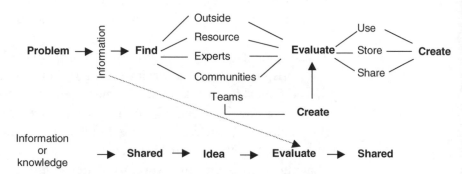

Fig. 7.2 *Information flows and problem solving. Source TFPL*

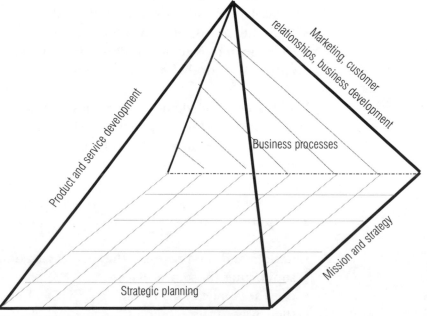

Fig. 7.3 *Key business decisions and processes*

From an organizational perspective the core requirement is for staff to be 'information aware', to understand the value of information within the context in which they are working. The foundation of the organization is the mission and strategy that determine the key activities and processes. The strategy itself is built on knowledge – of the marketplace and the capability and aspirations of key stakeholders (public authority, shareholders, management, staff, environmental groups). The strategy is the basis for planning – turning strategy into action – and plans determine the key activities. The nature of the organization determines the key processes. These elements are centred on information and knowledge. An understanding of information value is critical.

Built around the appreciation of information value are five skills that enable people to work effectively with information: finding, using, creating, organizing and sharing. Their relationship is shown in Figure 7.4.

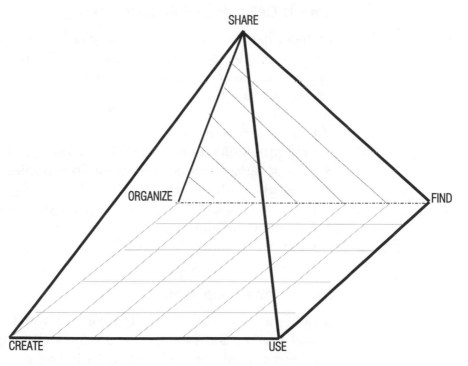

Fig. 7.4 *Information literacy pyramid (TFPL model)*

Information literacy competence

An appreciation of information and knowledge value must become embedded in the organization; information literacy competencies must become part of the core capability. It is possible to isolate the skills and competencies that create an information-literate organization able to support business activities and processes.

Awareness of the value of information and knowledge

A key competence underpinning information literacy. It requires an appreciation of the value that knowledge and information can add to business processes. It also requires an understanding of the business processes and the context in which they operate, the ability to understand the crucial information inputs and outputs of those processes and the knowledge that the organization creates and utilizes in carrying out these processes.

Finding information

Step 1: Define the information need

Problem definition is an analytical skill and requires the systematic definition of the information required to solve the problem including the level, depth and volume and the level of confidence needed in the information used:

- Identify the need.
- Recognize different uses for information.
- Place the information needed within a frame of reference (who, what, when, where, how, why).
- Relate the information needed to prior knowledge.
- Formulate the information problem using a variety of questioning skills.

Step 2: Initiate the search

Requires a basic level of searching skills – the ability to navigate (electronic) systems and sources, and a basic knowledge of the range of sources not available electronically including print, centres of excellence, people and colleagues. It also requires judgment on whether internal or external sources are required, an appreciation of which sources are most appropriate in the circumstances and when the integration of information from a number of sources will add value. The following questions should be posed:

- Is the information already available, relevant and sufficient?
- Is it available within the organization and, if so, how can it be obtained?
- Can it be, or should it be, created by in-house teams?
- Is it available from external sources?
- Is the cost of obtaining or creating the information equalled by its value in the context?

Step 3: Formulate search strategy

Requires a detailed knowledge of the most appropriate sources and their structure. In addition, subject skills will be needed. It will be necessary to:

- Brainstorm ideas – recognize a variety of inputs
- Select search tools
- Identify keywords, concepts, subject headings, descriptors
- Identify criteria for evaluating possible sources.

Using information

Use of structured information, which is consistently used in the same way, requires little more than the ability to follow pre-determined instructions and competence in using tools associated with that use. The design of systems is in itself an important element of the efficient operation of many business processes and the ability to use the systems may give rise to training requirements. This basic level of competence to use core information systems is part of an information literacy framework.

The effective use of more complex information requires the application of core professional, technical or organizational knowledge in order to recognize significance and meaning. It also requires the ability to:

- evaluate the information found
  - determine authoritativeness, currency and reliability
  - differentiate between sources
- assess its relevance, quality and suitability
  - skim and scan for major ideas and keywords
  - differentiate between fact, opinion, propaganda, point of view and bias
  - recognize errors in logic
- integrate information from disparate sources
  - classify, group or label the information
  - recognize interrelationships among concepts
  - identify points of agreement and disagreement among sources
- sift and select information effectively
  - the ability to reject information is as important as being able to find it
- select appropriate formats
  - integration of information may require expertise in using IT tools and report formats but, more importantly, will require an understanding of the comparability of information from different sources and the ability to present results in a meaningful way
- interpret the information
  - summarize, identify relevant facts and detail
  - synthesize
  - organize and analyse
  - compare with original problem – adjust strategies
  - draw conclusions.

Creating information

The creation of information is often a product of the business process and the results may not be recognized as 'information'. Documents of all kinds are written and distributed within organizations and sent to clients, suppliers, regulatory authorities, etc. Other information may be generated in the form of management information reports, and the data that feeds into these reports. Information will be created that is peculiar to the organization. The creation of operational data is generally predetermined, structured around particular tasks and reflects industry norms. Effective training in the use of organizational tools for these processes is part of the information literacy approach. Critical actions include:

- deciding on purpose
- identifying key content
- selecting formats (written, oral, visual) appropriate to audience and purpose
- assessing production guidelines and standards
- creating an original product – appropriate use of media – audio, video, software, etc.
- understanding legal and corporate constraints
- providing appropriate guides, mapping, documentation.

Organizing information

KM-related discussions focus primarily on behaviours – how to 'make' or encourage people to use information. This aspect is important and there is a set of skills to make it possible for people to do this effectively. 'Using' requires more than a willingness, it requires the capability to record information effectively, signpost and guide people to it efficiently and identify its status and fitness for purpose.

Lateral thinking is related to the ability to use information creatively, being able to view it within its domain but also to spot similarities and synergies. This requires an understanding of the influences that lie behind the interpretation or presentation by the information creator. A basic understanding of how data is collected and information is created is an information literacy competence.

Other core information literacy skills enable information to be stored effectively. These include:

- abstracting: the ability to write a succinct summary which gives the reader a clear impression of the relevance and significance of information available in a particular source, thus enabling colleagues to select relevant information
- indexing: using corporate indexing, classification, codes or taxonomies to enable information to be found when required
- structuring: signposting documents and expertise enhances both the alerting and finding process; this includes, among other things, the effective use of subject headers, document summaries, and the structure of (intranet) web pages
- providing retention, review and disposal information: including status, age, and version information about the item.

Sharing information

In KM environments the information- and knowledge-creation process recognizes that real value is created through the sharing of ideas, making connections between ideas, spotting the implications and opportunities through linking information from disparate sources and the ability to express, explore and exploit ideas. The key skills are communication, team working, IT literacy and lateral thinking.

In an information-literate organization communication skills include the ability to:

- express ideas clearly in writing, orally or in a presentation
- listen and evaluate the opinions and information contributed by others
- assess the most effective means for communication in particular circumstances.

Effective team working, that which results in the creation as well as use of information, requires the ability to:

- facilitate productive meetings, either virtual or actual, and communication between people
- record and build on outcomes of such interaction
- understand when team and community outcomes have significance for wider communities.

Understanding information management

Although there is a requirement for increased skills for information seeking and use, there is also a need for increased understanding of information management principles, throughout a KM environment. The recent emergence of corporate 'taxonomies' of varying quality, designed by people from a variety of functions, is an indication of a perceived requirement but also of the lack of an established body of knowledge in this area.

Specific KM, or IM, roles deal with the design of systems, procedures and processes to enable effective creation of and access to recorded knowledge. Within the context of systems design many decisions that affect information management are driven by technical and cost considerations, specific to the system. An understanding of basic information management principles is required by everyone in a KM environment in order to overcome barriers. At a very fundamental level, understanding the purpose of structured fields in document templates, for example, is likely to improve the quality of input. Similarly, designing the layout of web pages, normally seen as a purely technical function, needs input from information-literate users.

Information literacy skills are needed throughout the organization and need to be part of the daily skill set. Just as computer skills have spread throughout the workforce through primary, secondary and higher education we will eventually see an information-literate society. That is a long-term view; organizations need to create the capability now. Information skills must be actively and visibly valued by the organization and people given time, space and encouragement to develop them. People need to see their relevance to their work and understand the objectives and benefits of a more information-intensive way of working. It should add quality to their lives – not more burden. If core competencies can help them deal with information overload they will see an instant benefit.

Conclusions

The skills required throughout a KM organization are emerging as a strong discussion theme in the KM arena. So far the focus has largely been on knowledge-sharing behaviours and the ability to manage and survive in less hierarchically structured organizations. As organizations achieve success in these fields they recognize the next stage of skill development – information literacy. Discussion among support professionals, in particular those in HR and IT, is addressing the implications of the KM approach to their roles and skills.

Information sharing and utilization

The concepts of information sharing, utilization and creation, imply a level of information-handling skill that has been taken for granted but not explored in any depth outside the LIS academic arena, where there is an established interest in information-seeking behaviours.

Find, appraise, use

The process of problem definition, identification of relevant information and knowledge, evaluation and appropriate application, and feedback of results has been explored as part of the evidence-based healthcare approach. The lack of skills emerges as a major concern in KM environments where the value of the systems and activities developed is dependent on the eventual utilization of knowledge.

There is a requirement for an understanding of information management principles throughout the organization. The development of corporate 'taxonomies' indicates a recognition that the 'organization of knowledge' through structuring and coding is key to accessing relevant, filtered information. Similarly, the mechanisms in place to assist the recording of information, sharing of knowledge and navigation need to be understood by those using them in order that they may maintain quality and demonstrate benefit. IT literacy has had a high priority for a number of years in order that everyone can use IT tools as part of everyday working practice. The same attention to the integration of sound information management practice is required.

References

American Association of School Librarians, *Information literacy: a position paper on information problem solving*, available at www.ala.org/aasl/positions/ps_infolit.html

Bayliss, V (1999) How to determine a curriculum, *RSA Journal*, **CXLVII**, (3/4), 39–47.

Kahlthau, C C (1999) 'Accommodating the user's information search process: Challenges for information retrieval systems designers, *Bulletin*, **25** (3), Feb/March 1999, available at **www.ala.org/aasl/positions/ps_infolit.html**

Lesley, J (1999) Opening minds, *RSA Journal*, **CXLVII** (5489), 2/4, 18–23.

McGovern, G (1999a) *The caring economy: Business principles for the new digital age*, Blackhall Publishing.

McGovern, G (1999b) *Re-inventing human interaction in the 'e-age'*, presentation at the European Business Information Conference, Dublin, TFPL.

Marland, M (ed) (1981) *Information skills in the secondary curriculum: The recommendations of a working group sponsored by the British Library and the Schools Council*, Schools Council Curriculum Bulletin 9, Methuen Educational.

Owens, I et al (1996) *Information and business performance: A study of informa-tion systems and services in high performing companies*, Bowker-Saur.

Palmer, J (2000) 'Schooling and skilling health librarians for an evidence based culture', *Advances in Librarianship*, **23**, 145–67.

RSA (1999) *Opening minds: Education for the 21st century*, RSA.

Secretary's Commission on Achieving Necessary Skills (SCANS) (2000) *The SCANS skills and competencies: An overview*, The Workforce Skills Website, available at

www.scans.jnu-edu

Wiig, E H and Wiig, K M (1999) *Conceptual learning considerations*, Knowl-edge Research Institute.

Yung-Rng Cheng and Shaw, D (1999) Information seeking and finding, *Bul-letin of the American Society for Information Science*, (Feb/March).

Part 3

IM in KM – leveraging information management skills

8

The role of IM in KM – core skills in new contexts

Anyone in the organisation who is not directly accountable for making a profit should be involved in the creating and distributing of knowledge that the company can use to make profit.

(Browne, 1997)

A key feature of knowledge-based environments is the management and exploitation of information – its identification, acquisition, capture, structure, flow, use and maintenance. As we have discussed in earlier chapters this information is complex, wide ranging and is produced, acquired and held by many sources. It includes both external and internal information: external information being formally sourced and acquired from information providers and organizations, commissioned from third-party research and intelligence organizations and flowing into the organization through its working contacts and relationships; internal information being the product of the operational, tactical and strategic business of the organization, held in a variety of formats and records. Some types of information are mandatory, formal and controlled; others flow through and around the organization as part of the communication process and individual or departmental work processes. Internal information is often invisible to most people and equally often poorly managed and used. Realizing the value of this information is a key knowledge management objective and depends on its effective integration and use, calling for the application of a high level of information management skills.

Within most emerging KM environments the visibility of the

library and information professionals and the utilization of their skills have been low. Although increasing numbers are moving into KM-related posts few of these, with notable exceptions, have yet gained senior KM positions. There are undoubtedly many reasons for this, but a number of key factors need to be explored.

Barriers to entry

Peer groups

Firstly, the successful development of knowledge environments is almost always driven from the most senior levels of the organization. As we noted earlier, without the commitment of backing from the CEO or other influential senior managers it is an approach that will seldom succeed. A strategic planning team, however small, which can identify and demonstrate the potential benefits, wins this commitment. These teams typically involve senior people whose roles often include a responsibility for strategic developments within the organization. As such they are part of a peer group who identify each other as those able to plan and champion new ideas. Seldom are information officers/managers part of this peer group and thus they are not involved in that early strategic planning stage. The complexity of corporate information has resulted in many diverse roles being involved in its management, and the theoretical base and practical skills of the information profession have often not been recognized. This problem is compounded by the tendency of members of the LIS sector to gravitate towards and focus more on their professional groups than on broader environments.

Focus of KM approaches

Secondly, many of the approaches to KM discussed in Part 1 have not been based around information management. They have focused on changing cultures, facilitating and sharing information, recording best practice, organizational learning, group working and the application of information technology. All, of course, rely on effective information management, but it is often viewed as a support to the prime activity – not a central concern. Even those approaches that explicitly set out to leverage stored information and data collections tend to focus on technology solutions before facets of content management and organization of knowledge.

Senior management perception of LIS professionals

The complexity of corporate information and the fragmentation of information roles and functions also affect the way that the LIS profession is perceived. Despite the variety of roles that qualified information scientists and library managers hold in organizations the perception of most senior management is that the profession is fundamentally associated with the management of libraries. Even where this is translated into supply management for external information resources or the facilitation of virtual libraries it is still perceived as a support rather than as a core function. The valuable technical skills that information professionals possess are readily acknowledged. A number of leading KM personalities emphasize that more librarians and information specialists will be needed. Presenting at a TFPL conference in 1998, Ellen Knapp, then CKO of Coopers and Lybrand (now CKO of PwC), said

Information specialists are going to get rich.

At a conference in April 2000 David Snowden of IBM referred to the skills of librarians as valuable and undervalued, and the business guide *Liberating knowledge*, published by the CBI in association with IBM, includes a chapter on the art of classification.

For the most part senior management feel that KM skills need to be directed by people core to the business. Rightly or wrongly, information professionals do not appear to be seen as business managers or to have the necessary understanding of the organization to take key strategic roles.

The advent of KM has again brought into focus the apparent lack of effective marketing skills in the profession. Marketing in this context means the ability to communicate the potential impact of information skills on the organization and their relevance to the core business.

LIS professionals' perceptions and expectations

Perceptions obviously affect expectations. If senior management do not expect information professionals to participate in strategic planning, then senior information professionals do not expect to be involved. It becomes a self-fulfilling circle. When TFPL undertook its research into skills for knowledge management in 1999, it was alarming to discover a large number of corporate information professionals who felt that KM was a new term for what they were already doing. There were, of course, notable exceptions, but many felt the label was being used by other functions and professions as a means of capitalizing on the relatively new corporate interest in information. And it is certainly true that the KM approach has broadened and deepened the interpretation of information and information management, and in so doing it has also created far more competition for information roles. In the same way that Ben Gilad can suggest that the post of Competitive Intelligence Officer is best taken by an ambitious high flyer (Gilad, 1996), information management roles are beginning to be a seen as a potential route to a high-profile career. No wonder that some information professionals are beginning to feel insecure.

The danger is, of course, that while they are defending their corner they are also building walls round their own staff. Such attitudes in information managers contribute as much to the information department being kept in its box as do senior management expectations. A surprising number of LIS professionals associate their role with the management of external information although various research projects suggest that anything between 80–95% of the information used in an organization is generated internally. There appears to be little understanding of the integration of internal and external information discussed in Chapter 4.

A typical comment from a strategic planner on the effect of maintaining boundaries round any function was

If you manage people in boxes you get boxes.

The ability to work across organizational boundaries and the willingness to take opportunities to try different roles and ways of working are essential for information professionals in knowledge environments, but it requires an understanding of organizational dynamics and a particular mindset.

Mindset

In his presentation at EBIC99 Hubert Saint Onge suggested that the most important task for organizations developing KM is to change the mindset of their people (Saint Onge, 1999), and Figure 8.1 illustrates the relationship between capability, attributes and mindset.

When this is applied to the information profession he suggested that the change information professionals have to make is to think of themselves as part of the core business – not as a service to those who do the business. To understand the way that corporate information is created and used, and the crucial information flows, requires an understanding of the business process and an ability to map the knowledge processes that support it. The people who understand this best are the strategic planners, organizational developers and those who work in the core business. Few information professionals understand the full picture. They interface with document managers, builders of customer relationship databases, management information systems, operational data flows, etc, without being able to see the full picture. They are, therefore, not able to contribute easily to any radical thinking about its management. Even more frustrating is the fact that this lack of understanding of the total picture prevents many information professionals from being able to communicate the value of their skills in new applications.

Knowledge environments are clearly information centric and require first-class information management. They provide, therefore, a unique opportunity for members of the information profession to

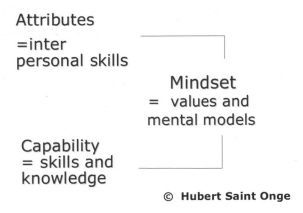

© **Hubert Saint Onge**

Fig. 8.1 *Capability, attributes and mindset*

become a core part of their organizations. In order to participate fully, however, it is necessary to buy into the KM philosophy and to recognize that working with strategic partners, initiating cross-functional projects and active membership of multidisciplinary teams is essential. IM is not KM, even though it is an essential element. Information professionals need to demonstrate that they not only understand this, and the role that IM plays, but also that they are able to adapt and grow with the organization. More than ever before the information professional cannot work in isolation.

Key mindset changes for information professionals

- Partnership – not service
- Contribution to key business processes – not professionalism
- Integration – of external and internal information
- Skills transfer – training, facilitation, coaching – not protection of the information delivery function
- Creation of strategic services and change.

The impact of professional information skills

So how can the expertise of the information professional best have impact and value in KM environments? Figure 8.2 illustrates five activities that underpin knowledge creation, flow and use and utilize the core skills of an information professional. They are skills that need to grow and develop alongside a real understanding of context – understanding the business and its processes; the development of management and organizational skills; and the application of experience. The ability to learn and apply that learning is the most valuable.

Identifying and acquiring internal information sources

A knowledge environment needs to identify its information resources. Its raison d'être is to leverage these resources, map where they are, how they are created and used, which are mission critical and how these are protected, and which create value. It requires an understanding of business processes and information flows, and the ability to assess the quality, reliability and relevance of the resources.

An information audit, or the creation of an information map, is a process which, through the analysis of workflow and processes:

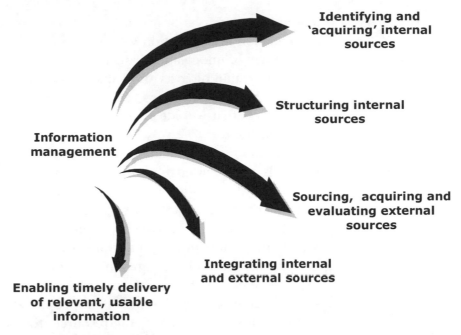

Fig. 8.2 *IM skills in KM environments*

- identifies the information needs of the organization, business unit and individual
- develops an understanding of where information is created
- creates an information assets register
- draws a map of information flow
- establishes the need for information integration
- assesses the effect of technical platform and organizational culture on the use of information.

The benefits of an information audit are:

- Evaluation of information assets
  - identification of key information related to business objectives
  - prioritization for creation, access, maintenance and protection
- Improved information flow, reflecting business processes
  - detection of information gaps and of unmet need
  - development of information and information resource sharing
  - improved quality of information
  - identification of 'quick wins' for early impact
  - information infrastructure made explicit

- Saved money
  - reduction in duplication
  - leverage of information assets
  - identification of costs and value.

It is a process that will ideally consider the need for, and availability of, external sources.

Undertaking an information audit requires information management skills and knowledge plus an understanding of information use and value. It also calls for a range of additional skills of which project management is the key to ensuring that the appropriate mix is available as required. Data collection needs the skill of a market researcher – interviewing, questionnaire surveying, facilitation of group discussions and focus groups, analysis of results and presentation – all are needed for an effective audit. The understanding of the corporate culture and the way that people work in that culture enables the auditor to identify the resources that are in silos throughout the organization. An understanding of work processes and the critical success factors for individuals enables the identification of the value of information resources to individuals and business processes.

The acquisition of these resources requires the ability to demonstrate their potential multiple use and the value of sharing. It requires an understanding of which resources are appropriate on the intranet, or via a portal (and what implications suggest maintaining these as current and reliable), and which may need to be accessed through alternative methods. It needs a mix of information theory and practice, an understanding of technology, an understanding of business processes and an appreciation of corporate culture. It also requires skills transfer. Training others to identify useful data and information, establishing methods and routines for information capture, the design of usable coding and indexing for information owners to apply to their data are all part of 'acquiring' internal information.

Core skills and competencies for the identification and acquisition of information are derived from the ability to:

- map and analyse internal information needs, assets, flows and sources
- propose mechanisms to improve information flow and sharing
- identify and demonstrate the potential impact and business value

- negotiate and persuade
- work in multifunctional teams.

Structuring internal information

The structuring of information is a core information management skill. It includes the design of both the form in which the record is held and its output, the selection or development of coding tools to enable effective navigation and retrieval, and management of metadata. The enterprise-wide use of shared information sources requires the use of software, well-structured information and intelligently selected indexing. Despite the development of software that will surf many information sources and employ 'fuzzy logic' and intelligent agents, the need to code and index internal sources to reflect the unique focus and work of the organization has fuelled the growth of corporate taxonomies. The ability to build subject structures, thesauri and classification schemes has much to offer. Its application to the construction of a corporate thesaurus, for example, is proving invaluable, facilitating a corporate approach to structuring the corporate language.

The design of databases, data warehouses, and a variety of data files may seem to have been taken over by IT and other professionals. But the design of effective structures depends on the understanding of the ultimate use of information – and that is an information professional's skill. For this skill to be effective it needs to be accompanied by the ability to communicate and work with those who manage information technology and design business processes.

Core competencies for structuring internal information sources include:

- an understanding of how information is used
- the ability to select and develop tools for coding and classifying information
- an understanding of IT applications, including intranet and portals
- an appreciation of information design
- the ability to work with other professions and disciplines.

Sourcing, acquiring and evaluating external information

Successful organizations are sensitive to the external world. They are open to ideas from all sources and are continually monitoring risks and opportunities. The flow of information from the external environment is important. It is on this area that the LIS profession has focused its attention, and is where it needs to make explicit the expertise it employs in this activity.

The knowledge of external sources and services is not to be undervalued. There are an increasing number of options, and picking the mix that will provide maximum value to the organization requires an understanding of the elements of cost-effectiveness. Supply management for information requires, as with supply management for any other resource, an understanding of needs and priorities, an in-depth knowledge of potential resources and their value to the organization, and an ability to evaluate their reliability and quality.

Supply management also requires the ability to negotiate contracts and partnerships to meet organizational requirements. As suppliers develop their markets and offerings it is crucial that information managers have the ability to make deals with suppliers and services that have high value and utility for the organization. Global organizations, for example, need contracts that allow them to use consistent information in all their operations without duplicating contracts or suppliers, while suppliers need to maximize their sales and contacts. The ability to negotiate with suppliers, and the many potential purchasers of their products within a global or multi-site organization, results in significant savings of cash, time and frustration.

Specification of delivery formats that translate well to corporate intranets or desktop sites is crucial to supply management. Information provided in a format that can be easily assimilated into the environment and task is twice as valuable as that which needs massaging and re-presenting. The understanding of its ultimate use, and the context in which it is to be used, is the task of the information supply manager. Organizing information feed requires more than a negotiation of price and technical platform – it needs a real understanding of the organization that will use it.

Monitoring supplier performance requires an understanding of the difference between price and cost. Prices can be benchmarked against other suppliers but the assessment of cost requires an evaluation of the use of the information supplied, its relevance and delivery. Assessing the real cost of one supplier against another requires an understanding of the value of the service to the organization.

And there are always new suppliers, new allegiances and new products on the market. Tracking these against established suppliers requires a balanced view of the information mix. Business units and influential individuals will continue to be targeted with new or alternative products and services. In the information technology arena, where the problem is equally, if not more, acute, outsourcing to a facilities management organization has become popular. The FM company picks up the problem of finding solutions to match organizational requirements and the organization is able to limit the numbers involved in supply decisions to a few experts. Few organizations have so far outsourced the supply of information services. However, as suppliers merge and form partnerships, thus creating the critical mass to orchestrate all the information supply sources an organization requires, it must eventually become an attractive option. In this scenario the corporate information manager is still in much the best position to understand the real requirements, and ensure that the FM company makes the best suggestions. Their role as the expert link between the FM company and the business should increase, not decrease, their value.

There are also copyright issues. The re-use of information that is supplied is a fact of organizational life. But the issue of protection of intellectual property and of the information purchased from external suppliers has to be understood and enforced. An understanding of re-use and of management issues is as crucial to information management as is the interpretation of the legal situation. The latter will prevent the organization being challenged in law. The former will help it assess its position as it develops its own information products.

Core competencies for sourcing external information include:

- an understanding of business processes
- an understanding of information impact, exploitation and use
- a knowledge of information suppliers and an ability to assess their credibility
- the ability to evaluate information for reliability and value
- negotiation and contractual skills.

Integrating internal and external information

The integration of internal and external information is key to knowledge environments. For those who work with and use information there is little distinction between the two. 'Internal' information is often 'external' information that has gone through an internal brain. It is a compilation of information:

- collected or gleaned (from service or sales staff for example)
- generated by daily operations
- fed in from news stories or the chairman's latest business meeting
- commissioned from external agencies of consultants
- supplied through an information centre or library.

Spotting the significance of the resulting mix of information is, as argued earlier, where information ends and knowledge begins. But where does internal end and external begin? There is a variety of sources that a user can access, some on the internal systems – which may also give direct access to some external sources – while other external sources need to be accessed differently. Integration means bringing these together or signposting their existence. The ideal is where the user can pose a question, be prompted to provide context, then receive the most pertinent information and be guided to other relevant sources, either internal or external. Portals are, of course, an example of this approach and are becoming commonplace in organizations and on the web. They provide easy access to a variety of electronic sources, point to people and organizations, provide links for forums and discussions, and provide additional value in tailoring this access to individuals, teams, groups, or departments.

To build such systems there has to be:

- an understanding of available sources, their quality, reliability, and comparability, and the applicability of intranet, groupware and other systems for information dissemination
- an ability to design information supply for consolidation with other information resources
- a mechanism to make visible relevant sources
- a system for maintaining the sources
- a means for editing and verification.

Core skills for managing the integration of internal and external sources include:

- an understanding of information impact and use

- an appreciation of information technology applications and developments
- information structure and design skills
- a knowledge of business processes and operations.

Delivering information

The delivery of information is the point at which the effectiveness of the system is judged. The information needs to be there when required – not sooner and not later. It must be just enough – not too much – but some people need more than others. It has to be focused and to the point – but also to stimulate thoughts and ideas. Delivery is, in fact, a demanding task. Desktop delivery via computer networks has changed perceptions. The ability to log on to the Internet, or to dial into information suppliers selected by the organization, appears to give everyone 'information at their fingertips'. The reality is that access to numerous information sources and the web can result in the acquisition of a great deal of information, very little of which can be used. Information overload is a result of having a great many interests and information feeds and no system for filtering or prioritizing.

Task-orientated, narrowly focused information can be effectively delivered as a generic product via the desktop. The first win for the information professional is in understanding this requirement and ensuring that it works well.

If everyone knew exactly what they wanted, and if it was available, there would be no problem. The next and more difficult challenge is to provide information that meets less well articulated or formulated requirements. This may be through the design of systems that identify related and 'almost relevant' information. These may be based on inference and insight, and may be electronic or manual. Whatever the system, it is about managing serendipity – that process that allows us to hunt for something that we will recognize when we see it and will put the most useful piece of information in front of us when we aren't looking for it. It is a process that contributes to creative and innovative working, but that can also bury you in information if it is adopted as a way of life. It may mean mediated desk research or the expansion of electronic and people networks. It is about managing the interface between people and information in a way, and within a timescale, that meets their purpose. It is where the science of information management has its most explicit impact.

Core competencies for enabling the timely delivery of information include:

- an appreciation of business, group and individual objectives
- an understanding of workflow and practices
- the ability to identify time- and business-critical information content
- an appreciation of the use of appropriate formats for re-use of information
- a knowledge of software and information supply developments such as textual analysis.

Powering information

Information management skills, as demonstrated in Figure 8.3, underpin essential activities in a knowledge management environment. But their value is only realized through the understanding that the 'sum of the total is greater than all the parts'. Each individual activity is crucial

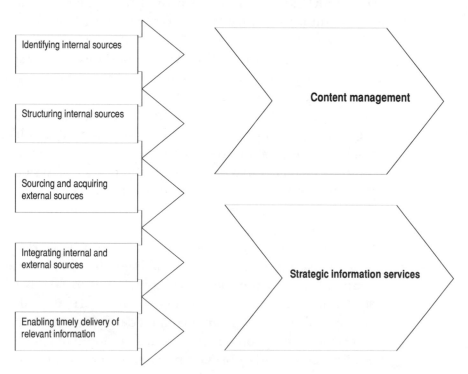

Fig. 8.3 *Creating an information-empowered organization*

but taken together we are talking about strategic objectives – content management and business-aligned information services – a model that is emerging in many knowledge-based environments.

Content management

Content Management is the Achilles heel of most KM initiatives.

An article in the journal *Financial Knowledge Management* used the above quote from an Ovum report to argue that content is king – but only if it is current, relevant and accurate – and used the Ovum definition of content management as

a set of rules, roles and processes to manage the content lifecycle through origination, publication, delivery and expiry of digital assets such that quality information is delivered to the right people.

(Woods and Madan, 1999)

The important point about the concept of 'content management' is that it does not limit the focus to either external or internal information, or to any part of the value chain. The focus is on the content, wherever it comes from, be it electronic journals, market data, operational data or internal reports. It is the efficient acquisition, effective packaging and delivery, and lifecycle management that are crucial. This requires an understanding of how content is created and used, its value and shelf-life, and an ability to integrate both with each other and into business processes. It is a core business activity, whatever the business. It is also a core information management activity.

Strategic information services

Information services package, develop and deliver value-added services to the business-critical areas of the organization. Their role is increasingly to:

* facilitate effective handling of the 80% of enquiries that can be predicted through help systems and call centres

- educate and train users to find, acquire, use and manage information
  - to make effective use of content
- manage the internal information flows that do not fall within the jurisdiction of content management
  - facilitation of meetings and forums (virtual or otherwise), for example
- provide the 20% of value-added information that requires a mix of research, analysis and consultancy skills.

Enabling an organization to obtain a high return on their investment in information requires information professionals to think strategically, to build strategic partnerships, and to understand and value their own information management skills.

Conclusions

A knowledge management environment needs excellent information management (IM). Although IM is not KM, knowledge is communicated through information, and the management of information creation, flow, storage and destruction is essential if individuals and groups are to share and build knowledge. The skills that facilitate the building of infostructures – the combination of information architecture, content management and information technology that enables individuals to access the right, reliable information at the right time, prevents information overload, and supports push- and-pull information delivery – are increasingly valued and sought by organizations. There is no doubt that the information profession has the theoretical basis and practical skills to provide this essential element of KM. However, the impact of the skills developed by many information professionals is diluted by a lack of business understanding, and of the ability to demonstrate an understanding of where their skills have strategic and tactical value. We believe that to add value to a knowledge-based environment, a library and information service needs to develop a range of interpersonal and business skills in its staff, and value itself as a core part of the organization. We suggest therefore that LIS professionals must:

- understand the organization they work for and its business drivers and process

- identify with, and be part of, that organization
- build strategic partnerships and work well in multidisciplinary teams
- understand the value of their own skills and the ways in which they can be applied across the organization
- innovate and ensure IM skills can be exploited
- avoid building barricades and protecting their patch
- recognize the strengths of others and work with them
- continue to learn and develop
- move from a service mentality to a partnership approach
- facilitate the development of information literacy throughout the organization
- think strategically about the development of information services and content management
- take risks
- enjoy the process of change.

References

Browne, Sir J (1997) 'Unleashing the power of learning: an interview with John Browne', *Harvard Business Review*, **75** (5), Sept–Oct, 147–88.

Gilad, B (1996) *Business blindspots: Replacing myths, beliefs and assumptions with market realities*, Infonortics Ltd.

Knapp, E M (1996) *Knowledge management: the key to success in tomorrow's economy*, Business Information Conference 96, New York, TFPL.

Saint Onge, H (1999) *Cultivating corporate culture towards a knowledge environment*, European Business Information Conference, Dublin, TFPL.

Woods, E and Madan, S (1999) *Knowledge management: Building the collaborative enterprise*, Ovum.

9

Stepping over the boundaries

> In the new knowledge economy, companies and individuals will thrive on the knowledge they hold; the skills they update to meet technological change; the flexibility they can deploy to meet changing circumstances; the creativity they can apply to tap new markets.
>
> (Rt Hon Tony Blair MP, CBI Annual Conference, October 1999)

The new economy presents unique opportunities for those willing and able to take them. There is nothing particularly new in this situation. Every generation is faced with opportunities that enable those with the right set of skills to move in a different direction, to enhance their careers, and enjoy the challenge. It has always depended on a mix of luck (being in the right place at the right time), foresight (acquiring new skills and experiences) and the capacity to enjoy change and risk. Each generation also has the choice of maintaining a more conservative career path, opting to develop along a well-tested route. The point is to retain the right to choice. Within the knowledge economy opportunities for information professionals have opened up in a way that is unprecedented – but competition for those opportunities is intensifying all the time, and traditional library and information roles are changing fast. It is then imperative that those members of the profession who want to develop with the opportunities make an assessment of their skills and how they can be applied, and devise a strategy for ensuring that those skills make an impact on the organization.

Great expectations

Take just one example of the opportunities – the one quoted above on page 161 – where a recent Ovum report claimed that 'content management is the Achilles heel of most KM initiatives'. And that example is just the tip of the iceberg. In 1987 Nick Moore published the results of his research which identified the many roles that had information content and could be potential opportunities for information professionals (Moore, 1987). Since then the impact of information skills in other roles has been felt, and the range of posts where information skills are applied in creative and imaginative ways have become diverse and increasing. They are essential, tactical posts; but the movement of information professionals into key senior posts outside the library and information sector has been minimal. Information professionals are valued members of teams and their essential contribution to the underpinning infrastructure is recognized. They are seldom the people who set the information strategy, still less the knowledge management strategy, at business level, or even determine the mix of resources to be allocated to building a robust information capability. There are notable exceptions, of course, but they are still the exceptions.

Does it matter?

We think that it does. Information has become a key corporate resource and its strategic management is beginning to move up the corporate hierarchy. As knowledge management and learning organization's philosophies become embedded into corporate life, as e-business gathers momentum, as content management becomes as crucial as the management of technology, then responsibility for information strategies and their development will move into the boardroom or to the senior management team. That is where the information profession should be represented. It is where the next stage in corporate development will be discussed and where it is possible to incorporate information into corporate strategies. It is where the challenges become crucial but exciting. It may not be everyone's cup of tea, but many could thrive in those positions.

It is as much about information professionals increasing their areas of influence as it is a question of skills transfer. It is worth noting that at least one organization is basing their reward system on the sphere of influence that a person has, a reflection of the importance of being in a position to contribute and persuade. Information professionals bring an equally valid perspective to corporate decision making and it is up to them to make sure it is taken into account.

So why isn't it happening?

This is a question that has been asked for at least three decades. We believe it is all about expectations. Undoubtedly there are information professionals with the potential to move into senior management. Not only are their basic skills good but we are seeing more confident and outgoing personalities, willing to think laterally about careers, an interesting and highly experienced workforce and a calibre of under- and post-graduates that can match any profession. We are also seeing a wave of people from many other professions and functions attracted to information/knowledge management as their future career. They are becoming serious competitors, not so much for the highly technical information management roles where the lack of appropriate skills is a real barrier, but for the management of services and resources.

The information professional's expectations

As TFPL found in its research of 1999, in the business sector few Chief Knowledge Officers, or their equivalents, have been appointed from outside the organization or the business sector. But then few top management posts go to people without an intimate knowledge of the industry in question. Again there are exceptions. Professional managers do move between sectors, but they are a very small minority. People in senior positions were not born with an innate understanding of their industry or organization. They acquired it throughout their career, just as information professionals do – or do they? Is that the difference – that those reaching top management positions never saw any barriers to doing so? Their training as an accountant, engineer, HR or OD professional didn't somehow set them apart from the business of their organization. They expected that there would be opportunities for them and they were ready to take them.

How many information professionals set out with the same attitude, or are ready to look for opportunities to extend their experience and influence? How many expect that they could, and should, succeed at senior management level?

Employers' expectations

The other side of the coin is the perception of the role of information professionals by potential employers. During the past two years we have written articles and given presentations that share the unwelcome findings from different research projects that employers perceive information professionals as possessing valuable skills, but as back-office workers who provide services and resources to the organization under the direction of real managers. The reasons given for this by employers include:

- a lack of business knowledge
- a lack of understanding of the interplay between information and organizational objectives
- poor team and leadership skills
- lack of management skills.

How far these criticisms hold water is questionable, given the development in library and information science education, and the range of professional and personal development that many in the profession undertake. However, the perception remains and we are convinced it influences the thinking that questions whether information professionals are the best people to develop corporate information resource strategies. Information services managed by a professional manager, rather than by an information professional, are not new. Neither are they necessarily less effective. It is the ability to manage resources for maximum positive impact on business objectives that matters, not the professional background. But why do employers still think that the information profession does not have that skill? Why do the senior KM roles, those that determine structure and strategy, go to people from a variety of disciplines but not to the discipline of information?

Why don't employers expect to see information professionals in top management? Is it because there are, outside the academic sector, few role models? Is it because they are aware that the entry requirements to LIS academic courses are comparatively low? Is our vocabulary a barrier or is it our insistence on a professional rather than a business identity? Is it because information professionals are poor at networking – at being where the employers are? Watch successful management consultancies, academics who make a name for themselves, people who get invited to join think tanks, people who make unpredictable career moves. They all have one thing in common – their networks. They spend a great deal of time increasing their sphere of influence and bringing themselves to the attention of potential employers.

Improving expectations

Changing expectations requires effort, and that effort has to come from individuals. Taking a look at what is possible, taking a few chances, challenging their own expectations, creating opportunities to extend experience and skills, are positive steps. Planning for portfolio careers is certainly a start. Moving out of a specific information role for a while doesn't necessarily mean leaving the profession. It could be the opportunity to acquire experience that enables professional expertise to be applied with more obvious benefit. There are at least three questions that individuals should ask themselves if they want to raise their own expectations.

1 Do I know this business and what makes it tick? Really know it? Do I know and understand corporate objectives and their implications? Do I know what decisions are crucial? Do I understand what it feels like to be a fee earner, a research director, a corporate planner? If not, how do I find out? Do I respect the organization and the people in it? If not, what am I doing here?

2 How much do I know about the information that supports the organization and the way it flows? Am I still thinking that external information is my area, internal information is a problem for someone else? Who else manages information? Is there a corporate community of information workers or a collection of people in discrete roles regarding each other with suspicion? Who is valuing information? Who is taking an enterprise-wide view? Could that person be me?

3 Can I think strategically? Am I thinking strategically? If not, what can I do about it? Training? Finding opportunities to work in strategy teams? Join the Strategic Planning Society? Read?

Strategy – whether personal or corporate – does not come easily. Many of us still equate it with some sort of Machiavellian activity rather that as a process for working out where you want to be and how to get there. Corporate strategies, which are very difficult to devise, are often regarded with suspicion and 'mission statements' with cynicism. But if you want to raise your sights, understanding the dynamism between information and corporate strategy is a good place to start.

Moving forward

The most essential element in building a career in the new economy is the recognition of the value of your information skills and their potential application. The first step in the run-up to crossing any boundary is the decision that you want to do so; the second step is an understanding of where you are starting from; the third is planning how to get where you want to go.

So start with an assessment of your core skills. What are they, and how good are they? Follow that with an assessment of how you use them. Where does the value lie? Are your skills being applied to core business processes – to the value-creating part of the organization – or are they somewhat less focused? Do you regularly reassess the mix and level of skill you require for different roles? Losing the reputation for having excellent online searching/research/help desk skills is the price many professionals pay when they move on to management positions. But those skills are the building blocks to understanding the difference between costs and prices when selecting vendors. The question is, do you need the technical skill, or the ability to recognize and use the skills, expertise and experience in others? The reference interview may be a technique that you use in order to provide an effective research service; as an information auditor the reference interview technique becomes a sophisticated tool in analysing corporate information needs.

A review of the essential skills of information professionals is not the topic of the chapter – and would provide the content of another book. The indicative list of skills in Table 9.1 is an invitation to consider how you are using yours to impact on your organization's value chain and how they could be applied in the roles emerging in the knowledge economy.

Table 9.1 *The core skills of an information professional – indicative*

Understanding user requirements	Managing information
Information auditing/mapping	Archives management
Information processes	Bibliometrics
Problem formulation	Cataloguing
	Codification
Sourcing information	Content management
Content management	Document management
External sources	Indexing
Internal sources	Informatics
Research skills	Information architecture
Search and retrieval	Information/document lifecycle
Vendor management	Metadata
	Records management
Dissemination and delivery	Taxonomies
Abstracting	Text analysis
Analysis	Thesauri
Editing/writing	
Information design	
Intranet/extranet management	
IT applications	
Synthesis	

Redefining roles

We have discussed the new roles that are emerging, but equally important in crossing the boundaries is to consider the existing role, or roles, you occupy. How far do you let your job title determine the role you play or how you are perceived? A notable feature of many of the organizations that have wholeheartedly adopted KM or other approaches is their resistance to job titles. They are, they will explain, more interested in what the post can achieve than what it is called, and a title can be constraining. It is a more difficult situation for most people than it seems. It throws the responsibility for defining the role on the person who has been given target outcomes. It requires them to build their work relationships and ways of working without having a job description that defines their level or sphere of influence. Most people still feel more secure with a closely defined role, but it is also liberating to be without it, and redefining information roles is one way of reassessing how skills are being applied.

Some examples

Information strategist

What does an information strategist do? They understand the strategic direction of the organization, analyse the information flows that underpin it and align information resources (content, processes and infrastructure) to corporate strategy. The role requires business understanding and strategic thinking, the ability to plan, and a thorough appreciation of all the elements of 'infostructure' – the mix of information and communication infrastructure, information architecture and content and the people and groups who work with it. An information strategist will utilize the information auditing and mapping techniques described in Chapter 4 and will be the person who influences the integration of information and knowledge management.

Information auditor/cartographer

Drawing a map of information flows and assets requires a mix of skills and experience. These include an understanding of business processes and business goals, market research techniques and communication and team working skills. None of these are new to the information professional. The redefinition comes in understanding the process as a key business one. If the flow of information underpins all processes, then understanding and designing effective flows moves from being an information project to being an essential business process.

Becoming a producer

Many information roles are essentially about providing a service or product that depends on a number of elements being brought together, requiring the cooperation and collaboration of a number of people. The information manager can seldom direct by right all the resources required to provide the level of service required, or even be assured that they will have corporate backing to provide the service. Take the management of an intranet, for example. Procuring the appropriate software and page designs pales into insignificance against the effort required to ensure quality and relevance of content, use of access and navigability, and avoidance of information overload. Such a complex task has been described by one experienced information manager as responsibility with no authority.

Thinking about it as a 'producer' is one way to stand back from the information role and to define it as a creative and managerial one. The stages of such a project are:

1 Consultancy/research/discussion phase
   This phase specifies the project in detail. In the film industry this would include the selection of a story, allocating the budget, etc. For a website it would include identification of technical platforms, structure maps, navigation methods, etc. It is the stage that defines the project and wins the resources.

2 Assembling assets
   This phase pulls together all the ingredients required. It is when the project goes into production. In filming this phase will include arranging the locations, coordinating the cast, etc. For a website it includes the identification of content, design of screens, application of standards, etc. It is the negotiation and team-building stage.

3 Building – Putting it all together
   This is the assembly stage. In filming it includes editing, adding music, etc. For a website it includes alpha stages – working models – beta testing, etc. It is about producing the pilots and demonstrating results.

4 Delivery
   This will include plans for operational maintenance and disaster recovery – duplication, back-up sites, etc.

Becoming a 'publisher' – making internal information accessible and usable

Thinking of libraries and library skills as part of the publishing cycle is not new, but the advent of e-content is driving the information professional to become an integral part of the cycle. Much of what we do is very much akin to the elements of the publishing cycle shown in Figure 9.1.

Information professionals need to understand their market, 'commission' the content, evaluate its value, distribute, manage, refresh and re-use.

Redefining roles is more than finding a new label – that is not what we are talking about. It is a means of assessing what your role really is in terms of value and process.

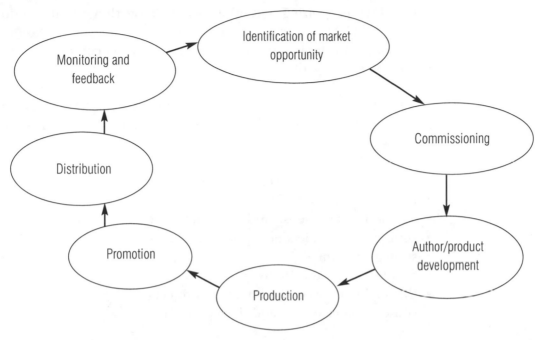

Fig. 9.1 *The publishing cycle*

Essential enabling skills

TFPL's research into skills for the knowledge economy identified a set of skills that are needed by everyone to enable them to feel comfortable and successful in environments that are restructuring to develop knowledge capabilities. These are essential for information professionals who wish their skills to impact on and influence the development of knowledge processes. During a recent Chief Knowledge Officers' Summit (2000) the leading practitioners from Europe and the USA identified some core skills and attributes that are key for those environments. High on the list are:

- the ability to learn: having curiosity, seeking new knowledge and taking responsibility for your own development
- self initiation: acting like a company of one – not waiting to be told or invited to participate
- collaborative working: being a team player with a positive regard for other people and their skills
- intellectual linking: seeing the big picture and patterns within it and making connections

- humility: recognizing that other people know things that you don't know and learning from mistakes
- the ability to think and do – with a focus on outcomes
- the ability to handle complex problems.

During the CKO Summit an exercise to identify the 'Dream Team' – the team that creates a knowledge environment – the key skills emerged as

- inquisitiveness and investigativeness
- journalistic skills
- a good business sense and the ability to question the status quo
- communication, leadership and negotiation
- strategic planning
- business process analysis
- the ability to design and manage projects
- content management and development.

These skills are not unique to the information professional but are, we argue, essential to anyone who wants to cross the boundaries of the profession they find themselves in. This is not the place to prescribe which skills need to be developed to which level, but there is a need for each individual to consider these issues in relation to their own abilities. To do this it is worth unpicking just what some of these desirable skills comprise.

Team working, for example, requires an understanding of how teams work, the different roles that people play and how teams can be developed. It is about understanding your own strengths and weaknesses and those of other people. It is about playing the strengths of the individual team members. The ability to influence requires skills for negotiation and persuasion. It is about understanding the audience, and being able to employ excellent communication skills. And communication skills themselves are complex, as is illustrated in Figure 9.2.

The art of facilitation, increasingly vital in environments where team and collaborative working is essential, requires good communication and the ability to relate context, objectives and people.

There are, in fact, a range of interpersonal and management skills that allow people to cross boundaries and create and take opportunities.

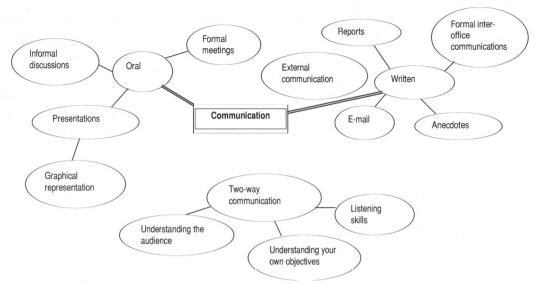

Fig. 9.2 *Communication skills*

There are also some specific skills that are gaining value in corporate settings. Examples of these are project management and journalistic skills. Project management skills have been explored in many texts and explicitly for information professionals by Liz MacLachlan who demonstrates the process outlined in Figure 9.3 (MacLachlan, 1998).

Fig. 9.3 *Project management process*

Journalistic skills have recently been more identified as key to knowledge environments and when examined in detail prove to be not so dissimilar to those of the information professional (see Figure 9.4).

Like information professionals, journalists define the problem, research the evidence, identify key points and communicate results and ideas – but they may also comment. The key difference lies in the willingness of the journalist to make a judgment and form an opinion.

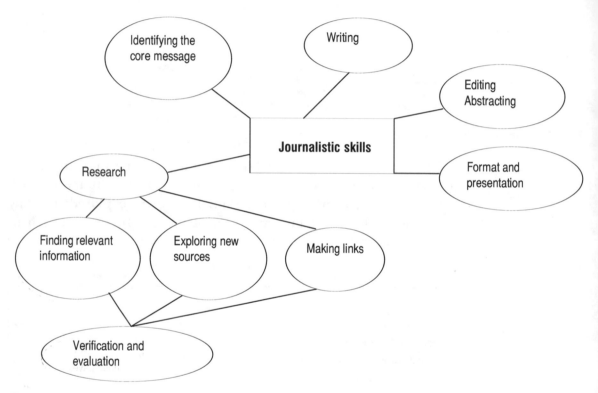

Fig. 9.4 *Journalistic skills*

Conclusions

The opportunities for information professionals are expanding, and the need for information skills in key management positions is becoming vital. But the competition for middle and senior management information roles is also increasing rapidly. Enjoying the opportunities and building on them require the ability to cross boundaries – organizational, professional, personal. In this chapter we have not attempted to define all the skills required to make this transition, but rather to discuss the range of approaches that need to be explored. We are convinced that the only real barrier to crossing boundaries is mindset. Increasing your own career aspirations will go a long way to increasing employers' expectations of information professionals. Understanding the value of information skills and the complementary skills that allow these to be applied in the organizational context is crucial, but getting involved and taking a few risks is probably the key.

To develop into the top manager of tomorrow's knowledge environments we suggest that you:

- Look at the world and recognize just how of it is based on information and its management.
- Understand your organization and the way it uses and values information.
- Take opportunities to acquire new skills and experience – broaden your horizons – but don't lose sight of your core expertise.
- Widen your sphere of influence and networks.
- Apply for that job if it appeals – even if you are not ideally qualified – you never know.
- Be prepared to learn continuously – and enjoy doing so.
- Recognize that the skills you have are the basis for an exciting career.
- Take risks and grow.

References

Chief Knowledge Officer Summit (2000) *Chief Knowledge Officer Summit, Dublin*. Sponsored by TFPL and Factiva (executive summary available from TFPL)

MacLachlan, L (1996) *Making project management work for you*, Successful LIS Professional series, Library Association Publishing.

Moore, N (1987) *The emerging market for librarians and information specialists*, LIR Report 56, British Library.

Woods, E and Madan, S (1999) *Knowledge management: building the collaborative enterprise*, Ovum.

Part 4

Case studies

10

The private sector response

We are convinced that knowledge management and sharing makes us more competitive – in concert with other development tools and philosophies.
(Jorg Schreibe, Roche Diagnostics, 1999)

The later part of the 1990s saw companies in all sectors exploring and developing management approaches and practical techniques to exploit their knowledge base. While the larger organizations initially led the field, firms of all sizes are now exploring how the concept can deliver benefits to them. This and the next chapter look at some of these organizations in the context of the sector in which they operate and Figure 10.1 illustrates some of the drivers behind their interest. These are not exhaustive case histories but stories to illustrate how and why some organizations have developed ways of competing with knowledge.

Financial sector

Financial institutions are knowledge and information based. Key business imperatives such as client relationship, cost efficiency, innovation, global reach, employee satisfaction, risk management, bank reputation and business intelligence depend upon strong knowledge performance capabilities (Moss and Thompson, 1998). They are essentially about managing risk. 'Fundamentally, risk management is about managing the complexity inherent in the trade-off between return and risk, through organisational knowledge, for the benefit of the firm's stakeholders' (Marshall, Prusak and Shillberg, 1997, 231).

Financial	• information based • highly regulated • risk management • competitiveness, fast reaction times		• multinational
		Manufacturing	• new competition • speed of products to market • changes in supply chain • customer focus • quality • changing relationships between manufacturers, retailers and customers
Professional services	• knowledge as a product • people as a primary source • mobile workforce • mergers		
Law	• people as creators of knowledge • increased competition • new markets and practices • mobile workforce	High tech	• global markets • customer driven • innovation • differentiation difficult
Process industries	• significant R&D • intellectual property • diverse products • global	Utilities	• change from public sector to private companies • competition • demand for value for money • regulation and watchdogs • extended markets • diversification in products
Oil	• global • fragmented • R&D • regulated		
		Air travel	• intense competition – new entrants • need for differentiation • partnerships, alliances, mergers • global and local
Pharmaceuticals	• global • high risk • R&D critical • regulated • controlled, but changing market • mergers, alliances and acquisitions	Public sector	• value of money • cost control • political objectives • customer focus • modernizing government
Engineering	• technical quality • innovation • reliability		

Fig. 10.1 *Examples of sectors and the drivers behind their knowledge initiatives*

Globalization and information technology have dramatically changed the market. People can now buy stocks in Hong Kong or in South Africa, interact with the financial market through intermediaries or directly with their personal computers. More volatile markets, and a wider choice of hedging vehicles such as derivatives have also contributed to increased competitiveness among financial services firms.

Skandia

Among the first to adopt KM was Skandia, an international financial services and insurance group, founded in 1855 in Sweden, with assets of approximately 600 billion kroner, annual sales exceeding 90 billion kroner and customers in more than 20 countries. 'Skandia's goal is to create sustained shareholder value. Skandia does this by providing customers innovative, world class services' (Interim Report Jan–June 1998). Its initial interest was in the difference between the market and book value of the company, which, they argue, represents its intellectual capital.

> Many Swedish companies on the Stockholm Stock Exchange are valued at 3–8 times their book value, i.e., the financial capital. This implies that there will be huge hidden value in such companies, which is not visible in the traditional accounting. Yet increasingly larger investments are being made in precisely these hidden assets. Such investments concern customer relations, information technology, networks and competence, for example.

Skandia's work on developing intellectual capital reporting began in 1991, when it defined 'Intellectual Capital' as 'Human Capital' + 'Structural Capital', thus introducing a new language into the corporate framework.

Skandia developed measures for intangibles: for customer relations, human resource development, future growth, management quality, etc, in order to reflect the potential of the company, its market standing, over and above the financial returns. It was probably the first company to report on intangible assets in the annual report. It has subsequently gone on to develop an 'intellectual laboratory', the Skandia Futures Centre, whose mission is to explore five key driving forces of the business environment – the European insurance market, demographics, technology, the world economy, and organization and leadership. Its current goal is to present a vision of the company's future to the Corporate Council of 150 top managers.

Skandia has undoubtedly been influential in increasing management awareness of ways of identifying and valuing intellectual capital. Whether it will be so influential in its approach to the creative use of physical environment and creative teams is yet to be assessed.

The World Bank

The World Bank is the largest provider of development assistance, committing about $20 billion in new loans each year. It also offers advice and an array of customized resources to more than 100 developing countries and countries in transition. Its mission is to reduce poverty and increase the quality of life in developing countries.

At the 1996 Annual Meeting, President Wolfensohn said that one of the Bank's goals is 'making the Bank's know-how accessible both to staff and to external clients, partners and stakeholders around the world'. At the Annual Meeting of 1997, it was said, 'By the year 2000, the Bank's know-how would be available for external users'.

The post of Programme Director of Knowledge Management for the Bank was created in October 1996, since when over 80 (internal) communities of practice (thematic teams) have been formed. In addition, multidisciplinary task teams and country teams have been created. Storytelling (successful case studies are collected and verbally disseminated) has been used as an agent for changing the culture at the World Bank, encouraging collaborative team work by explaining KM to staff and the Board. Recognizing that the best knowledge is exchanged via informal events, the Bank is providing support and tools and condones the value of human interaction by introducing event management as a component of KM.

The KM development in the Bank has been facilitated by the intranet developed in 1997 to provide access to a variety of information resources, including:

- help desks: facilitating access to expertise and technical support via databases of collective know-how
- online databases of policy papers, best practice papers, electronic forums, terms of reference, profiles of staff and consultants, and links to external resources
- a statistical database containing internal Bank data
- a clearing-house function for data available from other agencies
- a knowledge base on the economic aspects of human development, including good practice for economic analyses in project development; parts of this system, such as the new Early Child Development website, are available to clients.

The Bank has developed a number of other knowledge-based initiatives, such as the Education and Health Advisory Service which provides operational staff with customized information, advice on consultants and partners, and direct access to best practices from inside and outside the Bank, and the development of technology-based training and development. It is its use of 'communities' that has probably had most impact on other organizations. The linking of Bank staff, clients, consultants and other players to form a community to solve a problem has demonstrated the value of building virtual teams and the potential to deliver business benefits from the knowledge environment approach. For business benefits the Bank looks for, and is beginning to demonstrate, faster cycle time for clients, an increase in innovative proposals, and a more positive image among funding bodies and clients.

Natwest

NatWest, the UK-based bank, by contrast, has taken a more devolved knowledge management approach. The company consists of 70,000 employees at offices around the world. The company's development focus has been primarily on culture, supported by technology. Although there was a knowledge management project within the NatWest Markets subsidiary in 1997, the main focus of current initiatives is through the newly centralized training and development facility, the New Learning Organization (NLO). KM capability is intranet based, providing a sharing tool for the 350 staff employed by NLO in six sites throughout the UK and providing services to five NatWest business units. Although this KM initiative is not the only one within the bank, it is an example of the use of KM to support a particular function and as an exemplar for other parts of the organization.

Since this case study was written NatWest has merged with the Royal Bank of Scotland and the KM activities in both organizations are in the process of being integrated.

Thomas Miller

Thomas Miller is a global company specializing in shipping insurance. The Chairman of the firm developed their knowledge-based approach, which focuses on information sharing and corporate learning, in order to improve cross-fertilization of ideas and improved service to clients, and to extend market penetration. He initially appointed a Director of Information (with a good knowledge of the business and a solid understanding of technology) with a remit to create an information culture across the group and to improve the management of knowledge, internal and external, by individuals. A

Director of Learning was also appointed. There is an explicit inter-weaving of information and learning as a core strategy. A key feature of the approach was a move to open-plan offices for all staff with the Learning and Business Centre at their hub.

Clarica (formerly the Mutual Group)

Clarica is a retail insurance and financial services company based in Canada with over 100 agencies and offices across the country. The total number of staff, agents and managers, is approximately 7500, with a sales force of over 3000. The company has two million customers including about 10,000 corporate and institutional clients in Canada.

Clarica sees value creation as the basis of profitability and its knowledge strategy relies heavily on tapping into the tacit knowledge within the firm. Tacit knowledge is perceived as including the collective 'mindset' – people's own understanding of the firm. Based on this understanding and the belief that relationships, perceived as the key to knowledge value creation, are built through the values that individuals hold in common, Clarica undertook a project to identify the core values of its agents and employees. The resulting value maps were a precursor to a major cultural change initiative to create a company with three core values:

- stewardship: of time, money, resources and skills in the service of the customers to maximize value
- partnership: based on mutual accountability and respect to maintain high quality relationships
- learning: through sharing information, creating knowledge and innovating in order to serve customers and develop capabilities as individuals and as an organization.

To facilitate the learning process, Clarica created the Customer Knowledge Centre, designed to distil the learning gained through customer interaction. All information about customers comes under the Centre, including the library and research. Its aim is to make linkages between people who gather information, intelligence, etc. The Centre collects data, gives it meaning and distributes it.

The Community of Knowledge was created to generate organizational and individual capabilities to keep up with increasing customer demand. This initiative includes:

- the creation of Centres of Competencies (Communities of Practice) such as the Customer Knowledge Centre; agents are Centres of Competence as well
- recording of best practice
- use of an intranet as a learning platform in recognition of the need to be learning as work goes on
- recording of product knowledge, customer information etc, on the intranet
- availability of university modules on the intranet.

The Centres of Competencies have changed the boundaries of those who work within the organization, as everyone in the firm can now interface and communicate with the outside world. The Centres have meant a shift in organizational structure from a hierarchical structure to a team approach.

Each Community of Practice has its own Knowledge Manager. These roles are transitional in nature, and are occupied by high flyers within each knowledge community.

The significance of the Clarica approach is its focus on people and their values to improve the value creation process; within that value mapping led to practical, business focused outcomes. Figure 10.2 is a diagram of the current structure supporting KM activities.

Professional services

Professional services may not have been the first sector to adopt KM practices, but the early adopters in the sector are often quoted as examples of its practice and benefits. It is a sector whose main asset is quite evidently people. The ability of staff to learn and apply that learning, to use processes and methodologies while remaining creative and innovative, and to assess new situations and perceive links to other experiences, is the basis for competitive advantage in the sector. It is, therefore, a sector which invests heavily in training and development and places high demands on its staff in terms of performance and commitment.

It is also a sector of high staff mobility with an exceptionally high turnover rate being the norm, where fee-earners frequently work from remote and diverse locations. Many players in the sector are large global firms with offices and client in a broad range of countries. Many are also partnerships, and their global operations are

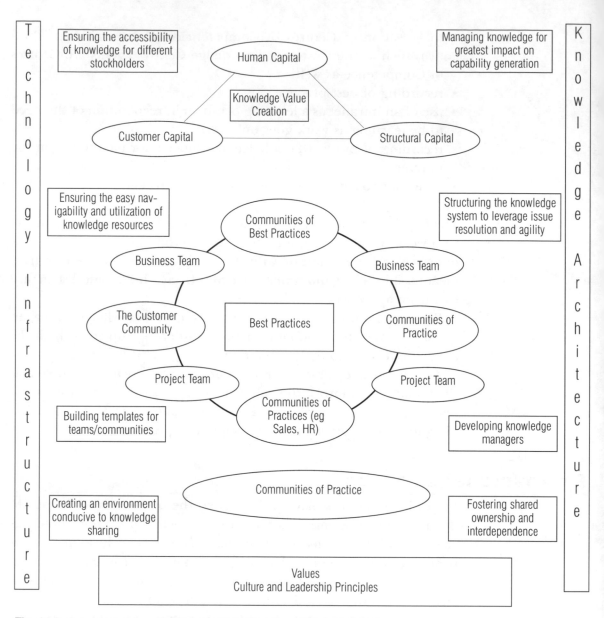

Fig. 10.2 *Schematic view of Clarica's KM effort (from Hackett, 2000)*

more like federations in structure than a single company. The challenge for the sector is to manage a competitive and individualistic workforce, retaining the benefits this brings while achieving consistency of approach and quality, within a structure where many senior staff have financial and directional power. Knowledge management is being applied primarily to enable systems and cultures to be developed to support the recording and sharing of lessons learned and experience gained. Hanson and Hope (1999) use consulting companies to illustrate their thesis that organizations take either a KM approach based on relationships or one based on codification. They argue that those practices whose business is based on applying standard processes to a client's problem will opt for a codified approach; while those who offer a tailored solutions approach based on the ability of consultants to apply the firm's experience to each situation, will opt for a relationship-focused KM solution.

PricewaterhouseCoopers

PricewaterhouseCoopers (PwC) is a global professional services firm. It employs approximately 150,000 people, spread among most of the countries of the world. Thirty-one thousand people are employed in management consultancy services (MCS). PwC's other business units are audit, assurance and business advisory services, business process outsourcing, financial advisory services, global HR solutions and tax and legal services. As it is a partnership organization, the profit motive and financial responsibility are widespread.

The organization is divided between three theatres of operation: the Americas; Europe, the Middle East and Africa (EMEA); and Asia/Pacific (APAC). They are united by global top management and extensive relationships between players in different theatres.

The sectors in which PwC operates are gradually being dominated by a few very large firms, formed through a series of mergers, of which PwC is one. PwC was formed in mid-1998 by a merger between Price Waterhouse and Coopers & Lybrand. Both organizations had their own cultures and their own KM initiatives, with different approaches, particularly in management consultancy services. The objectives of the current knowledge management programme of management consultancy services in the EMEA theatre are an illustration of the drivers in the consultancy sector:

- merging the abilities, expertise and histories of the two legacy organizations
- creating a consistent delivery of service across different business lines, sectors and territories
- meeting the need to train constantly replenished cohorts of consultants

- supporting the delivery of the MCS business strategy.

Although there are wide variations in employees' understanding of KM, the consistent view is that the process needs to be embedded in the business. KM at PwC encompasses:

- culture change, towards information and knowledge capture and sharing
- process change, towards innovation
- information management, via integration of resources
- information service delivery, through staff expertise in the business and in information retrieval.

The focus of PwC's KM activities was initially on explicit knowledge capture and cultural change oriented towards improving consultants' ability and willingness to contribute and re-use what they learn on assignments, resulting in three separate areas of KM activity:

- the 11 business units within MCS, each of which has its own Knowledge Manager
- a core MCS KM team, largely staffed from the UK and USA but working through all three theatres of operation
- a global KM team working for the whole of the organization, based in the USA.

In addition, the EMEA theatre has a central knowledge management help desk called Knowledge Point, based in London. There is a well-developed appreciation of the importance of taxonomy or classification, and many roles include a focus on information architecture.

The measure of success in a management consultancy is in delivering workable solutions to clients. The turnover of staff in management consultancy (not just at PwC) is very high, especially amongst the non-partner consultants, but the capability of a consultancy team is crucial. The significance of the KM initiative at PwC MCS is in its approach to:

- embedded knowledge-sharing behaviours within the business units through unit-based knowledge brokers working closely with the consultants

- support from the core team for 'rules and tools' to enable knowledge sharing
- the building of some elements of KM skills into the corporate competency framework.

KPMG

KPMG, the result of the first of the mega-mergers in professional services, aims to create competitive advantage through size, scope and geographical coverage in the field and this has led to the decision to integrate the knowledge of the company world-wide. It is one of the world's largest professional services firms, operating in more than 840 cities in 155 countries, with more than 100,000 partners and staff in total and 11,800 in 28 offices in the UK alone. It offers services in four areas: accountancy/auditing, tax, financial advisory services and consulting. It is organized by function (discipline) but goes to market through lines of business (industry sectors).

The KM programme is part of the process of internal alignment and is intended to mitigate the effects of the high turnover of consultants. In the UK the knowledge programme is focused primarily on cultural change – a 'project' to get into the hearts of 10,000 people in order to create a sharing environment. The Dutch and German offices, in contrast, are more technology focused.

KPMG did not set out to be a pioneer in KM but to be the best practitioner and soundly based, so it established links with academic institutions. In the UK the aim is to embed KM into business processes and to lose the KM label. The KM strategy reflects the four 'classic' areas of activity: People, Technology, Content, Process. Of these, the CKO believes content is the easiest to tackle and people the most difficult. A 'New Values' charter has been written, linked to the KM initiative, a skills matrix for the KM group developed, and KM issues are included in staff appraisals, framed by new competency guidelines for knowledge sharing and linked to rewards.

KPMG creates a number of new partners each year. Part of the KM strategy is to make potential partners a Knowledge Manager for a year – an intense sabbatical – thus giving them the best understanding of the firm's approach to KM before they become partner.

KPMG's technology strategy reflects the global/local approach to KM, with a global intranet, Kworld, providing world-wide access to corporate databases and European and US databases containing local knowledge. Content on the intranet is always owned by the originating line of business although the intranet development team issues guidelines and templates for how pages should look, and provides metadata to identify and control content. Business understanding has been placed at the centre of KPMG's knowledge management vision. KM aims to:

- create an environment where people have access to each other's knowledge
- capture learning from assignments, with signposts to the authors of captured information
- make it obvious that this is the right way to do business (there is currently an attitude that concentrates too much on moving straight on to the next project).

The KPMG general approach reflects that of the main management consultancies. Where it differs is in the involvement of its Library and Information Services Group, which formally became part of the KM Group in 1998. Although each line of business has a full-time Knowledge Manager, the LIS Group retains its central role in providing external information and, increasingly, developing the skills of consultants to find information in order to free up LIS skills for value-added work.

KMPG is currently considering separating its consultancy operation off from its other businesses as a separate legal entity.

Ernst & Young

Ernst & Young was formed with the merger of Arthur Young and Ernst & Whinney in 1989. The firm has since grown rapidly with revenues of over $10.9 billion and 85,000 staff in 132 countries, including 335 offices in Europe, 171 in the Americas, 60 in the Middle East and Africa, and a growing practice in Asia Pacific. The firm is particularly strong in the USA with over 30,000 professionals across 87 cities. In the UK there are over 8000 people in 23 cities. Roughly half of this number, as well as half the number of UK partners (over 400) are based in their London offices. The UK operation has grown by over 50% in the last three years. It is a highly dispersed workforce, even before taking into account the number of consultants who will be working on client sites.

The firm's services include assurance and advisory, tax and consulting services. Industry expertise is combined through multidisciplinary industry groups such as Energy, Financial Services, Consumer Products, Industrial Products, Health Care and Life Sciences, Insurance, Retail, and Technology, Communications and Entertainment.

Since 1993 there has been an ongoing change management programme and knowledge has featured as key to Ernst & Young's strategic plans and direction. There is a strong emphasis on demonstrating value to its clients by 'harnessing the skills and talents of all our people better than our competitors can or will – learning faster and sharing more'. At the core of its service are four values: client agenda based, co-developed solutions, value measured and knowledge rich service.

> We must constantly innovate to stay ahead of the curve [of the life cycle of intellectual capital]. But we must also deploy our ideas at lightning speed . . . That is why we must eliminate barriers to knowledge sharing . . . and enable our people to get what they need as quickly as possible.
> (John Peetz, Vice Chair, Knowledge and Technology, 1998)

> We wanted to be able to exploit more effectively the intellectual capital we already possessed as individuals, in order to provide greater value to clients and greatly decrease the amount of time it took to deliver that value.
> (Hanson and Hope, 1999)

There is a particular focus on implementing an industry-oriented strategy, identifying key industries and ensuring that its expert knowledge reflects these, and in maintaining a global approach. A global dimension has influenced the strategic thinking on how knowledge is managed. Ernst & Young's strategy in developing a knowledge-based business interlinks seven areas of activity, as shown in Figure 10.3.

Ernst & Young's fundamental strategy is to demonstrate to clients that its staff:

- build on shared knowledge and strive to push boundaries of best practice
- take relevant knowledge, experience and expertise to clients
- share experiences with clients and show understanding with own views
- 'provide robust challenge to help clients achieve relevant stretching agendas'.

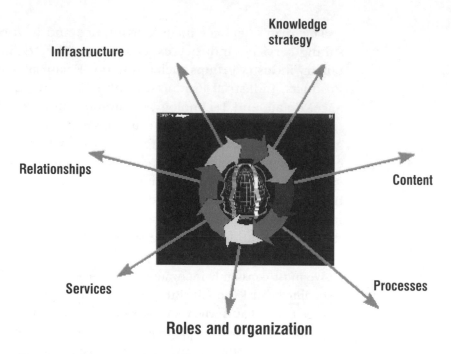

Fig.10.3 *Ernst & Young's KM areas*

The key features of the KM programme include:

- business needs analysis
- a knowledge architecture: a blend of different technologies known as Knowledge Web (KWEB), expert knowledge bases known as PowerPacks, discussion databases, external content; supported by a sophisticated taxonomy for categorization and searching
- acquiring content: there is now a collection of material such as leading practices, knowledge objects, client proposals, learning resources, intelligence reports, presentations and reports, held on various document repositories searchable via the KWEB; there are also vendor agreements with content suppliers to enable direct access to specific resources via the Internet
- Communities of Interest Networks (COINs): virtual communities, focusing on specific topics and enabling the sharing of tacit and explicit knowledge; Community HomeSpaces provide a navigational tool to internal and external knowledge resources, a discussion feature and the latest news on particular topics
- internal marketing and communications
- training programmes: a significant effort has been made to

develop a knowledge-sharing, innovative and learning culture
* measurement systems; incentives
* knowledge services (research and analysis teams).

Ernst & Young's Centres for Business Knowledge (CBKs) are responsible for the overall strategic direction and implementation of its knowledge initiatives, investing $125m per year or over 1% of revenue in the KM processes. They provide the core support team of 500 plus people world-wide. Their activities include identifying and tracking subject matter experts (SMEs) and ensuring their presence in sufficient numbers on industry and client teams; organizing the Communities of Interest Networks (COINs), setting up the skills and expertise database and the development of a knowledge architecture and taxonomy.

Ernst & Young maintains a number of centres as a means of developing its business. The Center for Business Transformation in Texas exists to develop, maintain and publish tools and methods for use by Ernst & Young consultants. The Center for Business Innovation, Boston (CBI), is responsible for the analysis of various business issues and the identification of trends in technology and management. Recent research has included measurement, customer connections, knowledge management and electronic commerce. While not the only management development think tank (Andersen Consulting has an Institute for Strategic Change), Ernst & Young's CBI has been influential in the KM thinking of many large organizations. Although it could be dismissed as a highly effective marketing tool for the Ernst & Young consultancy business a number of its staff and associates, such as Larry Prusak, were among the early gurus in the KM field, and the Center remains a conduit for thinking and ideas in the development of knowledge-based environments.

Law

Legal practices are becoming global and in recent years have experienced competition between practices and from corporate lawyers. They have moved from the world of 'gentleman's practice' and corporate retainers to one where the client is becoming more assertive and willing to change firms. Law firms see themselves as businesses, with business development and marketing functions. Knowledge of their markets, new and old, and of the competition has become important. In this scenario the utilization of the knowledge and expertise of the partners and fee earners is crucial; the ability to build on and re-use knowledge has become vital to the competitiveness of the practice.

As the competition for clients grows so does the competition for the best lawyers. Job mobility among younger lawyers means that ideas migrate from firm to firm, but knowledge is lost when staff leave. As with other service sectors, the partnership nature of the law firm has a particular effect on obtaining investment for new developments; the people who have to be convinced have generally been successful without the benefit of systems designed to help them manage their knowledge. While law firms are traditionally knowledge based they are also personality based – the individual's relationship with the client being paramount.

The legal sector has always been about knowledge and about interpreting and making judgments on information available. The value of a law firm has been associated with its expertise in making those judgments and in using available information more effectively than others. The challenge for this sector is the creation of environments where knowledge transfers more effectively between individuals and their practice or group, between practices and locations, between partners, senior fee earners and newly qualified staff.

Despite the difficulties know-how systems have emerged, particularly in the UK, during the 1980s, and have become a feature of many of the larger firms. The systems are designed to trap and manage evaluated information and its implications, documents and decisions for future use. Know-how collections are generally, but not always, databases and may contain precedent collections and checklists, client advice letters, instruction to counsel, internal memoranda, practice notes, etc. The content is selected and evaluated by legally qualified staff, know-how officers or professional support lawyers, working for a specific practice, sometimes working to a common model, often not. Although the legal sector was not among the early adopters of ICT, many firms have now invested heavily so that information can be shared between practices and locations. Know-how becomes a potentially shared resource. Almost always, the know-how activity runs alongside the library and information function.

Linklaters & Alliance

Linklaters is an international law firm with 212 partners, 1000 fee earners and 1000 other staff. Its core business is company and corporate law, property, litigation and tax. Its objective is to become one of the five major international firms.

As with many legal firms Linklaters does not use the term knowledge management, which is regarded as a trendy label in a sector where new 'fads' are not welcome. It considers that it has been 'doing KM' for years, particularly since the development of its know-how system, the history of Linklaters being described as '160 years of explicit know-how'. During the first 130 years, 1838–1968, when there were never more than 20 partners, everyone knew each other and what was going on. Following the Companies Act of 1967, which removed the ceiling on the number of partners, Linklaters grew rapidly and eventually senior partners included those recruited from outside the firm. This changed the information dynamic as the newcomers did not have experience of the firm and its know-how. Formal mechanisms for sharing information and know-how were introduced, with the installation of desktop computers in 1989 driving the development of tools and processes to underpin the system (Humphries, 1999).

These tools include:

- The Know-how Index: to letters of advice, opinion, documentation and experience on points of law. This is designed to answer the 'do we know anything about this point of law?' question, although face-to-face informal and formal meetings are still seen as primary means of information transfer. It is based on a series of databases with carefully controlled quality of input into the system. The author, date and thesaurus terms are important and a summary, written by a support lawyer, comments on and adds value to the document.
- The Transaction Index: to answer the question 'Have we done a similar transaction before?'; has a similar structure to the know-how index.
- Manuals of best practice (Linklaters Guide to . . .): which are becoming less important as Precedents (Standard forms) have developed.
- Precedents: which also have drafting notes against each clause explaining why the clause is there, when it can be deleted, etc.

- Internal publications: a means of sharing information, short and concise and drafted by a professional support lawyer and information staff, and turned into client publications by adding comment and analysis.
- The existence of formal groups of lawyers with a common interest either reflecting their business group or a specific topic.
- An intranet to link existing data sources.

The significance of Linklaters' approach is in the integration of two professions to build a knowledge management team. The know-how and information services teams require heavy investment in dedicated staff with a mixed skill set including legal, information management (workflow, document management, indexing, classification, intranet, research, call centre, database content, thesaurus) and information technology skills and an understanding of how the firm works. Know-how and information services have been integrated into the 'virtual' Legal Information Team operating within the practices throughout the firm. The Team coordinates know-how (which it defines as information that has been internalized by the firm) and information (the information from the outside world on which know-how is built and which also feeds much of a legal firm's practice). Information management skills have been applied to know-how, for example the thesaurus-based Know-How and Transaction Indexes and legal skills have been integrated into the provision of legal information services.

As already mentioned, Linklaters is a pioneer in the legal field having developed a know-how product, Blue Flag, to be sold over the Internet. The target market is very small and based on clients. The product focuses on keeping clients up to date about regulations that apply in different countries in one specific practice area. It demonstrates the recognition of knowledge as something that has tangible value and can be made explicit to the client without the presence of an expert.

Process industries

In the process industries cost control plays a key role in maximizing profits, globalization is not particularly new, and strong hierarchical organization has been the norm. Research and Development, although not highly visible, plays a significant part in the business and the day-to-day information problems of clients and staff are often technical. The exchange of experience and information through informal networks and between colleagues, clients and suppliers has been the way that many people in these industries have worked. They are industries where people tend to remain for most of their working life and thus know how things are done and how to solve problems, but such knowledge was in the past seldom formally captured.

The most frequently quoted example of an early knowledge management approach is that of Buckman Laboratories, a global speciality chemicals firm. Its approach has been mentioned several times and is not expanded on in this chapter. It is worth bearing in mind that, despite the many descriptions of their knowledge management programme, Buckman's CEO reminds everyone he speaks to that Buckman Laboratories sell speciality chemicals. That is the process the KM systems are designed to support. It was his perception that in order to add value in a competitive market Buckman Laboratories needed to help their clients solve their problems. It needed to be able to identify how Buckman chemicals could do that. The strategy was to put the technical and scientific skills directly in touch with the client and have decisions made by client-facing people.

Oil

As mentioned in an earlier chapter the oil industry includes one of the early exponents of the learning organization concept, Shell. Although an explicitly 'physical' industry, with evident machinery and processes to extract, process and distribute oil in all its forms and relying heavily on scientific and technical skills, it is also an industry that has management experience of operating globally in regulated markets influenced by political pressures and environmental concerns. It is an environment of mergers and acquisitions and of product diversity.

Shell UK

Shell UK Ltd is the UK arm of The Royal Dutch/Shell Group of companies with three main businesses:

- the exploration and production of crude oil and gas
- making and marketing the products refined from crude oil
- manufacturing and marketing petrochemicals.

It is the UK's biggest oil and petrochemicals company, producing more than one-fifth of the country's crude oil, 17% of its gas, 18% of its oil products, 16% of its petrochemicals and 20% of its petrol. In addition, it is the UK's fifth largest newsagent and retailer of sandwiches, through its chain of filling stations. The company employs 7000 people, plus 2500 more in its subsidiaries. Its main competitors in the UK market are British Petroleum and Esso (Exxon).

It is a company which, like many engineering-based enterprises, traditionally controlled those documents relating to regulated activities, such as the building of oil platforms, but did not put much emphasis on recording 'knowledge'. Loss of company experience and knowledge when people left the company was one of the primary drivers of KM in Shell. Its intranet forms the central tool for the exchange of explicit information. Work to improve knowledge capture and communication is supported by 'a five star model of a knowledge network' (Caralambous, 1999):

- the people network
- culture
- tools and resources
- managed knowledge base
- workshops and support systems.

A key component developed from this model has been the social network events:

- A half-day session every quarter to which all members of a team are invited to review the team's progress, which covers both technical and business issues.
- A one-hour meeting with no agenda that is discipline oriented. The discussion is convened by the Practice Centre Coordinator (see below) and focuses on the day's 'pain'; 60% of engineers in a discipline will regularly show up for discussion.

The knowledge that is generated or surfaces in social network events is captured using the following model:

- search for key issues
- capture major observations
- identify lessons learned

- understand the underlying logic
- generate the insights.

The captured data is published on the Shell intranet which also contains chat facilities, traditional information publications, 'how-to-do-it' pages, journal articles, books, contact e-mail addresses of local experts, and order forms for delivery of material from the internal library. There are standard HTML forms available to allow anyone in the company who wishes to disseminate their knowledge and expertise via the intranet to do so by creating their own web pages. Shell's data-sharing libraries have become an important focus. The company's areas of business interest are very data-intensive, so trusting a librarian to manage data for several people is regarded as very important.

Shell's approach depends a great deal on a role it calls the Practice Centre Coordinator or Practice Manager. This is someone who:

- is well respected in the specific field
- has a high level of social skills and is highly networked
- often has a background in training others in a specific area or technology.

These coordinators are located in their practice areas and retain their core competencies, keeping them and their knowledge management activities close to the heart of the business. Shell's knowledge strategy (see Table 10.1) is explicitly aligned with business strategy at Shell International (Charalambous, 1999).

Table 10.1 *Shell's knowledge strategy*

	Customer intimacy	Product leadership	Operational excellence
Business driver	Understanding of customers and markets	Differentiated products portfolio management, maximization of individual contributions	Strategic cost leadership
KM solution	Business intelligence	Communities (networked, practice, interest), virtual team working	Best practice replication, knowledge-shared services

While Shell is a highly technical company and draws on IT solutions, the underpinning theme of its approach to improving the management of its knowledge at all levels has been based on the belief in social networks and communities.

BP

BP has taken an approach to increasing its use and development of corporate capability that draws on the way in which groups of people learn from each other and shared experience improves the learning process. As mentioned earlier, the BP management of virtual teams to solve oil platform problems has provided an example for many of the need to build trust and a common understanding between members of teams if they are to be effective.

The need for a concerted 'learning' approach has increased further following the merger of BP and Amoco, and the recent acquisitions of ARCO and Burmah Castrol; BP has grown to employ 100,000 staff. Its people-oriented approach to knowledge management is based around a framework that includes:

- capturing and presenting explicit knowledge
- distilling lessons into knowledge assets
- creating tools for learning 'before, during and after'.

Learning before doing

> . . . the politics accompanying hierarchies hampers the free exchange of knowledge. People are much more willing to share and listen to their peers'.
>
> (Browne, 1997)

Learning before doing at BP has much to do with tools to enable people to make contact with those able to help them with their problem or task, the so-called Peer Assist. An intranet solution, Connect, allows people with appropriate skills and experience to be found, and communication to take place. Networks of people have been formed round common interests, supported by a home page.

Learning while doing

Continuous learning is supported by after-action reviews (AARs) with peers which look at what was supposed to happen, what actually happened, why there was a difference, and what can be learnt from it.

Learning after

Learning after is facilitated by a forward-looking meeting after the project has ended; objectives include the identification of best practice that can be repeated and mistakes that can be avoided.

Although BP's approach makes some use of technology, its focus is on developing a culture where people take time to learn, share and connect with each other in an environment that is highly performance orientated and where the results of every activity must be perceived as having bottom-line benefit.

Further information about the BP approach can be found at **http://www.sigmaconnect.com** and in a book appearing in January 2001 (Collison and Parcell, 2001).

Pharmaceuticals

The pharmaceutical sector is essentially global, although it includes national and niche players and is heavily research and development based. Enormous investments are made in the development of new products that take several years to reach the market. Despite their profits the financial risk is great. The sector has highly regulated markets which change as the funding of medicines and treatments in many countries changes. Patient and ethical pressures demand more and more information and influence attitudes to the large and 'powerful' drug companies.

The supply chain in the pharmaceutical sector has also become complex. Many of the large companies form alliances with academic institutions or boutique research organizations to contract out some of their discovery or development work. Specialist research companies, in the area of biotechnology, for example, have arisen. Recent years have seen mergers among the pharmaceutical giants. It is a climate of mergers, partnerships and alliances; of tight regulation and demand for more medical intervention in disease; of innovation and creativity together with higher standards of safety: a knowledge-intensive environment.

The business drivers for companies in this sector include:

- the need to reduce the time it takes to get a product to market
- issues of working with partners and alliances
- the need for effective integration of information from external and

internal sources throughout the drug lifecycle
- the need for development and maintenance of creative and innovative 'discovery' teams
- the need for the ability to make sound investment decisions
- the need for the utilization of expertise throughout all business processes – from marketing and sales, through development, manufacture and regulation to the discovery process.

Eli Lilly

Eli Lilly is an international pharmaceutical company, over 120 years old. It currently employs 31,000 staff and produces in excess of 150 products. Research and development activities are centred on seven research sites.

Lilly is confronted with increasing development time and costs, and increased average numbers of clinical trials, new drug applications and numbers of patients in trials. Against this background there are issues relating to the global regulatory, medical and organizational diversity. The company has to focus on unmet medical needs.

As would be expected in a knowledge-based industry, the company believes that is has transacted knowledge for a long time; that 'Knowledge is a powerful medicine' and that projects throughout the company in different functional areas are addressing issues associated with knowledge processes. A major challenge for the company is that teams need to communicate with multiple functions that may be globally dispersed and some of the activities Eli Lilly has undertaken to meet this challenge reflect the sector's approach. These include:

- creating a database of portfolio information about innovations and new ideas, to support the preview process – the decision about what to develop and how to prioritize
- 'facilitating the flow of information to those involved in global drug development' through Projects Management Workbench, an integrated project management tool, to improve communications between team members and functions, and with other teams, management, etc
- creating a web-based tool for team members, Team Information Access, for creation of team minutes, team plan, competitive information, discussions, to provide a consistent means of information creation and circulation

- creating an integrated solution, Scientist Profession Innovation Network (SPIN), to increase productivity and innovation among chemists through facilitating the sharing of expertise and providing better access
- a process of benchmarking R&D teams and finding out how teams learn
- streamlining the flow of information to and from the 5000 sales representatives
- providing knowledge-based solutions, from the process engineering area of the company, across manufacturing roles and teams
- orienting training and development specifically to increasing corporate competence and skills.

SmithKline Beecham (SB)

In his presentation to the Strategic Planning Society Knowledge Management Conference in 1999 Peter Haine, Director of Architecture Services at SB, said:

> Ensuring we make the best of our knowledge capital – through innovation, collaboration and shared learning/best practice – should be part of the way we all work in SB.

> (Haine, 1999)

His presentation went on to describe the company's knowledge-sharing processes as:

- optimizing and standardizing
- connecting people and expertise to processes
- achieving continuous process improvement at a global scale
- sharing problems, issues and solutions
- sensing, remembering and forgetting
- sharing knowledge in the community
- supporting innovation.

Significant in the SB approach is that it is bottom up, based on a community of KM practitioners. The KnowledgeAbility forum allows 60 or so people throughout SB interested in knowledge management to share best practice and lessons learned from KM-related projects, to promote knowledge management as a concept in SB and to work together to build reliable KM processes and means of measuring effectiveness.

AstraZeneca Pharmaceuticals

Before merging with Astra, Zeneca was among the top 20 ethical pharmaceutical companies in terms of size, with sales of £2.8bn in 1998. It manufactured products in 14 countries, marketed medicines in 130 countries and had 94% of its sales outside the UK. As was typical for leading pharmaceutical companies, around 30% of its products were the results of external investment (acquisition and licensing) resulting from a business process that incorporated complex activities and a variety of players, as shown in Figure 10.4.

The objective of this process was to convert business strategy into external investment targets, to implement a clear decision-making process about potential investments and to manage the resulting deals as projects. Key to the process was the ability to manage information and the building of appropriate skills throughout the Company, while operating internationally through multidisciplinary project teams. The basis for the process, shown in Figure 10.5, was an internal 'virtual' department which worked together through Concert – an enabling process and technology.

The guiding principles of Concert are ownership (process and project ownership), good information management, consistency in document creation and language, confidentiality and access, agreed benefits and metrics, and project and performance management. It is the acceptance and implementation of the principles that change the way that people work. Development of the process is based on consultation and communication at all stages, active champions, ownership, professional training and after-action learning. It is a system of process and people development.

Fig. 10.4 *AstraZeneca's external investment*

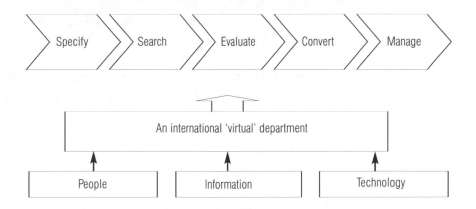

Fig. 10.5 *Zeneca's external investment process*

The success of Concert has been measured in terms of:

- cost saving: more effective screening of targets and resource utilization
- value: better deals and improved risk management
- speed: improved speed of response at all stages and time-efficient management of resources.

This is just one example of the knowledge management activities developed by Zeneca. It benefits from having clearly visible objectives and measurable results. The merged firm, AstraZeneca, presents the opportunity for propagation of the approach throughout the new company and for the application of Zeneca's KM approach to the challenges inherent in merging two cultures. A new generation Concert – now called Aztec – has subsequently been implemented throughout AstraZeneca's external investment community.

Hoffman LaRoche

Activities that focus on 'knowledge processes' – the creation, sharing and use of knowledge, as a means of improving business performance – can be identified in most pharmaceutical companies. Some are labelled KM but the majority are part of other business improvement activities or focus on one function. The Hoffman LaRoche example has targeted new product launches.

> For Hoffman LaRoche as with every other pharmaceutical company (and many other types of company), much depends on the speed of the new product launch. Industry observers estimate that the development of a new product takes, on average, five to eight years and costs over $250 million. Firms that can expedite the process stand to gain tremendously . . . In an industry like pharmaceuticals, where a firm's market standing is only as good as its current patents, fast and sure drug development is the key to survival.
>
> (Seeman, 1998)

A crucial process in getting drugs to market is gaining approval from the regulatory body, which can take months or years. Hoffman LaRoche's KM strategy targeted the new drugs application process where significant financial return could be expected if the process improved. As mentioned earlier, it put a figure of $1m a day on money saved, and as the firm has, at any time, approximately 30 drugs going through the process, this saving would have a real impact on profitability. A knowledge map was drawn to clarify the knowledge sources and flows, which, in its simplest form, provided a pointer to information and expertise, but also formed the basis for a tool that targeted expected questions, prompted questions and information flows and became a dynamic part of the new drug application process.

Engineering

Engineering companies are a paradoxical mix of innovation, creativity, caution and tradition. Safety issues and regulations impose a measured approach, the need for quality and reliability dictates many working practices and the industry competes on client satisfaction and the ability to innovate both product and process. It is an industry with large multinational companies and smaller local organizations, with competition between firms in one country matched by competition between countries. There has been both a skills shortage and an over-manning problem. In streamlining and flattening structures, in creating more cost-effective and slimmer companies the sector discovered how much of the know-how on which they operated lived in the heads of the people they had employed. It is also a sector in which partnerships and alliances have become a feature.

Attempts to build more sustainable and competitive companies

CHAPTER 10: THE PRIVATE SECTOR RESPONSE 209

have included all the approaches covered in Chapter 3 but many have focused on the learning organization approach to improve capability.

British Aerospace (BAe)

BAe went through many changes in the last quarter of the 20th century. Fluctuating market conditions, new technology and new partnerships meant various reorganizations, periods of labour shedding and periods of recruitment. Despite the problems BAe is one of the UK's largest exporters with 89% of its £8bn-plus sales being overseas in over 70 countries. In addition to its 46,000 employees, it also works with 29 international partners. The business driver for BAe is international competition in a technology-intensive industry that is increasingly information and communication driven. Knowledge and know-how have become key, with competitiveness based on people, ideas, markets, time to market, and customer responsiveness.

Within this environment the emphasis is on people development to enable faster sharing, cooperation and collaboration, making the corporate university the platform. BAe has formed alliances with universities as strategic partners and individuals are able to work through accredited programmes to achieve anything from apprentice qualifications to a PhD. Perhaps the most interesting aspect of the BAe approach is the concept of the firm as a campus. BAe's virtual university has faculties and centres and a Vice-Chancellor:

- A Faculty of Learning: to motivate and support personal and company-wide learning programmes for all types of employees, to ensure their skills and competencies.
- An International Business School: to support executive and management development, to support strategic decision making.
- A Faculty of Engineering and Manufacturing Technology: to develop and sustain excellence in core engineering capabilities and seek, acquire and transfer critical enabling technologies.
- The Sowerby Research Centre: a central resource for the identification, acquisition, adoption and delivery of technology in response to business needs.
- A Best Practice Centre: to secure maximum competitive advantage from benchmarking and knowledge sharing across BAe and its partners.

Manufacturing

Manufacturing companies, like engineering ones, have a reputation for being slow to adapt and adopt change. In theory they were the focus for quality improvement and flexible manufacturing initiatives in previous decades. They are less likely to adopt a management label than to adapt practical ideas and approaches. Their business drivers are predominately associated with productivity and cost control, but innovation and market intimacy play as important a part as in any sector.

Unilever

Unilever is a prominent multinational company involved in a broad range of business activities, principally the manufacture of food and household products. Unilever people move frequently, and often internationally. Networking is therefore important and the company builds this around its business areas.

Knowledge management principles have been adapted by Unilever through a model containing three sets of enablers – Organizational, Process and Technology. Successful knowledge management only comes from the appropriate integration of these three to suit each application. The model is shown in Figure 10.6.

Unilever focuses on value creation in its knowledge management programme and seeks to ensure that each KM activity addresses three business processes: knowledge creation, knowledge dissemination and knowledge exploitation. Projects that don't address each of these processes are unlikely to perform optimally or leverage company resources in the most effective way.

One of the techniques used builds on the company networking approach to share knowledge, to stimulate ideas and avoid costly mistakes. Knowledge workshops bring together a range of employees from different business areas but with a common interest, such as the production of tomato paste. They pool their knowledge of this part of the industry and create a knowledge map of the processes, in this case from tomato paste back to agriculture. Through the mapping process they discover what the company knows about the knowledge content of the product. These workshops help create a community of practice together with a shared language that defines the domain. Both of these help long-term knowledge development by making it

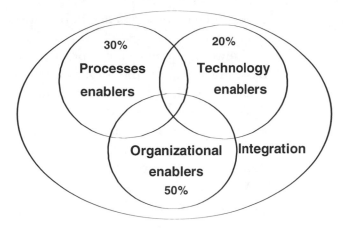

Fig. 10.6 *Unilever model of KM enablers*

easier for experts around the world to communicate with their colleagues without the usual formalities or barriers.

Xerox

The document company Xerox is the global leader in its industry, offering the widest array of document-related solutions, products and services for business productivity. Xerox provides expertise in the production and management of paper and electronic documents from the desktop to the network and from the home office to the global enterprise.

Xerox's approach to KM is to promote and facilitate the sharing of best practice across boundaries, both geographical and business.

Eureka is a dynamic central database of problems and service tips to capture new problems as they have emerged. Technicians are encouraged to add their stories and experience to the database. To maintain the quality of information and the structure of the database, technicians themselves not only build but also validate what goes into it. As a consequence of this filtering, the content reflects the leading edge of the collective understanding of the broad community of technicians engaged in shared practice, with a shared background and shared belief in what is useful and what is not. It represents a turnaround in Xerox from top-down to bottom-up KM. Business benefits include improved customer satisfaction, cycle time, productivity, efficiency and quality. To further facilitate the sharing and exchange of knowledge, Xerox has provided radios to their sales people so that they can chat and exchange information about customers at any time or place.

Knowledge management practices are now being used by all business units within the organization. The company-wide KM programme is driven by the Document Services Group which has designed a project called ICARE (Intellectual Capital Reuse) to help all business units to share knowledge more effectively. A central document management system called Docushare is used as a tool to facilitate knowledge capture and collaborative knowledge sharing.

Xerox also provides convenient places, called 'distributed coffee pots', where employees can get together, to chat and exchange ideas.

High tech

This is the sector of most obvious change, where the speed of innovation and time to market are of the essence. Markets are global and customer driven, competition intense and product differentiation difficult. While new products and the next technological breakthrough drive the sector, it is service and pricing that capture market share.

ICL

One of the early adopters of the knowledge management philosophy was ICL whose CEO has described the company as having changed from one that delivers boxes of technology to one that delivers services. In launching Project VIK (Valuing ICL Knowledge) in 1996 he sought to change the way that ICL staff thought about themselves and the way they worked. Knowledge that they gained in working on projects became knowledge assets, and eventually ICL employed journalists to help capture end-of-project learning. Teams tendering for major contracts considered what they had learned from past failures before embarking on a major bid. At the centre of this approach is Café VIK, an intranet-enabled service for access to and exchange of information. The 'café' label is important and reflects the style of the full-time catalyst team. It represents the conversation that goes on between peers when comparing notes, and the trust that builds up to enable real exchange of experience. Projects and virtual teams that include members from ICL's partners and clients underpin the knowledge-sharing process.

British Telecom (BT)

British Telecom is a successfully privatized former state monopoly with a current turnover of £18,223m and a series of high-profile international partnerships. It has 125,000 employees (95% in UK) and following privatization went through a period of expansion, followed by a period of contraction, which began to focus attention on the amount of corporate capability that resided in the heads of the people who worked for, then left, BT. There followed a period of knowledge-management-focused initiatives that set out to change from an individual-knowledge-based approach to one of a team-based or corporate approach. Initial activities focused heavily on changing behaviours, on finding mechanisms to embed knowledge sharing within work processes and on making the knowledge environment comfortable.

At the same time developments in technology meant that BT was developing sophisticated tools to assist knowledge sharing, such as the knowledge garden that is being developed for internal use, and BT Presence, a commercial offering that combines the use of audio conferencing and shared documents by virtual teams.

Within this fast-moving area mobile telecommunications has become a booming market and has provided a focus for a KM activity. A key strategic question is: 'How can "BT Group" capitalize more effectively on the combined knowledge and expertise of the people employed in all its mobile ventures?' (Tony Rubin, BT Programme Director – 'mobilityleaders', BT Group Strategy and Development (Rubin, 2000)).

As with any fast-moving, booming market there are limited skills and resources, and the competition for people is fierce. The market is made up of individuals – geography is not important, the business operates in cultural diversity, across different business practices and time zones. Information shared between partners in the mobile telecommunications area must move quickly while still relevant. The nature of the partnerships involved means that not all companies will be at the same stage of maturity.

The response to this challenge has been the development 'mobilityleaders': a multidimensional KM programme for a targeted community of mobile communications professionals which 'stimulated by effective use of the Internet, seeks to maximize the competitive advantage of members by increasing contact and collaboration at all levels within partner companies (Rubin, 2000).

BT supports the community with a website, the facilitation of face-to-face workshops and conferences, bilateral issue-related meetings, the provision of expertise, and the organization of exchange visits. There are 21 member companies and approximately 50 online workgroups, but the significance is that:

- the members include companies who may be both collaborators and competitors and key suppliers
- the commercial model recognizes the value of knowledge exchange and uses a financial tool to build an exclusive club from which people will seek to gain value through participation.

It is radical in its inclusive approach to suppliers and competitors.

Siemens Business Services (SBS)

This subsidiary of the German-based multinational built its approach to knowledge building round the nurturing and support of communities. Initially a core knowledge team of seven, including a CKO, supported the implementation of knowledge management activities. The team was multidisciplinary, comprising a knowledge leader (project manager), a marketing person, a journalist and an IT specialist supporting intranet applications. Their role was to develop strategy, coordinate and harmonize knowledge brokers in the lines of business, as well as to support specific KM projects.

Virtual teams came together to facilitate debriefing at the end of a project and evaluate the significance of information collected during the debriefing. Membership of the debriefing teams reflected the nature of the project and used an interview technique based on that used by the American army.

SBS also used the mechanism of communities of practice for knowledge building and, like other companies with dispersed knowledge practitioners, supported a knowledge community. Since the early implementation stage, a permanent CKO and dedicated team have been appointed.

Utilities

The utilities sector in the UK underwent a massive change during the

1980s when they moved out of the public sector to become commercial companies. From running organizations that had only to meet the demands of their regulators and the constraints of public funding, the industry was suddenly faced with competing for clients and meeting competition, both from within and outside the UK. Many of the new companies were formed through the merging of a number of smaller organizations, with all the issues of local loyalties, customers and practices that went with them. The missions of the new companies included becoming market leaders, development of overseas markets and being profitable.

Anglian Water

Anglian Water has already been mentioned, as has its use of a learning approach as a means of changing and developing its corporate culture. This change it describes as a journey, borrowing concepts from Lessem (1998), Nonaka and Takeuchi (1995) and Stacey (1992). This journey was intended to enable employees to:

*   increase their self-understanding
*   develop their ability to think 'out of the box'
*   be creative
*   explore empowerment without business risk.

At a conference in 1999 Peter Matthews of Anglian said that, while the benefits of the journey were difficult to judge objectively, it was felt by many people that it had helped them to develop and accept challenge and change (Matthews, 1999). At a later lecture at the RSA in early 2000 another representative from Anglian Water described the findings of market research prior to launching Anglian Direct, which revealed that within their geographical area the firm was 'trusted' by the community, not because of the purity of its water but because of the community work undertaken as part of the transformation journey.

Anglian Water now sustains a multidisciplinary knowledge management team to support and encourage KM activities.

Eastern Generation Ltd

Eastern Generation, part of the Eastern Group and the fourth largest

UK electricity generator, faced the same issues as the water companies. Its aims for KM activities were to:

- find efficient ways of sharing best practice, knowledge and experience across the portfolio
- improve commercial and competitive advantage by ensuring efficient knowledge transfer
- develop capability to lever KM across Europe as a mechanism to attract potential alliance partners
- find a new operating model that supported these aims.

Its approach was to focus on one of the key functions, asset management, and to develop activities that improved their performance in this area, identify key interfaces and information flows across the business and centralize some business functions while establishing virtual offices and teams for other groups of staff. The key was to establish flexibility and effective use of resources and to adopt best practice to improve the speed and quality of service provided. But the most important outcome has been the increased rate of innovation (Hyams, 1999).

Air travel

Our final example is another privatized company operating in a global, competitive market where clients have an increasing amount of choice and service is the main differential. Air travel is a large and growing industry, with growth predicted by the International Air Transport Association at 5% per year until 2010, for both personal and business travel. Customers have become increasingly discerning and airlines are having to invest heavily in the quality of service that they offer in order to compete. In Europe the European Union has ruled that governments should not subsidize loss-making airlines and elsewhere there is a move to privatization. Deregulation is also stimulating competition, and the industry has proceeded along the path towards globalization and consolidation through the establishment of alliances and partnerships.

British Airways (BA)

Prior to privatization in 1987 Sir Colin Marshall, then the Chief

Executive, set out the mission for British Airways 'to be the best and most successful company in the airline industry'. In 1997, it redefined its mission, values and goals to address four key areas:

- the global economic climate
- the challenge of competition
- what customers were asking for
- what employees wanted.

The mission became 'to be the undisputed leader in world travel' and the new values include to be seen as 'safe and secure', 'honest and responsible', 'innovative and team-spirited', 'global and caring' and 'a good neighbour'. The values reflect the current business imperatives of competitive advantage through stakeholder inclusion.

The development of 'the undisputed leader in world travel' is essentially a people-based business. The machines that carry the travellers may be the result of excellence in engineering and their safety and operation dependent on information and communication technology, but the success of an airline is completely dependent on its staff and BA have introduced a series of initiatives to improve and support learning and development. Culture, says Keith Rapley, is the biggest barrier to learning and sharing and BA have targeted culture change (Rapley, 1999). Their flagship in this area is the new headquarters building designed to use space to encourage and facilitate sharing and communication. Its 'village street', which forms the main thoroughfare of the building with cafés and meeting areas, open-plan offices and team rooms, has drawn many visitors to see how physical space can be employed to help build a knowledge environment.

This environment includes learning centres and a virtual university, teams to create an atmosphere where learning and sharing is natural and easy, and where newcomers can navigate their way round the corporate memory and contribute ideas and experience as easily as established employees.

References

British Airways
  http://www.british-airways.com
Browne, Sir J (1997) 'Unleashing the power of learning: an interview with John Browne', *Harvard Business Review*, **75** (5), Sept–Oct, 147–88.

Charalambous, I A (1999) *Knowledge and best practice sharing*, SPS Knowledge Management Conference 99, October 1999.

Collison, C and Parcell, G (2001) *Learning to fly: Practical lessons from one of the world's leading knowledge companies*, Capstone Publishing.

Hackett, B (2000) *Beyond knowledge management: New ways to work and learn*, USA, The Conference Board.

Haine, P (1999) *Making knowledge count*, SPS Knowledge Management Conference 99, October 1999.

Hanson, T and Hope, J (1999) Knowledge services: Where self service and value added services exist, *Business Information Review*, **16** (1), 38–43.

Humphries, J (1999) *Presentation to the CEST Knowledge Management Forum*.

Hyams, E (1999) *Practicalities of linking KM to business strategy: Practical implementation of a knowledge based strategy*, SPS Knowledge Management Conference 99, October 1999.

Lessem, R (1998) *Management development through cultural diversity*, Routledge.

Marshall, C, Prusak, L and Shillberg, D (1997) Financial risk and the need for superior knowledge management. In Prusak, L (ed), *Knowledge in organizations*, Butterworth-Heinemann.

Matthews, P (1999) *Best practice management & sharing*, SPS Knowledge Management Conference 99, October 1999.

Moss, M and Thompson, C (1998) *A new performance opportunity for investment banks*, IBM Consulting Group Report, IBM.

Nonaka, I and Takeuchi, H (1995) *The knowledge creating company*, Oxford University Press.

Peetz, J (1998) Internal document.

Rapley, K (1999) *Stimulating a learning culture in British Airways*, SPS Knowledge Management Conference 99, October 1999.

Roche Diagnostics (1999) Roche Diagnostics, *Annual Report*.

Rubin, T (2000) Case study of an inter-company knowledge sharing and knowledge management programme, *Journal of Communications Management*, **4** (3), February, 278–86.

Seeman, P (1998) *A prescription for knowledge management: What the Hoffman LaRoche case can teach others*, available at
http://www.businessinnovation.ey.com/journal/issue1/
Skandia
http://www.skandia.se

Stacey, R (1992) *Managing the unknowable: Strategic boundaries between order and chaos in organizations*, Jossey-Bass Management Series, Jossey-Bass Publishers.

11

The public sector response

New management ideas and approaches are, it may be argued, taken up and discarded more quickly in the private than the public sector. The reasons are not surprising. The success of a company depends on its ability to change and adapt in fast-moving markets and environments. Strategy and tactics may be carefully thought through before implementation but the ability to react quickly and flexibly to changing circumstances is key to survival. Managing such organizations requires that new and innovative management practices are evaluated, piloted and adopted as appropriate. The risk of not being prepared to consider new management ideas is almost as great (or greater in some eyes) as the risk of investing in the wrong management innovation.

The drivers for public sector organizations are different and reflect their three groups of stakeholders: the policy makers, those who determine the funding, and the wider public. Public sector organizations seek to understand and minimize risk, reflecting their public accountability and a wider spectrum of objectives than the need to make a profit. The opprobrium attached to the failure of an initiative is usually greater than in the private sector, and there may be greater restraints on the availability of funding for major initiatives. For these reasons the sector has traditionally been slower to change management and strategic processes and has a record of exploring new approaches at a more mature stage of their development. In recent years, however, the public sector has been subjected to continuous change as different governments have sought to improve its efficiency and image through the adoption of private sector ideas and the application of radical management thinking to public administration. Government agencies are now committed to a business approach in providing government services. The UK NHS (National Health Service) operates an internal market and now faces increased competition from the private sector. Academic institutions compete fiercely for funds and students, and both the education and law enforcement sectors have seen the introduction of private companies to carry out certain functions. Central and local government are increasingly operating in environments that are strongly influenced by global events and international regulation. The public sector, as all others, deals with an increasing volume of information and has staff who need to gain new experience, a significant staff turnover, a small but increasing number of staff working at home, and complex supply and client chains. The UK government has taken a strong lead in the development of the knowledge economy, heralded by the Competitiveness White Paper in 1998 (Department of Trade and Industry, 1998):

> Government needs to learn and innovate as much as the private sector and it must create new mechanisms for sharing ideas and best practice.

The Modernising Government White paper published in 1999 (Cabinet Office, 1999) set out an agenda which includes the need for all parts of government to work better together – 'joined-up government'. The agenda also includes:

> Smarter knowledge management across government, which increasingly enables government to harness its data and experience more effectively, and to work in new ways.

The government has underpinned its commitment to supporting the knowledge economy by appointing a minister of e-commerce and an e-commerce envoy.

While the private sector has led the way in the implementation of knowledge management concept, the take-up within the public sector has not lagged far behind. Changing environments and organizations are undoubtedly factors influencing the public sector, coupled with the rapid development of information technologies and the increasing individual access to, and publication of, information.

Central government

> The role of government today is to equip people and business for the new economy in which we are going to live and work. To encourage innovation and entrepreneurship; to improve education; stimulate competition; broaden access to the new technology; and to encourage a spirit of entrepreneurship and innovation in the public sector too. All of us need to embrace change, not to let the forces of conservatism stand in the way of what has to be done to prepare us for the future.
>
> (Rt Hon Tony Blair MP, Prime Minister, CBI Conference, 11 February 1999 (Blair, 1999))

Even before the Competitiveness White Paper was published in December 1998 there was a growing interest in some UK government departments in the KM concept. The Government Advanced Technology Circle, part of the Central Computer and Telecommunication Agency (CCTA), held a seminar on the subject in the previous September which attracted delegates from most government departments and which was not primarily technology focused. The CCTA has continued to encourage cross-departmental thinking in this area, facilitating meetings with KM themes and keeping a watching brief. The UK government's stated aim to move rapidly to electronic government, with 25% of its business transacted electronically by 2002, puts the CCTA firmly at the centre of information and knowledge sharing. As the primary publisher of guidelines on IT procurement and management for government departments it is possible that they will eventually produce KM guidelines, although the Department of Trade and Industry has an equally large stake in the area, being the flagship for the UK knowledge economy

A CCTA Foundation Briefing on the KM market produced in June 1999 summarized the progress being made in the public sector at that time (CCTA, 1999). It will be interesting to see how projects outlined in the Modernising Government White Paper, such as the 'Business Register', which sets out to enable a single point of entry for all transactions a firm conducts with government, develop within a KM climate. Initiatives such as these, although based on information and data management, cut across the structures of all government departments and require the shift in thinking and approach that KM requires.

The Department of Trade and Industry (DTI)

A requirement of the Competitiveness White Paper (Department of Trade and Industry, 1998) was that the Department of Trade and Industry establish a Knowledge Management Unit (KMU) to put the Department at the forefront of knowledge management. The KMU came into being in March 1999 with the objectives of building systems and processes to encourage the capture and sharing of knowledge, both within the Department and with customers. Central to its objectives was bringing about a culture change, and many of its efforts have been focused on creating an awareness of KM principles and practice, and providing a strategy to ensure that the Department continually improves as part of the drive to modernize. Facilitated, participative workshops and other awareness campaigns aim to involve DTI staff at all levels in the development of ideas and initiatives, reflecting the key messages that the KMU identified at the initial KM seminar (again a direct result of the White Paper):

* the requirement for a shared set of values for DTI/the government in general
* the necessity for culture and attitude change at all levels
* the need to build relationships of trust between colleagues at all levels
* the emphasis on social infrastructure and not technology.

The KMU works with other groups to identify and develop cross-department projects within the DTI that will produce short- and long-term benefits, thus connecting the portfolios of projects that have KM potential. The responsibility of the Competitiveness Unit, for example, is external to the Department, specifically the implementation of the Competitiveness White Paper (CWP), but it is also interested in promoting KM within the Department and it spearheaded the publication and dissemination of the CWP Implementation Plan as a KM initiative. The Future Unit, a group formed in 1999 with the vision of making 'consideration of the future a conscious aspect of decision making throughout the DTI (Department of Trade and Industry, n.d.), identified knowledge and expertise within the Department as part of their report *Mapping the future* (Department of Trade and Industry, n.d.). The Innovation Unit, which initially pioneered KM within the Department, continues to monitor and provide information on KM practices outside government. The DTI's intranet is designed and managed by the Information Management & Process Engineering Directorate (IMPE) and the intranet strategy of February 1998 was commissioned with the creation of a KM knowledge-sharing environment as a key element. The IMPE and KMU work closely together to provide an appropriate KM infrastructure.

The KMU currently consists of approximately eight people with a diverse range of skills, experience and backgrounds. Their role is essentially that of advocates of KM, building links between people and projects, and pioneering approaches that build a KM culture. Their plans for the future are ambitious and not yet prioritized, but include the development of human resource activities to support the culture change, a skills database, a DTI virtual university and a DTI client data exchange. Their success in achieving these objectives may depend on their ability to win the hearts and minds of the Department's top management. As the government's flagship for the knowledge economy, the DTI KMU stands a very good chance of succeeding.

The Department of Health (DOH) and the Department for Education and Employment (DfEE)

Both Departments are focusing on a Department-wide intranet as a knowledge sharing infrastructure, but are also addressing processes and procedures for disseminating best practice, raising awareness of Departmental activities and for sharing information across business units.

The DOH has developed a number of key knowledge management activities based on

- a Department-wide intranet
- databases to support policy making, providing links between various policy initiatives
- a package of guidance and training to help staff use information effectively
- a promotional campaign to encourage business units to share information
- a strategy to replace manual practices with electronic documents and records management procedures.

The intranet links internal and external information sources supported by a Departmental thesaurus, a subject index to those Internet and NHS websites relevant to DOH work, and a number of internal websites for information sharing across business units. 'As a basis for the intranet, a range of information management standards have been developed to ensure structure and access is uniform' (CCTA Foundation, 1999). The guidance and training in information use includes 'intranet maintenance, electronic publishing via external networks, information management skills and general information/web searching' (CCTA Foundation, 1999).

The DfEE 'has chosen to address key areas where improvements will assist better KM, such as reducing information overload, improving corporate communications, better use of its knowledge base for policy development, and improved sharing' (CCTA Foundation, 1999). It is also focused on sharing best practice with the Department's partners such as the Local Education Authorities, Training and Enterprise Councils, educational institutions, funding agencies, etc. The intranet provides access to policy materials, sites providing essential facts, case studies, prominent initiatives and a who-does-what directory. It also 'operates "learning sets" –a number of self-managed groups used by Divisional Managers to share experience and learn from their peers' (CCTA Foundation, 1999) and the Department is exploring the concept of communities of practice. Regular seminars are run to keep staff informed about aspects of the business of the Department, and to provide insights from outside speakers on the subject of leadership. Interestingly the Department also provides guidance on facilities such as the principles and practice of e-mail and shared areas, dealing with issues such as e-mail overload, management of folders and files, etc.

Government agencies
Higher Education Funding Council for England (HEFCE)

HEFCE was established as a Non-Departmental Public Body under the Further and Higher Education Act 1992. The Council's mission is by working in partnership to promote and fund high-quality, cost effective teaching and research, meeting the diverse needs of students, the economy and society. Its principal task is to distribute funds made available by the Secretary of State for the provision of education and the undertaking of research by higher education institutions in England, and for the provision of higher education in further education institutions. The Council is legally responsible for ensuring that the quality of education is assessed in the universities and colleges and also advises the Secretary for Education on the funding needs of the higher education sector.

(Civil Service Yearbook, 1996)

HEFCE is a highly networked organization. Its external partners include government departments, academic establishments, advisory bodies, research organizations and contractors and education experts. Its own staff consist of a headquarters team and advisors in the field. It is a contributor to education policy. It collects large quantities of information and data, commissions research and produces information. It is an organization of professional experts bringing a diversity of experience and working with a range of educational researchers, practitioners, administrators and policy makers. It is a knowledge-based organization which in 1996 recognized a need for an information strategy and set up a project for its development. This quickly became a knowledge management strategy, with the first draft being produced in 1997. The drivers for this strategy were seen as:

* the growing complexity and scope of its activities and associated problems of information overload
* a need to move from a reactive approach to long-term planning
* the need to make more effective use of information from institutions and to improve feedback to institutions
* a need to clarify information needed for projects and its availability, and to move from an over-reliance on internal material
* a need to consolidate knowledge gained from projects.

The purpose of the KM strategy was to enable HEFCE to more clearly define its role as a knowledge-based organization and the ways of achieving its objectives. The strategy set explicit objectives, including that of becoming the most knowledgeable and reliable source of information and the leading player in the understanding, development and promotion of higher education. This would be achieved through knowledge sharing, knowledge generation and management, effective use of IT and the promotion of corporate goals.

The development of a KM approach in HEFCE has been led by

senior management but based on cross-functional teams identifying tactics that would produce the changes required. Earlier, problems were identified as those common in new and dispersed organizations. Knowledge was associated with individuals and held in their heads, information collections were local or individual, there was a lack of resources for central records functions, problems of convergence of print, verbal and electronic communications, and a perception of resistance to information sharing.

The implementation of the KM strategy included a number of defined actions within two main themes:

- The development of a central Knowledge Centre to manage knowledge resources and the appointment of a Knowledge Manager. The purpose of this appointment was to create standards, systems and infrastructure to meet the information and knowledge requirements of staff; to facilitate good information practice and to improve awareness of internal and external information sources.
- The development and reward of staff to enable the Council to become a learning organization.

The focus on people, their tacit knowledge and development was underpinned by the change agenda set in place by the Chief Executive with the following explicit aims for change to enable the Council to meet its objectives:

From	To
Structured	Flexible
Teams	Networks
Activity	Outcomes
'Need to Know'	Openness
Regulator	Partner
Precedent	Innovation
Cynicism	Commitment
Blame	Help

To achieve the change a set of expectations were agreed between staff and management (Figure 11.1) which reflect the KM philosophy of developing shared values.

HEFCE expects you to add value by:

- showing respect and working effectively with people
- taking and giving responsibility
- showing and encouraging initiative
- seeking and delivering challenging objectives
- taking responsibility for developing appropriate skills and knowledge.

And in return, you can expect HEFCE to:

- show you respect
- give you responsibility
- reward your initiatives and delivery of challenging objectives
- assist you in developing appropriate skills and knowledge.

Fig. 11.1 *Expectations in HEFCE*

Supporting these expectations are a set of competencies defined to clarify behaviours and attitudes needed in order to achieve corporate objectives, help define training and development needs, and provide a basis for performance review.

DERA

DERA is an agency of the UK Ministry of Defence (MOD), incorporating the bulk of the MOD's non-nuclear research, technology, test and evaluation establishments. It is one of Europe's largest research organizations with a turnover of approximately £1 billion and about 12,000 staff. It offers a unique range of services, from the highest level of operational studies and analysis, through the various categories of basic and applied research, to consultancy advice on the procurement process and the test and evaluation of specific equipment in both the development phase and during actual operations. In 2000 the government announced that a substantial part of DERA would be privatized in order to exploit its commercial opportunities, with a section of core research work being retained in a new public agency

While DERA exists primarily to support the MOD, it is encouraged to seek work on commercial terms from other government departments and other governments and industry, provided such commercial developments lie within the framework of its corporate and business plans as approved by the Secretary of State. DERA has six business divisions plus a small corporate headquarters for core functions including the Technical Directorate.

DERA's success depends on its ability to give informed, impartial advice based on first-class science and the ability to acquire, create, use and disseminate knowledge effectively. It has strong links with industry and academia and has been extensively involved in international collaboration and exchange. Many aspects of knowledge management are core to best practice in science and engineering. A more formal approach to KM started at DERA when the Technical Directorate needed to understand the fundamental uniqueness of DERA in order to write a technical strategy; this led to the first KM strategy in 1996. This was revised and developed by a core KM team in 1998, leading to the appointment of a Board-level Chief Knowledge Officer.

DERA treats KM as a change programme, alongside a number of other initiatives, with the objectives of increasing productivity and improving profitability as the agency approaches potential privatization of much of its activities. The approach is closely aligned to how DERA measures its success so KM projects support the quality of service to clients and the working environment of the staff, and the effectiveness of identifying and transferring available technology and developments into the DERA knowledge base. The initial KM focus was on the identification of expertise within and without DERA, on the establishment of a knowledge-sharing culture and on increasing the visibility of, and access to, the corporate 'warehouse' of information. As the strategy developed, a wide range of organization-wide actions were identified as crucial to the promotion of effective KM. These are summarized as the BEST programme:

- **B**ehaviour: the creation of a trusting culture where staff naturally share
- **E**nvironment: building a physical, organizational and secure environment to support knowledge sharing
- **S**ystems: the development of intuitive and user-friendly IT systems to provide the infrastructure for knowledge sharing and utilization
- **T**argets: metrics and targets that allow the organization to measure and improve the efficiency and effectiveness of its processes.

The KM focus in DERA is on improving technology and processes, on improving organizational culture and environment, on changing behaviours and developing people, on the better management of explicit knowledge among three groups – scientists, information scientists and management – and on the development of metrics to monitor the effectiveness of processes. One of the activities identified as key to the success of knowledge management has been that of information management. The Information Resources Department manages the organization's intranet, providing standards and rules for the creation of web pages. Information scientists trawl for and filter information for the specialist teams charged with identifying significant scientific and engineering developments in the external world. The ability of individual scientists and engineers to access and manage information is perceived as crucial enough for information management skills to be included as a competency in the DERA competency framework.

An additional challenge for the two arms of DERA following privatization will be managing knowledge flow between the two resulting organizations within confidentiality and security constraints.

The academic sector

Academic institutions exist to generate knowledge. They do so by teaching, by developing the ability of individuals to learn, to apply what they learn within the context in which they work, and to increase their own knowledge and that of the groups within which they move. They also contribute to the expansion of knowledge through research both within subject disciplines and, increasingly, in areas that are interdisciplinary and at discipline boundaries. Academic institutions are seen by government as the natural home of blue-sky research, but much of their research is guided by commercial requirements and paid for by the organization who will take the findings to market. They therefore attract people whose interests and objectives focus on the expansion of the boundaries of knowledge and who, while communicating their knowledge widely, also protect their position as experts. Academic rivalry is not a new concept. Being 'first in class' brings the funding for blue-sky and near-market research.

Competition between academic organizations has increased during the past two decades. Funding for core teaching is related to student numbers and research grading. Distance learning and alternative means of access have created new approaches to qualification and self-development. At the same time the success of the institution may be judged as much on its connections with the commercial and industrial world as on the quality of its graduates. As with all organizations, academic institutions have recognized that their strength in the market may in future hinge on their ability to build collaborative and strategic partnerships. While partnerships with employers have been nurtured to increase the relevance of their graduate and postgraduate courses and to create centres of excellence in research and training, there is now a push for collaboration between the institutions. The White Rose Consortium of Leeds, Sheffield and York universities for example has a powerful research capability and has been hugely successful in attracting funds. Such collaboration also takes place across international boundaries for the delivery of academic courses and collaborative research.

Through the European Union requirement for cross-national partnership in their major research programmes, academic institutions have learnt a lot about international collaboration both private and public. In the USA and Europe partnerships with interest groups such as the Knowledge Management Consortium, and with corporate bodies developing their own education programmes, increase the ability of academic institutions to tailor and deliver materials and programmes to meet specific requirements.

Within these environments a paradox seems to exists. Many institutions teach new business skills and urge the sharing and maximization of knowledge. Some are developing knowledge management courses. However, many are still internally organized as competitive and autonomous faculties. Introducing new ways of working requires the cooperation of very individualistic and talented people with competing drivers and objectives, a challenge in knowledge management terms.

The development of modular courses and qualifications increases the interaction between faculties and schools. Starting with the provision of cross-faculty modules, and perhaps led by the cross-discipline approach of the Open University, the integration of teaching programmes has seen the emergence of centres and learning programmes that rely on multidisciplinary input. There is still little crossover in some institutions between the research activities and their teaching capability. The skills of many academics are often only apparent within their own department or school. Some are better known outside their own institution, in other countries even, than they are in neighbouring departments and schools. Research funding is generally project based. The PhD students and contract staff who undertake the core research work take what they have learned about the networks within and without the organization with them when they leave.

As expansion of the higher education sector took place, the Follett Committee (Joint Funding Council's Libraries Review Group, 1993) identified the core role of information technology in facilitating this expansion through the electronic creation and delivery of course material and information, and access to support through campus-wide communications. The Follett report led to significant investment in the IT infrastructure. The provision of the infrastructure enabled a re-evaluation of 'student-based learning' and the full range of support that staff and students require. This resulted in a move towards converged services and the further development of Learning Centres. In universities such as Sheffield Hallam, North London and Hertfordshire purpose-built Learning Centres have enabled all the functions that support students and staff to come together: information sources, production of materials, access to learning materials and teacher development. The provision of such services requires inter-disciplinary teams with library managers and information specialists, computer and applications support, media and production facilities, teacher support and assessment of new means of learning.

The core issues for academic institutions are associated with:

- knowledge transfer from research activities to teaching and learning programmes
- knowledge and information sharing within the institution
- knowledge and information sharing between themselves, their academic collaborators, funding organizations and private sector partners
- promoting knowledge sharing while maintaining a regard for the commercial confidentiality associated with private sector funding and their own competitive position.

University of Leeds

The University of Leeds has tackled these problems from a knowledge management perspective. It has established a record of success in the development of its 'reach-out', collaborative activities with business and the community. These are progressively embedded alongside teaching, learning and research as a core part of the strategic mission of the University through a Third Arm Board chaired by the Vice Chancellor. The University is engaged in a series of major, linked initiatives that present challenging issues of knowledge management within and between projects. Examples include:

- Institute for Corporate Learning: to establish an enhanced interface with corporate partners and provide a focus for new activities and a vehicle for their delivery
- Innovation Centre: a joint venture to establish a centre for start-up high technology businesses, spun-out from, or allied with, university research
- The Virtual Science Park (VSP): developed initially within the research-driven Centre for Virtual Working Systems and, more recently, through the University spin-off company Virtual Working Systems Ltd. The VSP provides a desktop computer-based virtual working environment that addresses the needs of organizations to manage and utilize their distributed knowledge resources in more effective and efficient ways. The web-based VSP tool suite includes:
  — a variety of 'rooms' that provide intuitive environments to support tacit knowledge exchange and access to expertise directory services
  — resource rooms for multimedia document management
  — discussion forums
  — integrated collaborative working tools for application sharing, one-to-one video conferencing and shared whiteboards
  — powerful search tools for cross-searching databases
  — the opportunity to create personal working environments and alerting services
- REPIS (Research Expertise and Publications Information System): a major university knowledge management project, which combines information about people's expertise and experience with validated publications and project information. It provides services to individual researchers, resource centre managers and senior executives for research strategy development.

REPIS now provides an expertise matcher through the VSP and is being further developed through a HEFCE-funded project to demonstrate the use of knowledge management good practice to support 'reach-out and third arm' activities in higher education institutions

- PETIS (Packaging Executives Training and Information Service): as part of the Faraday Centre of Excellence in packaging technology, a consortium of universities, companies and trade associations piloting 'executive tutorials' for translating academic expertise into insight for senior executives and an environment for research students to contribute to this process

- NEST (Network for the Exploitation of Science and Technology): aims to improve UK competitiveness by enhancing the dialogue and promoting partnership between R&D users, providers and enablers to achieve a significantly higher 'hit' rate of successful UK-led innovative ventures. This is being achieved by creating a national NEST gateway allowing access to information on research capabilities. The Office for Science and Technology and Research Councils funded the first stage of the project to create an integrated database of research expertise across all universities and all Research Councils in the UK

- ADVISER (Add Value Information Services for European Research): a European funded project to provide access to research expertise and research results from Framework 4 funded projects in the telematics area.

These initiatives have overlapping missions, activity and information development. The University recognized at an early stage the potential for adding value through integrating IT and knowledge platforms in the VSP. The technology and platforms developed in Leeds are used in knowledge sharing, expertise matching, online consultancy, information brokerage, collaborative networking and graduate/professional education. For example, the VSP is used to support a range of information gateways, particularly focused on research information systems, support for distributed collaborative projects such as the virtual centre for industrial process tomography (ten major industrial companies and three universities) and environments for online learning, eg the BBC Online masters degree in media management.

Sheffield Hallam University

The Learning Centre at Sheffield Hallam University was formed in 1996, and integrates library and information services, user computing and multimedia production with the University's Learning and Teaching Institute. The department occupies the Adsetts Centre, a £14m building on the University's main city centre campus.

The department was planned as part of the University's strategy to deal with changes affecting higher education: for example, institutions have experienced significant increases in student numbers at the same time as a reduction in the funds for teaching. Two particular trends were identified that would impact on work with students: the continuing shift from tutor-centred work towards more independent work by students and the potential of new technology for learning.

The Learning Centre was designed to create a flexible learning environment which would both anticipate and lead changes in higher education. The department integrates a range of provisions to support the various teaching and learning styles, from traditional lectures and guided reading to group work with multimedia and the creation of web-based resources for project assignments.

The development of new staffing arrangements was critical to the success of the department. The Learning Centre brought together staff with a variety of backgrounds: librarians, computing staff, media designers, educational developers, researchers and administrators. The integration of staff has been achieved through a new scheme for front-line staff, the adoption of a flat staff structure based on teams and the introduction of a staff development framework that enables individuals to develop a portfolio of skills.

The new staffing scheme integrates support for library, information and computing provision. It includes information assistants, information advisors, senior information advisers and information specialists. By accommodating individuals with a variety of qualifications and experience, it has enabled teams to develop a common culture based on common responsibilities and seamless support to students.

The introduction of this staffing scheme was underpinned by an intensive staff development programme which allowed individuals to develop their skills across the information and computing areas. Subsequently, a dual approach to staff development has evolved, with

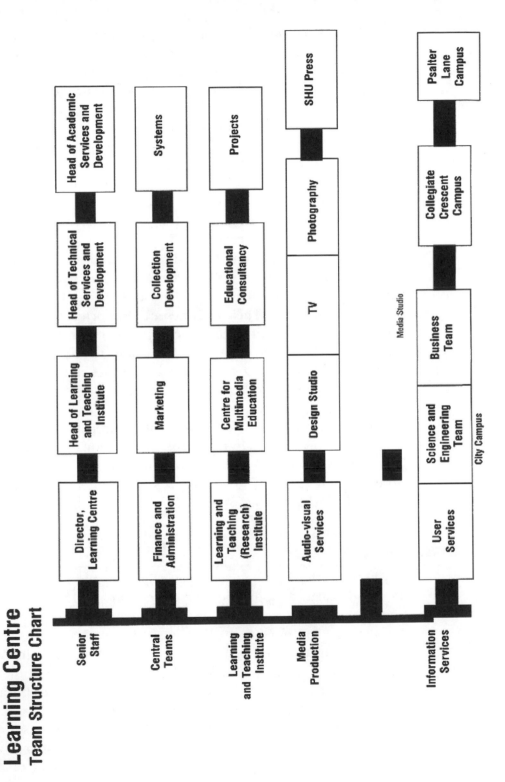

Sheffield Hallam University

**Learning Centre
Team Structure Chart**

Fig. 11.2 *Sheffield Hallam University: Learning Centre team structure chart*

individuals being supported both in the development of skills in their core professional area and also in the development of a portfolio of skills across the key areas of the department's work.

A team structure (see Figure 11.2) provides individuals with a base for their work, and allows services to be managed with a clear focus on users. The flat structure is also designed to encourage individuals to work collaboratively across the entire department so that the full range of skills and expertise can be harnessed to deal with enquiries and projects. The development and evaluation of multimedia course-ware for students, for example, has involved a variety of staff: educational developers, multimedia designers, information advisors, systems specialists and researchers.

Considerable energy has been directed at the development of a strong culture and sound working arrangements. Teams and individuals are encouraged to have a strong user focus and to take responsibility for their work. Their activities are supported by departmental frameworks and central teams which place decision making close to the activity. The departmental culture is also to value all staff, with diversity being seen as a strength that provides an opportunity for staff to develop new skills and to think outside of the limits of traditional professional boundaries.

Information about the Sheffield Hallam University Learning Centre is available on the website (**http://www shu.ac.uk/services/lc/ index.html**). Graham Bulpitt has written a useful case study of the Adsetts Centre (Bulpitt, 1998), and a RIBA Conference of 1995 provides another (RIBA, 1996).

The health sector

The health sector is undeniably knowledge rich and relies on the ability of individuals to apply their experience and skill to the identification of the cause of outward systems, the appropriate intervention, and the care and nursing of the patient. It is a sector that has been based on a hierarchical system of professionalism, with individuals occupying 'star' positions supported by teams of healthcare workers, and where the interdependence of the various skills in healthcare has not, until recently, been explicitly acknowledged. It is also a sector that has experienced a great deal of change in mechanisms for funding and administration and where there is a desire on the part of government to make more use of the experience of all members of the healthcare teams, but where the culture of hierarchy makes this difficult.

The UK's National Health Service (NHS) is one of Europe's largest employers with over one million employees from 100 professions, and spends over £40 bn per annum. All residents of the UK are eligible for healthcare through the NHS, and there is an ongoing tension between providing high-quality care to the majority of the population and delivering a cost-effective service. Services are provided through numerous channels, from general practitioners in local area partnerships to large teaching hospitals. A recent paper by Fraser and Godbolt outlines the climate of change within the NHS:

> Health practitioners work in hospital trusts, in health authorities and community settings such as local clinics and pharmacies. Increasingly they work across sectoral boundaries with local authorities, voluntary organisations and higher education.
>
> (Fraser and Godbolt, 2000)

A number of common thrusts emerge from the policy papers produced by the current UK government which have implications for the development of information and knowledge management. Fraser and Godbolt summarize these as:

- patient-centred services
- primary care-led services
- delivery of evidence-based care and treatment
- seamless services based on collaborative working across health and social care
- multidisciplinary team working including education and training
- focus on health information for the public.

> These policies outline a clear strategic direction for a more unified NHS in the future with an overall raising of quality of services on offer.
>
> (Fraser and Godbolt, 2000)

Or, as the White Paper on the NHS describes it,

> knowledgeable patients advised by knowledge professionals supported by up-to-date information and information technology.
>
> (Department of Health, 1997a)

The key development supporting these policies has been the development of a seven-year information strategy for the English NHS to ensure that good quality information is available to patients, professionals, members of the public and planners, and one of its most ambitious targets is the National electronic Library for Health.

The National electronic Library for Health (NeLH)

The key objectives of the NeLH are to

- provide easy access to best current knowledge
- improve health and healthcare, clinical practice and patient choice.

Conceived as a virtual library, NeLH is being developed with three core 'floors':

- Knowledge and Knowhow – research evidence and clinical guidelines
- Patient focused information – developing as NHS Direct Online
- Learning Opportunities – under discussion as an NHS virtual classroom.

The main body of knowledge will be lodged in the Knowledge and Knowhow floor with a pilot service launching at the end of November this year (2000). NeLH will actively support communities of interest in the health sector by developing Virtual Branch Libraries (VBLs) in key areas such as Mental Health and Cancer.

NHS Direct and NHS Direct Online have begun to set the trend for much greater consumer participation in healthcare delivery. NeLH will link closely to NHS Direct Online which is expected to be the first port of call for patients and the public seeking information.

(Fraser and Godbolt, 2000)

Evidence-based health care

The goal of quickly translating clinical research findings into medical practice was expressed by the UK government at the beginning of the 1990s. This presented the challenge of identifying the best means of raising awareness of best practice and paved the way for the adoption in the UK of evidence-based healthcare in the mid-1990s. This approach aims to facilitate the rapid application of research findings to everyday medicine and health care by making the findings readily accessible, and by educating all members of health care teams to use the findings. This is the re-use of knowledge on a large and significant scale, and has required the systematic recording and dissemination of research findings and the training of health teams in activities identified as key to the process. Training requirements identified include:

- problem definition and the identification of information requirements
- finding and evaluation of relevant information
- the recognition of the difference between too little and too much.

South Thames Regional Office of the NHS Executive

The 1997 Strategic Framework for the NHS research and development funding changed the basis for allocating NHS research funds, favouring project-funding linked to national objectives:

> Instead of making funding available only to well-established teaching hospitals, every hospital became eligible to receive funding. Each group had to propose projects and compete for funds. They would be held accountable for the results through annual reviews.
>
> (Department of Health, 1997b)

With research funds potentially available to a greater number of hospitals, each unit had to decide how best to incorporate and foster knowledge-enabled R&D efforts. Drawing from organizational design theory, several units have used a methodology to evaluate their options to becoming a knowledge-based organization.

South Thames Regional Office sponsored projects focused on evidence-based practice, which studies the actual delivery of healthcare services, much influenced by a study by David Sackett and William Rosenberg (Sackett and Rosenberg, 1995). They followed a group of doctors on their rounds, evaluating situations to correlate whether new findings would have modified the doctors' final patient evaluation/prescription.

The biggest surprise of the study was that doctors who claimed that they would not need this type of R&D information more than two or three times a week were shown that 16 patient evaluations would have changed given the new findings. Only 30% of the information about these scenarios was in place in the workplace. Most doctors complained of the disorganization of content contained in journals and the out-of-date nature of textbooks, thus justifying their reason for not consulting paper-based resources when in need of an answer (Rowland, 1998). Instead, most doctors consulted other practitioners.

South Thames wanted to develop better methods for incorporating research findings, not relying on word of mouth. They sponsored a project to define what a knowledge-based healthcare organization would look like, including roles, responsibilities, processes and leadership. They developed a model and then used questionnaires and focus groups within each group to determine what it would actually look like in practice.

As more units worked with this model, several trends emerged, and training and quality became integrated with R&D implementation. Although most hospitals do not have extensive collaborative IT infrastructures, they saw more effective use of IT systems as a means of promulgating these findings.

NHS Lewisham Hospital

The University Hospital of Lewisham saw the new R&D strategy as an opportunity to achieve more from R&D. Their proposals focused on getting nurses involved in doing research, and on teaching practitioners to assess research findings critically and to enact sound research methodologies. According to the Academic Director, R&D was about raising the profile of best practices:

> For example, clinical research shows that you decrease the likelihood of subsequent hip fractures in elderly people when you prescribe drugs to increase bone density upon discharge. These patients, however, first see an orthopaedic specialist whose main priority is treatment of the initial problem. A battery of nurses see to their daily needs, and interns, who change roles every six months, handle their discharge. Because of turnover, stress, and the overwhelming nature of the interns' jobs, they often forget to prescribe their medication. We wanted to study the best implementation method for incorporating these types of R&D findings into daily practice. We currently have a project underway to study whether a one time lecture, a monthly course, or the incorporation of this practice into ward protocol will be the most effective means of getting interns to remember practices.
> (Rowland, 1998)

Lewisham set up an 'academic board' of people from different disciplines across the hospital, which would evaluate research proposals and progress. Raising the profile of best practices in health care delivery also entails providing access to research through libraries or systems, and the training of use in these tools. Teaching, staff development and R&D were seen as almost as important as treating the patients.

The police

Surrey Police

Among the early KM innovators in the public sector was Surrey Police, an organization with 2500 employees spread across 42 locations. The project had its origins in document management when in 1993 an inspector in R&D began to review retention schedules with the objective of improving access to information required for cases, and recognized that a great deal of benefit could be gained from improving the management of information at the beginning of its life-cycle rather than concentrating on what existed at the end of the process. This approach led to the development of a new approach to information collection that includes the incorporation of experience and knowledge with hard evidence, and the birth of SPIKE, the Surrey Police Information and Knowledge Environment.

The purpose of SPIKE is to

provide facilities that will enable the creation of a virtual organisation:

• That is not constrained by geographical limitations or organisational rigidity
• Where organisational structures can be established and changed to suit business requirements
• Where people can interwork in the manner that best suits their particular requirements
• Where the customer is unaware of where the people he/she is dealing with are located, but who appear to all intents and purposes to give the service a warm feeling of being locally based.

(Smithsonian Institute, 1999)

It is essentially an information management initiative that makes innovative use of IT and takes into account the culture and people aspects of information collection and sharing. Run by the Information Services arm of Surrey Police, its project approach enabled the service to develop structures and processes, and the skills and focus to develop and support SPIKE as an ongoing facility.

In simple terms the objectives of SPIKE are to deliver 'the right information to the right person at the right time in the right place'. It recognizes, however, that the recipients of information are part of the knowledge process and that 'employees have a personal obligation to access information sources to find out what they need to know and when they need to know it' (Smithsonian Institute, 1999). It is not, therefore, a passive approach to information management: it is an approach that puts information at the heart of every employee's work experience.

The technology platform of SPIKE provides all staff with an information utility for the provision of all information and messaging requirements, supporting internal and external e-mail, facsimile and telex, as well as giving intranet and Internet access and access to all operational and support applications. It also extends services to local communities relevant to the police such as Neighbourhood Watch and Business Security, through the Surrey Police website.

The core of SPIKE is an information architecture designed to express the relationship between data, applications, context and views and to support the technology to provide universal access. The benefit from the architecture is obtained from an information strategy based on a number of underlying principles:

1. Information is a corporate resource to be made available to all who require it in order to perform their duties. All members of staff have a responsibility to seek out and use information pertinent to their daily tasks.
2. Information Resource requirements and value are best informed by users of the information.
3. Information should be readily available to complement decision making. The timeliness of information is critical to its usefulness and its accuracy must be maintained.
4. The acquisition and maintenance of information resources represent a cost to the organisation which must be justifiable.
5. Information must be acquired, processed and managed in a planned, integrated and economic way.

6. Information is a valuable resource for all staff and its importance to the Force should be recognized through appropriate resource allocation and skills development.

(Smithsonian Institute, 1999)

This strategy includes the development of basic information rules and standards and help to apply them, in order to maintain quality and relevance of content, and the development of a toolkit to help audit information and skills requirements.

As the strategy and tactics take effect, the benefits of information availability to workstations or via personal mobile data terminals has become apparent, as officers are able to send information as easily as they access it. Information concerning incident control, criminal investigations or observations is trapped at the point of its occurrence. Information support for decision making is improved and confidence is growing in the quality of information available via the intranet. The benefits are now perceived as outweighing the considerable effort and commitment needed to establish an information strategy and the need for an Information Resources Director. The issues that have been raised by the implementation of the project are similar to those found in other organizations and include identifying the skills needed to interact with the information 'process': skills that enable people to understand and evaluate the information they are presented with, to know how to filter, assess relevance and apply context, to use IT applications and to know when enough information is available to make a decision, skills that are a mix of IT, information management and decision making.

Surrey Police is continuing to develop information-based solutions and services to its staff and local community. SPIKE has undoubtedly been made possible by investment in sophisticated technology but the success lies in the strategic approach taken to information as a core resource by a manager who understood how information is and could be used as part of the knowledge kit of the Force. Police officers are used to working in teams, to meeting and exchanging information, to assessing situations and collecting evidence. What Surrey Police has done through its KM approach to information management is to build an information exchange system of use in everyday operations.

The Surrey Police initiative has won a number of awards and was nominated for a Smithsonian Institute award in the 1999 government and non-profit section. More information about the initiative can be found in the archives on the Smithsonian website (**http://innovate.si. edu**), which was nominated for an award in 1999.

Conclusions

This chapter has reviewed just a few of the public sector initiatives in the UK that have been influenced by KM concepts. There are more in the UK and many more in other countries, some of which are reviewed by Eileen Milner in her book on IM and KM in the public sector (Milner, 2000). As this book was being prepared for publication, the European Union Heads of State were meeting in Lisbon with the knowledge economy as a main agenda item. At the same time the European Commission is developing internal KM projects in addition to launching projects with KM themes. The KM approach to organizational development is helping to close the gap between the public and private sectors.

References

Blair, T (1999) *Prime Minister's speech to the CBI conference*, Birmingham, 11 February 1999, available at
http://www.number-10.gov.uk

Bulpitt, G (1998) *The development of the Adsetts Centre* [Sheffield Hallam University], based on an interview with Graham Bulpitt, Director of the Learning Centre. In *Deliberations on teaching and learning in higher education*, available at
http://www.lgu.ac.uk/deliberations/lrc/sheffield.html

The Cabinet Office (1999) *Modernising government*, Cm 4310, The Stationery Office.

CCTA Foundation (1999) *An overview of the knowledge management market*, June 1999, restricted circulation.

The Civil Service Yearbook (1996) HMSO.

Department of Health (1997a) *The new NHS modern, dependable*, Cm 3807, HMSO, available at
http://www.official-documents.co.uk/

Department of Health (1997b) *Strategic framework for the use of the NHS R&D levy*, NHS.

Department of Trade and Industry (1998) *Our competitive future: building the knowledge economy*, Cm 4176, HMSO, available at
http://www.dti.gov.uk/comp/

Department of Trade and Industry (n.d.)
   http://www.dti.gov.uk/future-unit
Fraser, V and Godbolt, S (2000) Building a first class NHS: developing networks in the health sector, *Laserlink*, Autumn/Winter 2000, 6–7.
Joint Funding Council's Libraries Review Group (1993) *A report for the Higher Education Funding Council for England, Scottish Higher Education Funding Council, Higher Education Funding Council for Wales and the Department of Education for Northern Ireland*, HEFCE. [Follett Report].
Milner, E (2000) *Managing information and knowledge in the public sector*, Routledge.
RIBA (1996) *The development of learning resource centres for the future.* Proceedings of a Conference held at the Royal Institute of British Architects, 10 October 1995, SCONUL. [Includes case study of the Adsetts Centre].
Rowland, H (1998) Building a knowledge based health service, *Knowledge Management Review*, July/August 1998, 16–19.
Sackett, D L and Rosenberg, W M (1995) On the need for evidence based medicine, *Journal of Public Health Medicine*, **17** (3), 330–4.
Smithsonian Institute (1999) 'Innovation' site. Nomination for an award in 1999 Government & Non-profit section, available at
   http://innovatew.si.ed (search archives)

Bibliography

Hard-copy and electronic journals

Journals are a rich source of case studies and evaluation of techniques and case studies. There are numerous journal titles but the following are probably the core hard copy titles to scan for practical reports of who is doing what and the application of tools.

Fortune
    Time Inc, Switzerland
Harvard Business Review
    Harvard Business School Press, USA
13 Update
    David Skyrme Associates, UK
    http://www.skyrme.com/updates/updates.htm
Information Outlook
    Special Libraries Association, USA
Information Strategy
    The Economist Group, UK
The International Knowledge Management Newsletter
    Management Trends International, UK
The Journal of Knowledge Management
    IFS International, UK
Journal of Systematic Knowledge Management, Canada
    http://www.mcb.co.uk/journals/knowledge/welcome.htm
KM World
    Knowledge Assets Inc, USA
Knowledge and Process Management: the Journal of Corporate Transformation
    John Wiley & Sons Ltd, UK

Knowledge at Work
   Knowledge Management Associates Inc, USA
   http://www.knowledge-at-work.com/
Knowledge Inc
   Quantum Era Enterprises, USA
Knowledge Management
   Ark Publishing, UK
Knowledge Management: the Magazine for Knowledge Professionals
   Biz Media, UK
Knowledge Management Review
   Melcrum Publishing Ltd, UK
Knowledge Manager
   European Management Group, UK
   http://www.emgltd.com/
Managing Information
   ASLIB, UK
Sloan Management Review
   MIT School of Management, USA

There are also a number of electronic newsletters including knowledge@wharton.upenn.edu

General

Albert, S and Bradley, K (1997) *Managing knowledge: experts, agencies and organisation*, Cambridge University Press.

Allday, D (1998) *Spinning straw into gold: managing intellectual capital effectively*, The Institute of Management.

Allee, V (1997) *The knowledge evolution: expanding organisational intelligence*, Butterworth-Heinemann.

Auckland, M (1999) Competing through knowledge, *Knowledge Management Review*, **6**, 14–19.

Baker, M et al (1997) Leveraging human capital, *The Journal of Knowledge Management*, **1** (1), 63–74.

Balcombe, J (1993) Knowledge is the only meaningful resource today, *Aslib Information*, **21** (10), 378–80.

Barclay, R O and Pinelli, T E (1998) A strategic imperative, *Knowledge Management*, **1** (6), 1, 3–6.

Bednar, C (1999) Effective ways to capture knowledge, *Knowledge Management Review*, **2** (7), 26–9.

Blosch, M (1999) The new knowledge management supermodel, *Knowledge Management Review*, **8**, 22–5.

Boisot, M (1998) *Knowledge assets: securing competitive advantage in the information economy*, Oxford University Press.

Brown, J S and Duguid, P (1998) Organising knowledge, *Knowledge Management*, 1, 6, 6–9.

Buckley, P J and Carter, M J (2000) Knowledge management in global technology markets, *Long Range Planning*, **33** (1), 55–71.

Chase, R L (1997) The knowledge-based organisation: an international survey, *The Journal of Knowledge Management*, **1** (1), 38–49.

Chase, R L (1997) Knowledge management benchmarks, *The Journal of Knowledge Management*, **1** (1), 83–92.

Chase, R L (1999) *Creating a knowledge management business strategy to deliver bottom-line results*, Knowledge Management Report Series, Management Trends International.

Coles, M (1999) Knowing is succeeding, *Director*, **52** (8), 60–3.

Conference Board (1997) *Value-creating growth: goals, strategies, foundations: a conference report*, The Conference Board.

Conference Board (1998) *Managing knowledge in the new economy*, Conference Board Report No 1222-98-CH.

Conference Board (2000) *Beyond knowledge management: new ways to work*, by Brian Hackett, Conference Board Research Report No R-1262-00-14.

Cranfield University (1998) *The Cranfield/information strategy knowledge survey: Europe's state of the art in knowledge management*, Information Strategy, The Economist Group.

Cranfield University (2000) *Knowledge: releasing the value of knowledge: a Cranfield School of Management and Microsoft© survey of UK industry*, Cranfield University
www.microsoft.com/uk/knowledgereport

Cully, M et al (1999) *Britain at work: as depicted by the 1998 Workplace Employee Relations Survey*, Routledge.

Cutcher-Gershenfeld, J et al (1998) *Knowledge-driven work: unexpected lessons from Japanese and United States work practices*, Oxford University Press.

Davenport, T H et al (1998) Successful knowledge management projects, *Sloan Management Review*, **39** (2), 43–57.

Davenport, T H and Marchand, D (1999) Is KM just good information management?, Part Six: Knowledge management, *Financial Times*, 8 Mar, 2–3.

Davenport, T H and Prusak, L (1997) *Information ecology: mastering the information and knowledge environment*, Oxford University Press.

Davenport, T H and Prusak, L (1997) *Working knowledge: how organisations manage what they know*, Harvard Business School Press.

Dawson, R (2000) *Developing knowledge-based client relationships: the future of professional services*, Butterworth-Heinemann.

de Geus, A (1997) *The living company: growth, learning and longevity in business*, Nicholas Brealey.

Demarest, M (1997) Understanding knowledge management, *Long Range Planning Review*, **30** (3), 374–84.

Department of Trade and Industry Future Unit (1999) *Work in the knowledge-driven economy*, DTI, available from **www.dti.gov.uk/future-unit/**

Despres, C and Chauvel, D (1999) How to map knowledge management, Part Six: Knowledge management, *Financial Times*, 8 Mar, 4–6.

Drucker, P F (1995) *The post capitalist society*, Butterworth-Heinemann.

Economist (2000) Economist survey of the new economy, *The Economist*, **356** (8189), 23 Sept., Supplement.

Eisenstadt, M and Vincent, T (1998) *The knowledge web: learning and collaborating on the net*, Kogan Page.

Frick, V (1998) Creating business value with knowledge management, *Technology Update*, **3** (5), 20–2.

Fruin, W M (1997) *Knowledge works*, Oxford University Press.

Hansen, M T et al (1999) What's your strategy for managing knowledge?, *Harvard Business Review*, **77** (2), 106–116.

Holtham, C and Courtney, N (1998) The executive learning ladder: a practical process for knowledge management, *Proceedings of the 'Knowledge: Intellectual Capital and The Value Chain' conference*, London, 14–15 July 1998, Unicorn Seminars.

Houlopoulos, T M, Spinello, R and Toms, W (1997) *Corporate instinct: building a knowing enterprise for the 21st century*, International Thomson Publishing Company.

Johnson, C (1997) Leveraging knowledge for operational excellence, *The Journal of Knowledge Management*, **1** (1), 50–5.

Jordan, J and Jones, P (1997) Assessing your company's knowledge management style, *Long Range Planning Review*, **30** (3), 392–8.

Kim, W Chan and Mauborgne, R (1997) Fair process: managing in the knowledge economy, *Harvard Business Review*, **75** (4), 65–76.

Kleiner, A and Roth, G (1997) How to make experience your company's best teacher, *Harvard Business Review*, **75** (2), 172–7.

Knapp, E and Yu, D (1999) Understanding organizational culture, *Knowledge Management Review*, **7**, 16–21.

KPMG (2000) *Knowledge management research report*, KPMG Consulting.

Kransdorff, A (1998) *Corporate amnesia: keeping know-how in the company*, Butterworth-Heinemann.

Leonard-Barton, D (1998) *Wellsprings of knowledge: building and sustaining the sources of innovation*, Harvard Business School Press.

Liebowitz, J (1998) *Knowledge management handbook*, CRC Press.

Liebowitz, J and Beckman, T J (1998) *Knowledge organizations: what every manager should know*, Saint Lucie Press.

Lissack, M and Roos, J (1999) *The next common sense: mastering corporate complexity through coherence*, Nicholas Brealey.

Lloyd, B (1996) Knowledge management: the key to long term organisational success, *Long Range Planning*, **29** (4), 576–80.

McGovern, G (1999) *The caring economy: business principles for the new digital age*, Blackhall Publishing.

Malhotra, Y (2000) *Knowledge management and virtual organizations*, Hershley, Idea Group Publishing.

Marchand, D A (ed) (2000) *Competing with information: a manager's guide to creating v=business value with information content*, Wiley.

Morten, C (1998) *Beyond world class*, Macmillan Business.

Nonaka, I (1991) The knowledge creating company, *Harvard Business Review*, **69** (6), 96–104.

Nonaka, I (1994) A dynamic theory of organisational knowledge creation, *Organizational Science*, **5** (1), 14–37.

Nonaka, I et al (2000) SECI, *Ba* and Leadership: a unified model of dynamic knowledge creation, *Long Range Planning*, **33** (1), 5–34.

Nonaka, I and Takeuchi, H (1995) *The knowledge creating company*, Oxford University Press.

O'Keefe, J (1999) *Business beyond the box: applying your mind for breakthrough results*, Nicholas Brealey.

Oliver, D and Roos, J (2000) *Striking a balance in complexity and knowledge landscapes*, McGraw-Hill.

Our competitive future: building the knowledge driven economy (1998) The Stationery Office.

Oxbrow, N and Abell, A (1997) Knowledge management: competitive advantage for the twenty-first century, *USA and Europe in Business*, 143–9.

Peters, T (1992) *Liberation management*, Macmillan.

Pfeffer, J (1994) *Competitive advantage through people: unleashing the power of the workforce*, Harvard Business School Press.

Probst, G, Raub, S and Romhardt, K (2000) *Managing knowledge*, John Wiley & Sons Ltd.

Prusak, L (1996) Pursuing the knowledge advantage, *Strategy and Leadership*, **24** (2), whole issue.

Prusak, L (1997) Enemies of knowledge, *Knowledge Management*, **1** (1), 14–15.

Prusak, L (ed) (1997) *Knowledge in organisations*, Resources for the Knowledge-Based Economy Series, Butterworth-Heinemann.

Prusak, L (1999) Making knowledge visible, Part Six: Knowledge management, *Financial Times*, 8 Mar, 10–11.

Prusak, L and Matarazzo, J (1992) *Information management and Japanese success: a special report*, Special Libraries Association.

Quintas, P, Lefrere, P and Jones, G (1997) Knowledge management: a strategic agenda, *Long Range Planning Review*, **30** (3), 385–91

Rajan, A et al (1998) *Good practices in knowledge creation & exchange*, CREATE.

Rock, S (ed) (1998) *Knowledge management: a real business guide*, Caspian Publishing.

Ruggles, R L (ed) (1996) *Knowledge management tools*, Resources for the Knowledge-Based Economy Series, Butterworth-Heinemann.

Seelcy, C and Dietrick, B (1999/2000) Creating a knowledge management strategy; Parts 1–3, *Knowledge Management Review*, **18** (21), **18** (22), **18** (23).

Skyrme, D (1998) *Knowledge networking: creating the collaborative enterprise*, Butterworth-Heinemann.

Skyrme, D and Amidon, D (1997) *Creating the knowledge-based business*, Business Intelligence Ltd.

Special Libraries Association (1997) *Knowledge management: a competitive asset*, State of the Art Institute, Special Libraries Association.

Thurow, L (1999) *Building wealth: the new rules for individuals, companies and countries in knowledge-based economies*, Nicholas Brealey.

Tissen, R et al (1998) *Value-based knowledge management: creating the 21st century company: knowledge intensive, people rich*, Addison Wesley Longman.

Treece, D J (2000) Strategies for managing knowledge assets: the role of firm structure and industrial context, *Long Range Planning*, **33** (1), 35–54.

Trompenaars, A et al (1997) *Riding the waves of culture: understanding cultural diversity in global business*, 2nd edn, Nicholas Brealey.

van der Spek, R and Spijkervet, A (1997) *Knowledge management: dealing intelligently with knowledge*, Knowledge Management Network.

Wiig, K M (1995) *Knowledge management: the central management focus for intelligent-acting organisations*, Knowledge Management Trilogy, Volume 3, Schema Press.

Wiig, K M (1995) *Knowledge management foundations: thinking about thinking – how people and organizations represent, create and use knowledge*, Knowledge Management Trilogy, Volume 1, Schema Press.

Wiig, K M (1995) *Knowledge management methods: practical approaches to managing knowledge*, Knowledge Management Trilogy, Volume 3, Schema Press.

Wiig, K M (1997) Integrating intellectual capital and knowledge management, *Long Range Planning Review*, **30** (3), 399–405.

Woods, E (1998) *Knowledge management: applications, markets and technologies*, Ovum.

Yapp, C (2000) The knowledge society: the challenge of transition, *Business Information Review*, **17** (2), 59–65.

Zack, M H (1999) Developing a knowledge strategy, *California Management Review*, **41** (3), 125–46.

Case studies

Abbott, R (1999) An overview of the role of digital intelligence in healthcare and pharmaceuticals, with a focus on innovation, *The Journal of AGSI*, **8** (1), 22–30.

Bergeron, B (1998) The evolving role of knowledge management in medicine, *Knowledge Management*, **1** (6), 25–8.

Boyle, T (2000) Taking the knowledge challenge at BT: getting people to share knowledge across functional silos, *Knowledge Management Review*, **12**, 14–19.

Buchanan, L (1999) The smartest little company in America, *Inc.*, **21** (1), 43–54.

Butler, Y (1998) Six months in a leaky boat: issues for Australian and NZ law librarians, *The Law Librarian*, **29** (4), 229–33.

Carr, C (1997) Competency-led strategies based on international collaboration: four case studies of Anglo-Japanese cooperation, knowledge and process management, *The Journal of Corporate Transformation*, **4** (1), 49–62.

Choate, J (1997) Microsoft librarians: training for the 21st century, *Information Outlook*, **1** (3), 27–9.

Coles, W (2000) Learning from our mistakes: the General Motors story, *Knowledge Management Review*, **12**, 14–19.

Collison, C (1997) Greater than the sum of its parts: knowledge management in British Petroleum, *Knowledge Management*, **1** (1), 1–5.

Collison, C (1999) Connecting the new organisation, *Knowledge Management Review*, **7**, 12–15.

Covin, T J and Stivers, B P (1997) Knowledge management focus in UK and Canadian firms, *Creativity and innovation management*, **6** (3), 140–50.

Davenport, T H (n.d.) *Teltech: the business of knowledge management case study*
http://amigo.bus.utexas.edu

Doyle, D and du Toit, A (1998) Knowledge management in a law firm, *Aslib Proceedings*, **50** (1), 3–8.

Graham, A and Pizzo, V (1997) Competing on knowledge: Buckman Laboratories International, *Knowledge and Process Management*, **4** (1), 4–10.

Guest, M and Webster, D (1998) *Knowledge management in the pharmaceutical industry*, Financial Times Professional Ltd.

Henderson, J (1998) Age of know-how, *The Lawyer*, 10 Feb., 20.

Jubert, A (1998) The internet connection, *Knowledge Management*, **2** (1), 20–3.

Kennedy, C (1998) The roadmap to success: how Gerhard Schulmeyer changed the culture at Siemens Nixdorf, *Long Range Planning*, **31** (2), 262–71.

Kennedy, M L (1997) Building blocks for knowledge management at Digital Equipment Corporation: the Web Library, *Information Outlook*, **1** (6), 39–42.

Lank, E (1997) Valuing ICL knowledge: a case study, *Knowledge Management*, **1** (1), 16–19.

Saint-Onge, H (2000) *Shaping human resource management within the knowledge-driven enterprise: Clarica Insurance Company*, American Society for Training and Development. In publication.

Collaboration, teams and communities

Bennis, W and Beiderman, P W (1997) *Organizing genius: the secrets of creative collaboration*, Nicholas Brealey.

Senge, P M (1997) Communities of leaders and learners, *Harvard Business Review*, **75** (5), 30–2.

Human resources

Ashton, D (1998) Geography lessens, *People Management*, **4** (6), 46, 49.

Chatzkel, J (2000) A conversation with Hubert Saint-Onge, *Journal of Intellectual Capital*, **1** (1), 101–15.

Conference Board (1997) *The value of training in the era of intellectual capital*, Conference Board Report No 1199-97-RR.

Conference Board (1998) *Transforming the HR Function for Global Business Success*, Conference Board Report No 1209-98-RR.

Davenport, T H and Nohira, N (1994) Case management and the integration of labor, *Sloan Management Review*, **35** (2), 11.

Gourlay, S (1998) Knowledge management and HRM, *Employee Relations Review*, (8), 21–7.

John, G (1998) Share strength, *People Management*, **4** (16), 44–7.

Jones, A (1998) Wired guidance, *People Management*, **4** (24), 27.

Kamoche, K (1996) Strategic human resource management within a resource capability view of the firm, *Journal of Management Studies*, **33** (2), 213–33.

Lank, E (1998) Café society, *People Management*, **4** (4), 40–3.

The information professional and KM

Abram, S (1997) Post information age positioning for special librarians: is knowledge management the answer?, *Information Outlook*, **1** (6), 18–26.

Barker, P and Van Brakal, P A (1998) The role of the information professional in the 'knowledge economy', *The Electronic Library*, **16** (6), 373–6.

Bates, M E (1997) Outsourcing, co-sourcing, and core competencies: what is an information professional to do?, *Information Outlook*, **1** (12), 35–7.

Broadbent, M (1998) The phenomenon of knowledge management: what does it mean to the information profession?, *Information Outlook*, **2** (5), 23–37.

Butcher, D and Rowley, J (1998) The 7R's of information management, *Managing Information*, **5** (2)
http://www.aslib.co.uk/man-inf/mar98/article1.html

Cropley, J (1998) Knowledge management: a dilemma, *Business Information Review*, **15** (1), 27–34.

Griffiths, J-M (1998) The new information professional, *Bulletin of the American Society for Information Science*, **24** (3), 8–12.

Hartel, J (1997) Knowledge navigation or why I taught tango lessons, *Information Outlook*, **1** (1), 10–12.

McFadden, L M and Hubbard, K L (1998) Team concepts for emerging organisational architectures, *Information Outlook*, **2** (12), 18–25.

McPherson, P K (1995) Information mastery, *Managing Information*, **2** (6), 33–6.

Marshall, L (1997) Facilitating knowledge management and knowledge sharing: new opportunities for information professionals, *Online*, **21** (5), 92–8.

Morris, B (1997) Knowledge and co-operation: what librarians are good at, *State Librarian*, Spring, 31–8.

Mutch, A (1997) Information literacy: an exploration, *International Journal of Information Management*, **17** (5), 377–86.

Nelken, M (1998) *Knowledge management in Swedish corporations: the value of information and information services*, TLS, The Swedish Society for Technical Documentation.

Orna, L (1999) Using knowledge and information to manage and master change, *Managing Information*, **6** (1), 42–5.

Oxbrow, N (1998) The Chief Knowledge Officer: a new career path?, *Knowledge Management, Supplement to 'The Information Advisor'*, **2** (2), 1–4.

Remeikis, L (1995) Knowledge management: roles for information professionals, *SLA Business & Finance Bulletin*, **100/101**, 41–3.

Remeikis, L (1996) Knowledge management: the third 'era' the information age?, *Infomanage*, **3** (10), 1–5.

Srikantaiah, T K and Koenig, M (eds) (2000) *Knowledge management for the information professional*, Information Today Inc for the American Society for the Information Society (ASIS Monograph Series).

Stewart, C (1998) Building the desktop environment, *Library Association Record*, **100** (4), 192.

Willard, N (1997) Knowledge management: what does it imply for IRM?, *Managing Information*, **4** (8), 31–2.

Innovation

Amidon, D M (1997) *Innovation strategy for the knowledge economy: the ken awakening*, Butterworth-Heinemann.

Butler, R J et al (1998) Organizing for innovation: loose or tight control?, *Long Range Planning*, **31** (5), 775–82.

Coombs, R (1998) *Knowledge management practices for innovation: an audit tool for improvement*, CRIC Working Paper, No.6.

Intellectual capital

Bradley, K (1996) The value of intellectual capital, *Financial Times*, 26 Jul, 11.

Edvinsson, L (1997) Developing intellectual capital at Skandia, *Long Range Planning*, **30** (3), 366–73.

Edvinsson, L and Sullivan, P (1996) Developing a model for managing intellectual capital, *European Management Journal*, **14** (4), 356–64.

Edvinsson, L and Malone, M S (1997) *Intellectual capital: realizing your company's true value by finding its hidden brainpower*, HarperBusiness.

Fruin, M W (1997) *Knowledge works: managing intellectual capital at Toshiba*, Oxford University Press.

Lank, E (1997) Leveraging invisible assets: the human factor, *Long Range Planning Review*, **30** (3), 406–12.

OECD (1996) *Measuring what people know: human capital accounting for the knowledge economy*, OECD.

Roos, G and Roos, J (1997) Measuring your company's intellectual performance, *Long Range Planning Review*, **30** (3), 413–26.

Roos, J et al (1997) *Intellectual capital: navigating in the business landscape*, Macmillan Press Ltd.

Saint Onge, H (1996) Tacit knowledge: the key to strategic alignment of intellectual capital, *Strategy and Leadership*, **24** (2), 10–15.

Skandia (various) *Annual Reports*, available from **www.skandia.com**

Stewart, T A (1997) *Intellectual capital: the new wealth of organisations*, Nicholas Brealey.

Learning and development

Bontis, N and Giradi, J (1999) *Teaching knowledge management and intellectual capital lessons: an empirical examination of the Tango Simulation*. **http://www.celemi.com/articles/leveragingknowledgeman**

Conference Board (1997) *The Value of Training in the Era of Intellectual*

Capital, Conference Board Report No 1199-97-RR.

Garvin, D A (1993) Building a learning organisation, *Harvard Business Review*, **71** (4), 78.

Kim, D H (1993) The link between individual and organisational learning, *Sloan Management Review*, **35** (1), 37.

Sanchez, R and Heene, A (eds) (1997) *Strategic learning and knowledge management*, Strategic Management Series, John Wiley & Sons.

Senge, P M (1994) *The fifth discipline: the art and practice of the learning organisation*, Doubleday.

Measurement of value

Barchan, M (1999) The means of measurement: adding knowledge to the balance sheet, *Proceedings of the 'Knowledge Management: The Information Management Event' conference*, London, 24–25 March, Learned Information Europe Ltd.

Bukowitz, W R and Petrash, G P (1997) Visualising, measuring and managing knowledge, *Research-Technology Management*, 24–33.

Horne, N W (1998) Putting information assets on the board agenda, *Long Range Planning*, **31** (1), 10–17.

Huang, K (1998) Capitalizing on intellectual assets, *Systems Journal*, **37** (4),
http://www.almaden.ibm.com/journal/sj/374/huang.html

Leonard, D (1997) Mining knowledge assets for innovation, *Knowledge Management*, **1** (1), 11–13.

Lester, T (1996) Accounting for knowledge assets, *Financial Times*, 21 Feb., 11.

Skyrme, D (1998) *Measuring the value of knowledge: metrics for the knowledge-based business*, Business Intelligence.

Sveiby, K E (1997) *The new organisational wealth: managing and measuring knowledge based assets*, Berret-Koehler.

Organizational development

Blackler, F (1995) Knowledge, knowledge work and organizations: an overview and interpretation, *Organization Studies*, **16** (6), 1021–46.

Bonaventura, M (1996) The benefits of a knowledge culture, *Aslib Proceedings*, **49** (4), 82–9.

Coulson-Thomas, C (1997) The future of the organization: selected knowledge management issues, *Journal of Knowledge Management*, **1** (1), 15–26.

Davenport, T H (1998) Integrating knowledge management and the business, *Knowledge Management*, **1** (4), 1, 3–5.

Grant, R M (1996) Towards a knowledge-based theory of the firm, *Strategic Management Journal*, **17** (Winter), 109–22.

Grant, R M (1997) The knowledge-based view of the firm: implications for management practice, *Long Range Planning Review*, **30** (3), 450–4.

Gregory, F (1995) Soft systems models for knowledge elicitation and representation, *Journal of Operational Research Society*, **46** (5), 562–78.

Myers, P S (ed) (1996) *Knowledge management and organisational design*, Resources for the Knowledge-Based Economy Series, Butterworth-Heinemann.

Roles and skills

Abell, A and Oxbrow, N (1997) Knowledge pioneers, *Information Strategy*, (October), 23–6.

Chase, R L (1998) Knowledge navigators, *Information Outlook*, **2** (9), 17–26.

Cope, M (2000) *Know your value? Value what you know: manage your knowledge and make it pay*, Financial Times & Prentice Hall.

Corcoran, M and Jones, R (1997) Chief Knowledge Officers?: perceptions, pitfalls & potential, *Information Outlook*, **1** (16), 30–8.

Corrall, S (1998) Defining professional competence: skills and prospects for the information profession, *State Librarian*, Autumn, 48–63.

Davenport, T H (1996) Coming soon: the CKO, *CIO Magazine*, 1 April, available at
www.cio.com/archive

Earl, M and Scott, I (1998) What is a Chief Knowledge Officer?, *Sloan Management Review*, **40** (2), 29–38.

Earl, M and Scott, I (1999) The role of the Chief Knowledge Officer, Part Six: Knowledge management, *Financial Times*, 8 Mar., 7–8.

Funes, M and Johnson, N (1998) *Honing your knowledge skills*, Butterworth-Heinemann.

Gurteen, D (1999) Evangelising knowledge management, *Proceedings* of the 'Knowledge Management: The Information Event' conference, London, 24–25 March, Learned Information Europe Ltd.

Prahalad, C K and Hamel, G (1990) The core competencies of the corporation, *Harvard Business Review*, **68** (3), 79–91.

Javidan, M (1998) Core competence: what does it mean in practice?, *Long Range Planning*, **31** (1), 60–71.

Knowledge management websites

The following websites were all active at the end of November 2000. The first list are those used regularly at this time – the others occasionally. Favourites, however, are very subjective and change with the focus of interest.

Favourites

America Productivity and Quality Center
   http://www.apqc.org/best/km
Arthur Andersen KnowledgeSpace
   http://www.knowledgespace.com/
Buckman Laboratories – Knowledge Nurture
   http://www.knowledge-nurture.com/
Business Processes Resource Centre
   http://bprc.warwick.ac.uk/Kmweb.html
CIO Magazine: Knowledge Management Research Center
   http://www.cio.com/forums/knowledge/
E-knowledge Center
   www.e-knowledgecenter.com/
The Ernst & Young Center for Business Innovation
   http://www.businessinnovation.ey.com/
European Km Forum
   www.knowledgeboard.com/
FT: Mastering Information Management
   http://www.ft.com/mastering/
ICASIT – KM Case Studies
   http://www.icasit.org/km/kmcases.htm
International Knowledge Management Network
   http://kmn.cibit.nl/bench.htm
Kenniscentrum CIBIT
   http://www.cibit.nl/web/cibit-engels.nsf

Knowledge Management Case Studies
   http://www.bus.utexas.edu/kmrg/
KM Knowledge Management Table of Contents Page
   http://www.bus.utexas.edu/kman/toc.htm
KM World
   http://www.kmworld.com/
KMC: Knowledge Management Consortium
   http://www.kmci.org/
KMI
(focuses on Greece and other Southern European countries)
   www.kmi.gr/
Knowledge Connections
   http://www.skyrme.com
Knowledge Innovation (ENTOVATION International)
   http://www.entovation.com
The Knowledge Management Forum
   http://www.km-forum.org/
Knowledge Management Magazine
   www.destinationcrm.com/
Sveiby Knowledge Management
   http://www.sveiby.com.au/
TFPL: Knowledge Management
   http://www.tfpl.com/
Unit for the study of innovation knowledge & organisational networks (IKON)
   http://users.wbs.warwick.ac.uk/ikon/
WWW Virtual Library on Knowledge Management
   http://www.brint.com/km/

Occasional use

Aegiss On-Line
   http://www.aegiss.com
AIIM International
   http://www.aiim.org/
Effusion.net: new consulting for the new economy
   http://www.effusion.net/
EPSS.com
   http://www.epss.com/index.htm

Global Knowledge Exchange
  http://www.gke.com/
Instructional Management Systems Project
  http://www.imsproject.org/
KM Websites
  http://www.walshcol.edu/~mrutkow/KMsites.htm
Know>: knowledgecreators.com
  http://www.knowledgecreators.com
Knowledge Ecology
  http://www.KnowledgeEcology.com/
The Knowledge Exchange
  http://www.knowledgexchange.com/
Knowledge Inc.: the Execute Source on Knowledge, Technology and Performance
  http://knowledgeinc.com/
Knowledge Management
  http://www.xs4all.nl/~ktutein/kema/index.htm
Knowledge Management: Corporate Clients
  http://www.bt.com/youcan/
Knowledge Management Associates
  http://www.knowledge-management.com/
Knowledge Management News
  http://www.kmnews.com
Knowledge Matters
  http://www.knowledge.com/
Knowledge Nurture: knowledge library
  http://www.knowledge-nurture.com/
Knowledge Online
  http://www.knowledge.org.uk/
Knowledge Passion
  http://www.knowledgepassion.com/
Knowledge Research Institute Inc
  http://www.knowledgeresearch.com/
Knowledge Transfer International (KTI)
  http://www.ktic.com/
Lotus Development Corporation: Knowledge Management
  http://www.lotus.com/home.nsf/welcome/km
Netacademy on Knowledge Media Homepage
  http://www.knowledgemedia.org

OUBS Management of Knowledge and Innovation Research Unit
   http://oubs.open.ac.uk/research/mkiru/index.html
   Requires OU password
Paradigm Shift International
   http://www.parshift.com/
Teleos
   http://www.knowledgebusiness.com/
UCSF Center for Knowledge Management
   http://www.ckm.ucsf.edu/

A short glossary of terms used in knowledge management

Benchmarking

The practice of reviewing the performance of an organization, department, function or activity, by assessing it against the performance of 'best in class' organizations, industry standards or internal departments.

Best Practice

A process or methodology which has been identified inside or outside the organization and is recommended as a model. Also known by terms such as Better Practice in some organizations.

Business Process Redesign

An examination of key business processes in order to identify radical changes in order to achieve improved results

Capability

The skills, competencies, resources and processes available to an organization or individual to enable them to meet their objectives

Chief Knowledge Officer – CKO

A generic term used to describe an individual tasked with overall responsibility for managing the organization's knowledge.

Community of Interest – CoI

A group of people, often drawn from different functions within the organization, who share a common interest and who work together to enhance their understanding and knowledge. *See also* **Community of Practice**.

Community of Practice – CoP

A group of people, often drawn from different functions within the organization, who work on similar processes or in similar practice areas, and who share experiences and knowledge. *See also* **Community of Interest.**

Competence

The ability to handle a situation through the application of knowledge, skills, relationships, values, will and commitment.

Content

The intrinsic information and data contained in a variety of formats, including bibliographic data-sets, statistical and qualitative data, moving and still images, sound, textual resources and manuscripts.

Content Management

The management of all aspects of content in line with the business objectives of the organization or business unit, including demand and supply management.

Core Competence

The set of skills, experience and attributes recognized by an organization or organization as critical to their success.

Corporate Memory

The collective tacit or explicit understanding of the people, processes or products within an organization. **Corporate Memory** is strategically important, but it can also be a serious liability if it inhibits an organization from adjusting quickly to the changing environment.

Customer Capital

The value of the organization's relationship with its customers.

Data

Facts, observations and data points.

Data Mining

Software tools that allow users to examine large volumes of data to discover hidden patterns and cross-correlations.

Document

A set of formatted and related information, either physical or electronic.

Document Management

A process for managing the life cycle of a document, from inception, version creation, publication, storage, retention and disposal. This usually refers to electronic documents and uses specific document management software.

Enterprise portal

A means of presenting a business professional with clear, consistent and ordered access to multiple information sources and/or applications via a corporate intranet.

Expert System

Branch of artificial intelligence that develops computer applications to simulate human decisions.

Explicit Knowledge

Explicit knowledge is formal and systematic, and can be easily captured, codified and conveyed to others. *See also* **Tacit Knowledge**.

Groupware

Networked system applications that facilitate information/knowledge sharing and exchange.

Human Capital

The competence and capabilities of an organization's employees.

Information

A collection of data that has been organized within a context and translated into a structure that conveys meaning.

Information Assets

Collections of information which can be exploited by the organization for business value.

Information Audit

A process which reviews and maps organizational information need, creation, use, flow, and storage; identifies gaps, duplication, costs; and value; and uncovers the barriers to effective information flow. *See also* **Knowledge Audit**.

Information and Communications Technology – ICT

Merging of computing and high-speed communications links carrying data, sound and video.

Informatics

A discipline developed from the synergy between software engineering, mathematics, computer science and, in the case of the pharmaceutical industry, scientific data. **Informatics** is not a feature in company discovery, development and commercialization programmes.

Information Literacy

Employees' competency in using information and knowledge.

Information Management

An umbrella term for the various activities that contribute to the effective production, co-ordination, storage, retrieval and dissemination of information, in whatever format, and from internal or external sources, leading to the more efficient functioning of the organization.

Information Mining

Tools and techniques for finding and analysing electronic textual information stores designed to identify trends and patterns within the data/information. *See* **Data Mining**.

Information Overload

A state where the individual is no longer able effectively to process and make use of the amount of information to which he or she is exposed.

Information Quality

Measures of the reliability, accuracy, currency and usability of information.

Information Technology – IT

IT is a term that encompasses the physical elements of computing, including servers, networks and desktop computing and enables digital information to be created, stored, used and shared.

Infostructure

The information, technology and communication architectures that enable the effective creation of information and dissemination of information for re-use.

Innovation Capital

Renewal strength in a company, expressed as protected commercial rights, intellectual property, and other intangible assets.

Intangible Asset

The non-financial assets of an organization which contribute to its success.

Intellectual Capital

The sum of human capital and structural capital.

Intellectual Property

Intellectual assets that qualify for legal or commercial protections, eg patents, trademarks, copyrights, trade secrets.

IT literacy

The employees' competency in using information technologies.

Leverage

To realize the inherently value of an asset, physical or knowledge-based, beyond what is currently exploited.

Knowledge

The combination of explicit data and information to which is added tacit expert opinion, skills and experience to result in a valuable asset which can be used to make key decisions. The essential factor in adding meaning to information.

Knowledge Audit

A review of the knowledge required by an organization, department or group in order to carry out its objectives effectively. It will include a needs analysis, information; competencies and communication audits, and a review of interactions and knowledge flow. *See also* **Information Audit**.

Knowledge Base

The fundamental body of knowledge available to the organization.

Knowledge Management

The creation and subsequent management of an environment which encourages knowledge to be created, shared, learnt, enhanced, organized for the benefit of the organization and its customers.

Knowledge Maps/Mapping

A process to determine the knowledge requirements of the organization and its processes, its knowledge assets and knowledge flows. *See also* **Information Audit**.

Knowledge Management Typology

A framework that segments knowledge management into four key categories: intermediation; externalization; internalization; and cognition.

Learning Organization

An organization that views its future and subsequent competitive advantage based on continuous learning and adaptive behaviour. It develops a culture and processes to improve its ability to learn and share both at an individual and organizational level.

Lessons Learnt

Lessons Learnt are concise and insightful descriptions of experiences which may be communicated through mechanisms such as storytelling, debriefing, team learning, etc, and/or summarized or abstracted in databases.

Market Value

Market capitalization = Number of shares × Share Price. Used in the calculation of intellectual capital.

Metadata

Metadata, or 'data about data' describes the content, quality, condition and other characteristics of data in order to facilitate efficient and effective searching of that data.

Metatag

A single information element of **Metadata**.

Organizational Capital

Systematized and packaged competence, plus systems for leveraging the company's innovative strength and value-creating organizational capability.

Organizational Learning

The activity, by which knowledge is generated, captured and leveraged for the benefit of the organization. The form of capturing the knowledge must be in a form whereby the knowledge can be replicated, ie so that the knowledge does not have to be re-learnt in isolation from the original learning.

Story Telling

A technique employed in knowledge management environments to describe complicated issues, explain events, communicate **Lessons Learnt**, or bring about cultural change. The technique is based on established processes of constructing stories to communicate information, learning and values.

Structural Capital

Assets not directly related to the presence of employees – what stays behind when employees go home – including databases, customer lists, manuals, trademarks and organizational structures.

Tacit Knowledge

Highly personalized knowledge that is hard to formalize and communicate. **Tacit Knowledge** consists of know-how, mental models, beliefs and perspectives largely based on experience. *See also* **Explicit Knowledge.**

Taxonomy

A high level device constructed to enable the user to get an understanding of, and to navigate round, the intellectual capital of the enterprise.

Thesaurus

Thesaurus is a organized language used for inputting and searching information systems which predefine the relationships between terms and concepts used in its vocabulary.

Values

An expression of beliefs that will express and serve the cause, ie in the ultimate sense what will help to survive.

Value Chain

A concept developed by Michael Porter to illustrate an organization's value-creating ability and expressed as flow.

Virtual Organization

An organization without permanent facilities, eg building, and without many permanent employees. It relies on contractual relationships with suppliers, distributors and a contingent workforce.

Virtual Team

A team whose members are not co-located and who utilize electronic networks for communication, collaboration and work processes.

Workflow

The logical sequence of activities to achieve an outcome.

Index